I0793351

IMAGES
of America

FLORIDA GOVERNORS
LASTING LEGACIES

On The Cover: The Collins family poses outside of the original executive mansion. The previous fall, Leroy Collins won a special two-year term as governor. The entire family originally lived next door to the mansion, in the historic Grove house.

IMAGES
of America

FLORIDA GOVERNORS
LASTING LEGACIES

Robert Buccellato
with a foreword by Gov. Wayne Mixson

ARCADIA
PUBLISHING

ISBN 978-1-4671-1369-4

Published by Arcadia Publishing
Charleston, South Carolina

Printed in the United States of America

Library of Congress Control Number: 2014950769

For all general information, please contact Arcadia Publishing:
Telephone 843-853-2070
Fax 843-853-0044
E-mail sales@arcadiapublishing.com
For customer service and orders:
Toll-Free 1-888-313-2665

Visit us on the Internet at www.arcadiapublishing.com

To Steph and Barry, for all of those summertime trips to the historic capitol

CONTENTS

FOREWORD

Florida is blessed with a unique geography, great natural beauty, and a sunshine climate that attracts millions of visitors from other states and other countries each year. Millions of these have accepted our invitation to make Florida their permanent home. Public policy through the years has supported permanent settlers and economic growth. More than half of Florida governors were among these immigrants. Many were educated in other states. Some brought knowledge and experience in business, and some served in state and local government. No other state has been so enriched with such immigrant experience.

They were seeking economic opportunity and life under the sun for their families. Few, if any, came with the idea of seeking high office. Challenges from Florida's rapid growth, varied ethnic groups, languages, geography, and climate have been met by vision, timely leadership, and imagination by its able and dedicated governors, legislators, and courts through its history.

Florida, the nation's third-largest state, has been recognized for its modern and responsive governance. It has properly taken its place as a leader among the nation's states.

—Gov. Wayne Mixson

Acknowledgments

As always, to my wife, Stephanie, thank you for yesterday, today, and tomorrow. Thank you to my parents and Anna, for reminding me the value of hard work, and Nick and Shari, for reading each draft. A thanks also goes to Gov. Wayne Mixson and First Lady Margie Mixson for their boundless confidence, good will, and support. Thank you to Lt. Gov. Jim Williams and Ralph Turlington for all those wonderful phone conversations. I thank my grandparents, for those first books on the presidency, and Mama and Poppy, for your determination. I am grateful to Richard for advice and notes.

This book is the creation of many individuals who selflessly searched through mountains of forgotten folders and cabinets to bring these images to you. Some of them were actual witnesses of the state's past during its most historic moments. Specifically, I would like to thank Dr. and Mrs. Mixon, Rep. Walter Young and Dottie Young, the Florida Museum of History, the Historical Society of Jacksonville, the families of Gov. Leroy Collins, Gov. Daniel McCarty, and Gov. Buddy MacKay, and the family of Jim Williams. I would also like to mention the efforts of the State Archives Photo Lab, and Michael Croom, Charlie Reed, and Mark Foley, as well as the St. Lucie County Regional History Center.

Finally, to my project manager and editor at Arcadia, Maggie Bullwinkel, whose guidance made this book possible.

Unless otherwise noted, the images in this book appear courtesy of the Collection of the Museum of Florida History (MFH), the Jacksonville Historical Society (JHS), St. Lucie County Regional History Center (SLC), State Archives of Florida (SAF), the private collection of Gov. Wayne Mixson (WM), and the author's collection (AC).

INTRODUCTION

To define the state of Florida is as difficult a task as charting the wide expanse of the sea. The state has grasped the imaginations of countless individuals in every generation of exploration. It has been discovered, settled, conquered, divided, and even drained, but it has never stopped evolving. It has served as the fictional location of the fountain of youth and the base of operations for man's quest to reach the stars and land on the moon. It is where Thomas Edison first made motion pictures and Walt Disney dreamed of developing a new form of suburban living. Many have claimed it is really four states on one peninsula, with such a constant pattern of progression and change that it can never be controlled or ruled. However, this book is about those often ambitious, sometimes brilliant, usually wise, and always Floridian individuals who have met the challenges of governing the state.

For reasons unknown, this is the first book to solely document all the governors of Florida, from Andrew Jackson to Rick Scott. The purpose of this book is by no means to provide a definitive account of the nearly 200-year history of the state's governorship. Instead, it serves as a starting point for those interested in learning more about this exciting state and these interesting individuals.

Florida has a rich and diverse history, with a wealth of exciting events and colorful characters that form a brilliant narrative for any lover of history. The images presented in this book will hopefully add a new dimension to these long-neglected personalities. The book is titled *Florida Governors: Lasting Legacies* so that it can account for both the officeholders and the process of governing. Readers of all ages are given a condensed view of these compelling governors and their actions that have helped shape it into a paradise for millions.

One

Presidential Patronage

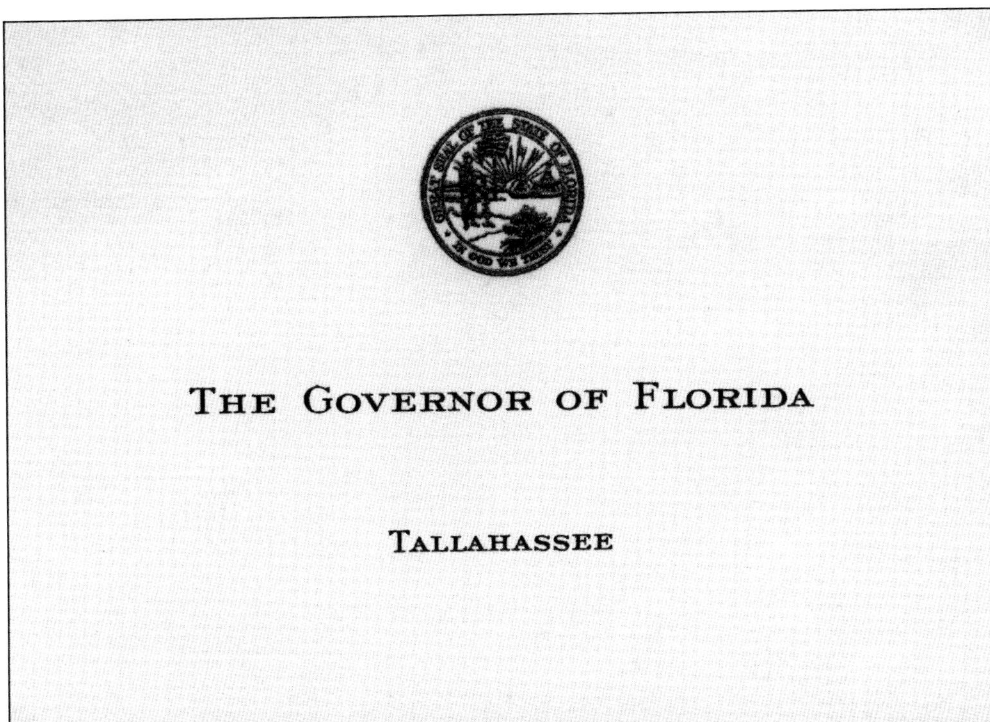

A governor's calling card, one of the perks of the job, contains only the title and the capital city, an indication that the officeholder needs no introduction. This modern trapping of the governorship shows just how far the office has come. From its humble origins as a presidential appointment, the governorship of Florida has been elevated to a position of national leadership. (AC.)

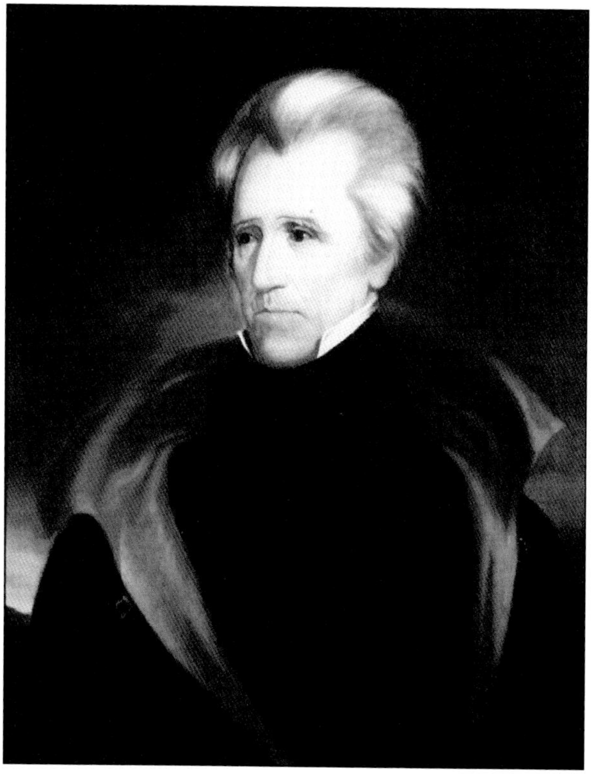

Future president Andrew Jackson served as commissioner of the United States and governor of the territories of Florida. Jackson was sworn in at Plaza Ferdinand in Pensacola, and his brief tenure proved to be eventful, as he used combative methods to settle the native Spaniards and Seminoles. His appointment orders were purposely ambiguous to provide maximum cover for Pres. James Monroe. (AC.)

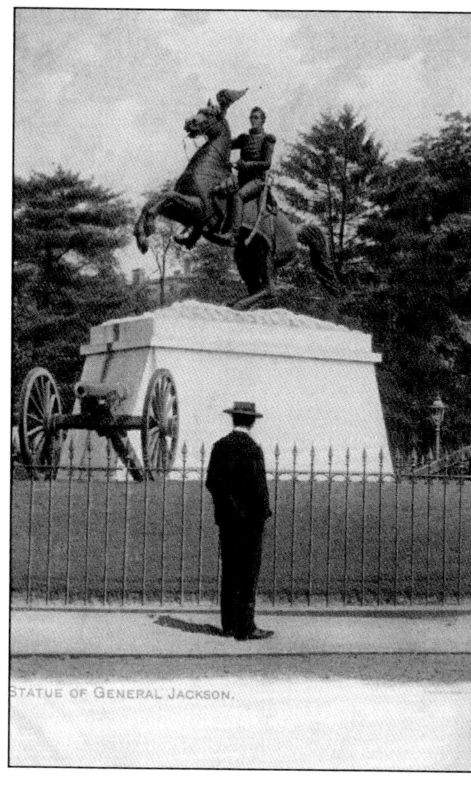

A statue of Gen. Andrew Jackson is located directly across from the White House. The bronze used for this statue was cast from cannons captured during his military campaigns in Pensacola and New Orleans. The impressive equestrian statue cost more than $50,000 and is surrounded by actual Spanish guns from the War of 1812. (AC.)

John Quincy Adams, shown here as secretary of state, went to great lengths to protect Andrew Jackson following the general's executions of two British citizens at St. Marks. Perhaps the greatest American diplomat of his age, Adams's successful acquisition of Florida has become legendary. Sadly, Jackson and Adams would become bitter rivals in the presidential elections of 1824 and 1828. (AC.)

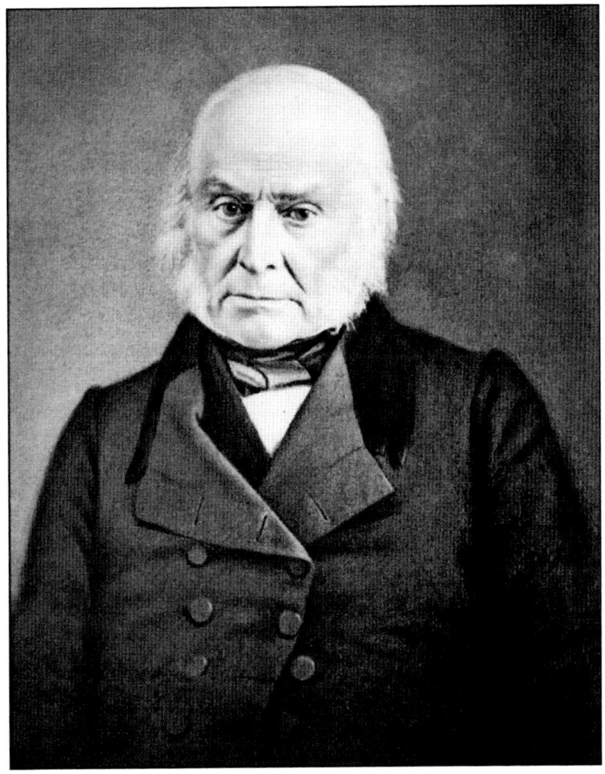

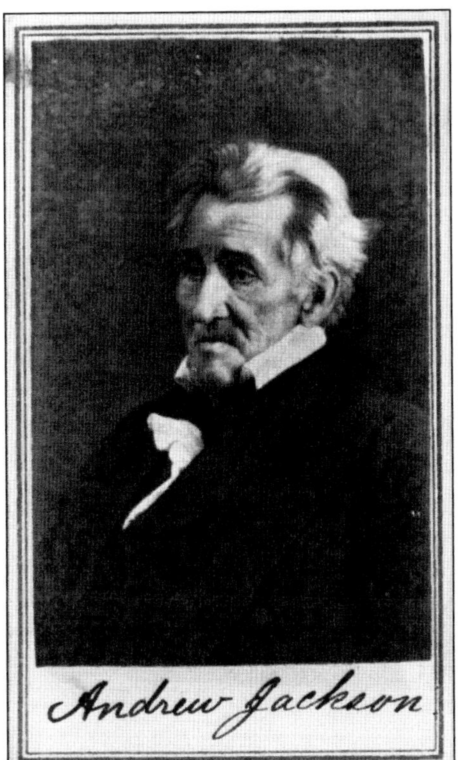

Jackson declined the governorship at least once and only accepted it on the condition that he would be permitted to resign as soon as the territorial government was organized. Departing West Florida in October, he sent the president a resignation letter almost as an afterthought in the fall. Until a successor was appointed, two territorial governors were appointed to serve as executives for west and east Florida. (AC.)

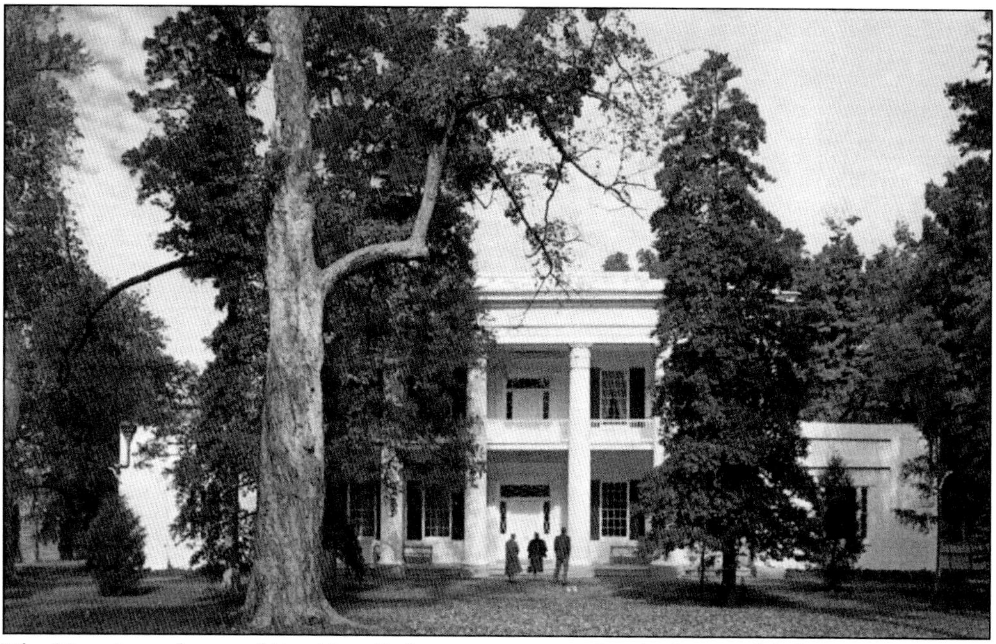

The Hermitage, home of President Jackson, was restored to look as it did during his lifetime. Despite his brief tenure as Florida's governor, Jackson's influence has proved far-reaching. When the legislature voted to build another executive mansion to replace the outdated structure, builders quickly turned to Old Hickory's beloved plantation for inspiration. (AC.)

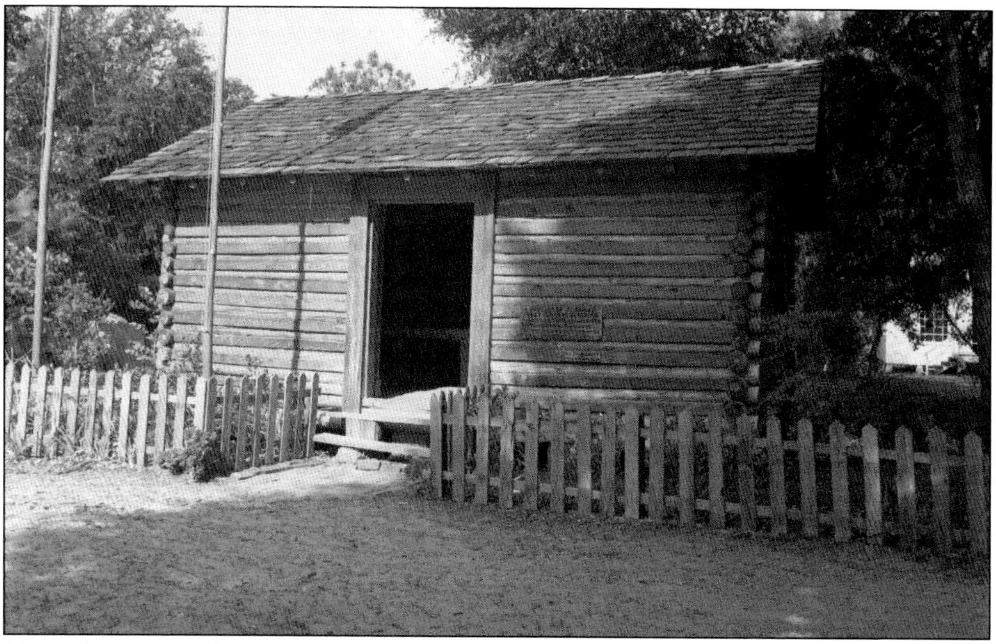

Shown here is a replica of Florida's first capitol building. This now-fabled log cabin was one of three structures built to accommodate the legislative council. The necessity for a permanent capital city was due primarily to the shocking death toll of council members during the annual commute between Pensacola and St. Augustine. These two populated towns served biennially as the territory's capital. (SAF.)

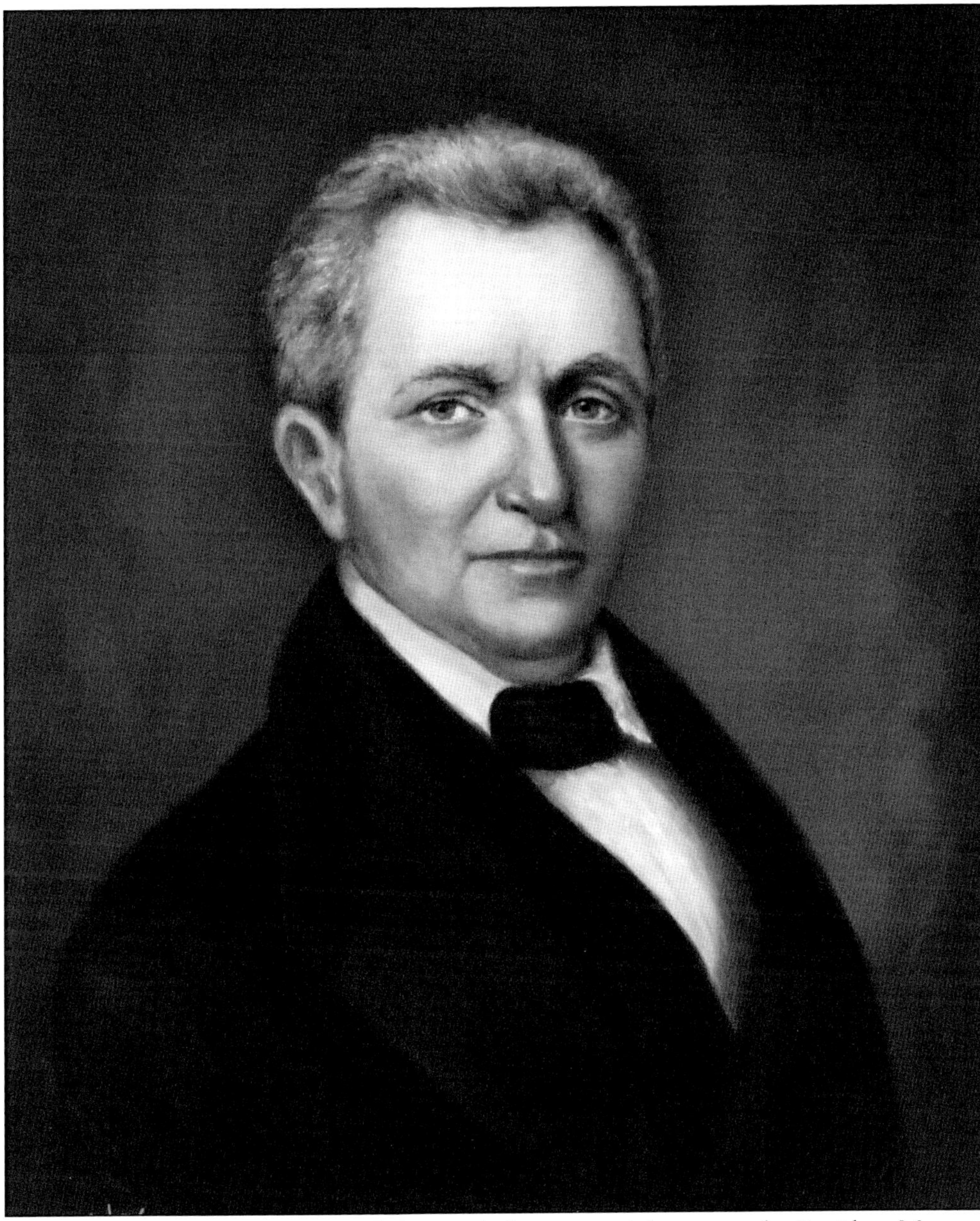

William Pope Duval was appointed the state's first territorial governor by President Monroe. His friendship with secretary of war and future vice president John C. Calhoun resulted in his reappointment to the governorship by Presidents Adams and Jackson. His nearly 12-year administration resulted in the establishment of Tallahassee as the state's capital and improved relations with Native Americans. Duval's house, built in the late 1820s, was later moved to become part of Florida A&M University. Duval was a renowned storyteller and host, and this official residence was the site of many lively gatherings. His administration was responsible for the founding of many public institutions and the formation of a commission whose sole responsibility was finding a suitable location for a new capital. During his governorship, Duval divided Florida into four territories, established the local court system, and served as the inspiration for Washington Irving's character Ralph Ringwood. (MFH.)

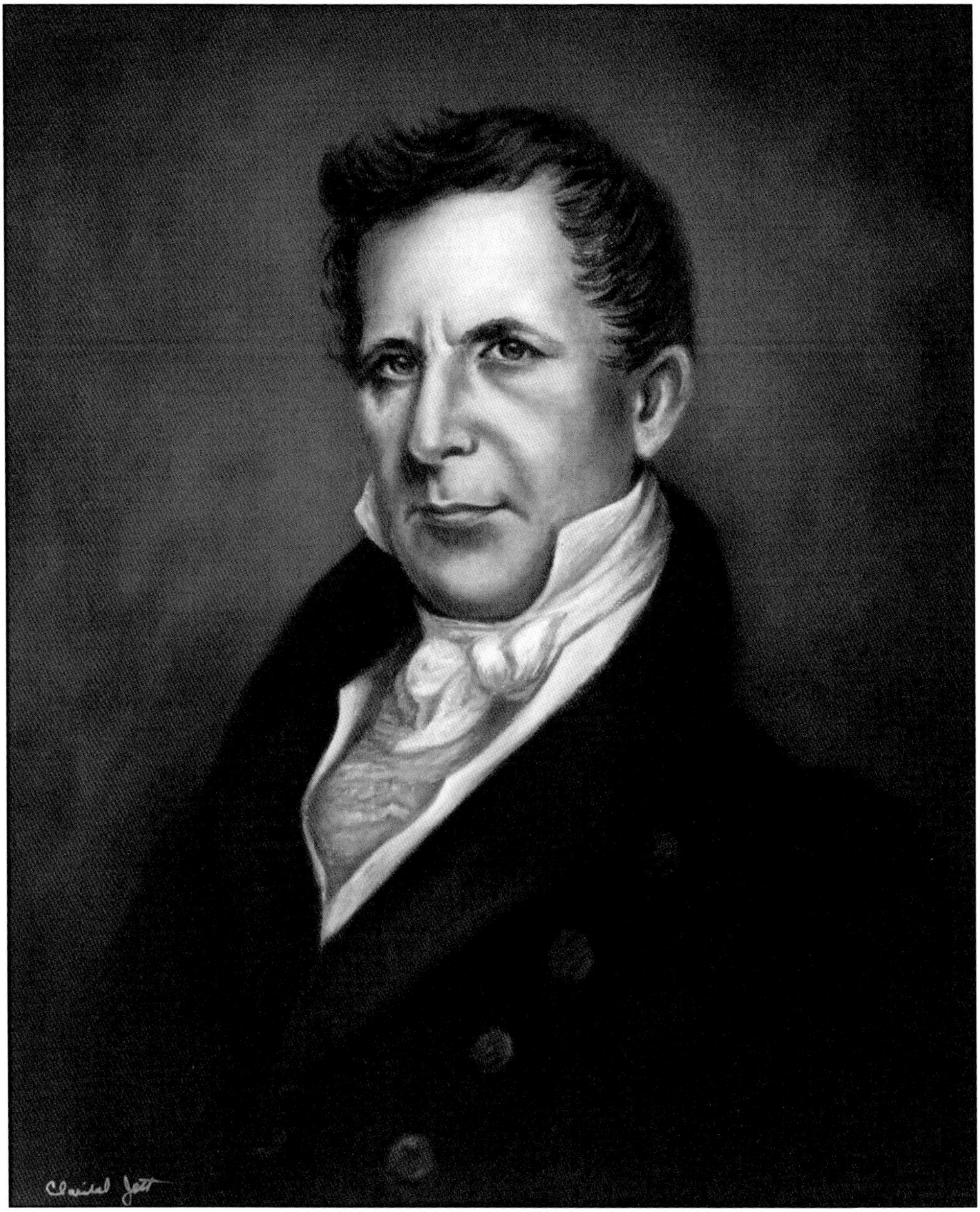

John Eaton, Florida's second territorial governor, was the youngest individual ever elected to the US Senate, taking the oath of office at age 28. As a member of President Jackson's cabinet, Eaton's second marriage to Peggy O'Neale would cause such a firestorm that it resulted in the resignation of several cabinet members. The Eaton affair, or the Eaton malaria, as the scandal was also known, caused the eventual removal of Vice Pres. John C. Calhoun from the presidential ticket. This was due to the Second Lady Floride Calhoun's role as the chief instigator of the anti-O'Neale movement in the cabinet. Jackson appointed his good friend to the Florida governorship primarily to distance him from the harsh Washington gossip. John Henry Eaton would serve as governor only from 1834 to 1836, before his appointment to the far more prestigious title of ambassador to Spain (1836–1840). (MFH.)

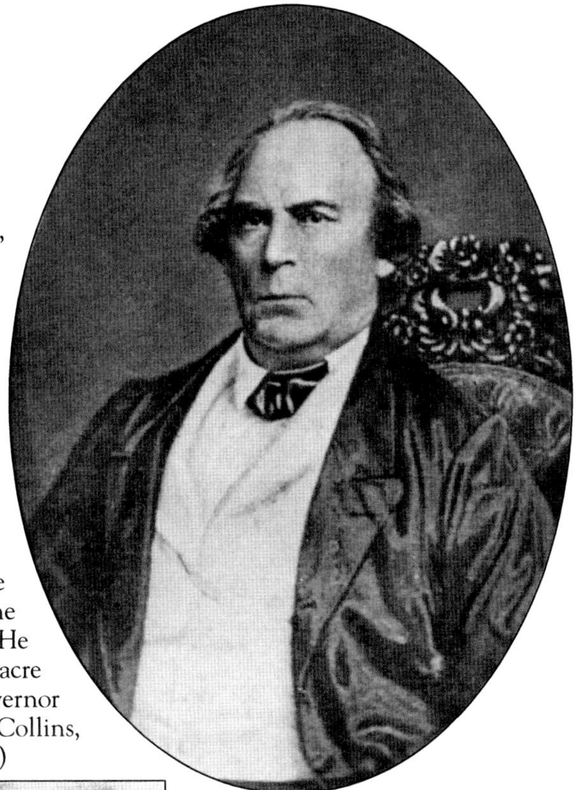

Richard Keith Call was born in Virginia, made his fortune in Tennessee, and found lasting fame leading the territorial government for a pair of three-year terms. During his tenure as Florida's third and fifth territorial governor, slavery was firmly established, and the Seminole Indians were settled. The territory experienced a great increase in commerce and population, and Call claimed credit for his desire to stop talk of secession in Florida. Governor Call's official residency was the Grove Plantation (below), built throughout the 1830s on the outskirts of Leon County. He would eventually cultivate it into an 800-acre estate with over 100 slaves. Florida governor Leroy Collins and his wife, Mary Call Collins, would later own the Grove. (Both, SAF.)

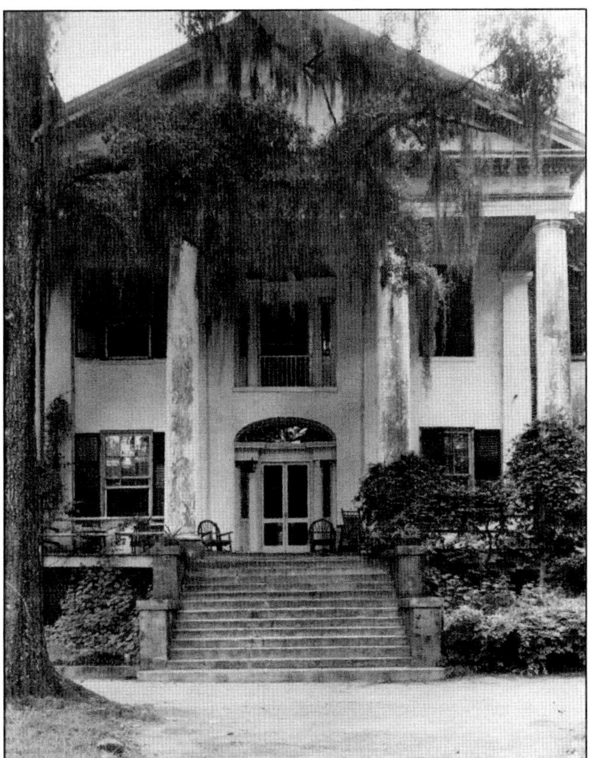

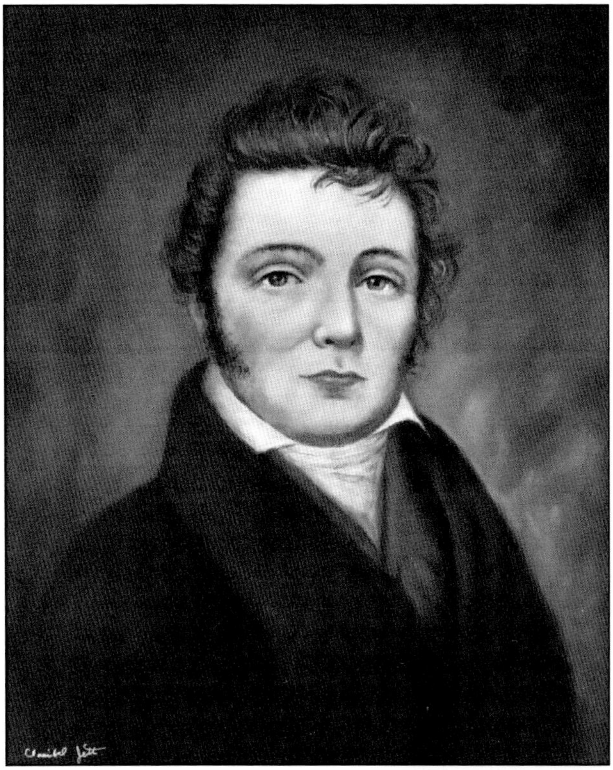

Robert Reid served briefly as the fourth territorial governor in a 15-month term sandwiched between Richard Call's two administrations. Reid's life was rocked by tragedy, with the deaths of two wives and several children. A judge for many years, he excelled as presiding official over the convention that drafted Florida's constitution. In weak health upon leaving office, he died in the yellow fever epidemic of 1841. (MFH.)

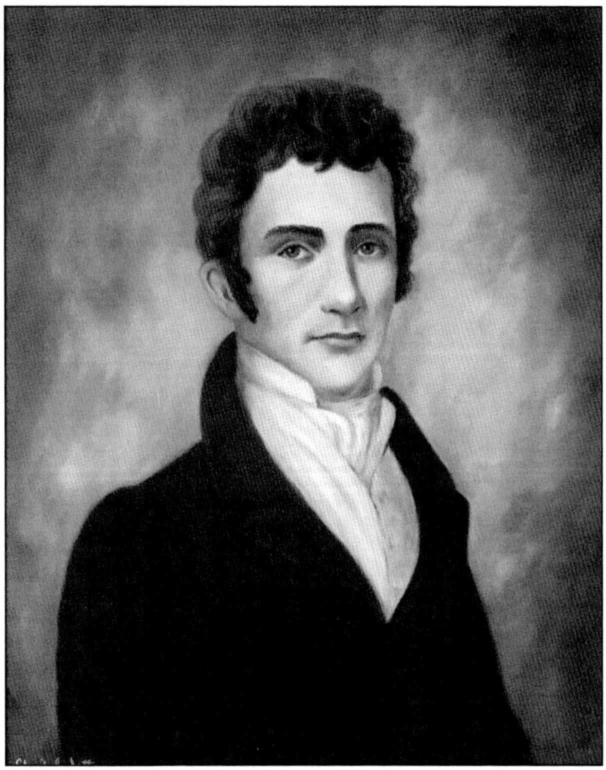

John Branch, appointed in 1844, is the only individual to serve as both governor of North Carolina (19th) and the territorial governor of Florida (sixth and last). Appointed as Jackson's secretary of the Navy, Branch was one of the cabinet members to resign over the Peggy O'Neale scandal. He would serve in both chambers of Congress and establish the Live Oak Plantation. (MFH.)

Two

STATEHOOD

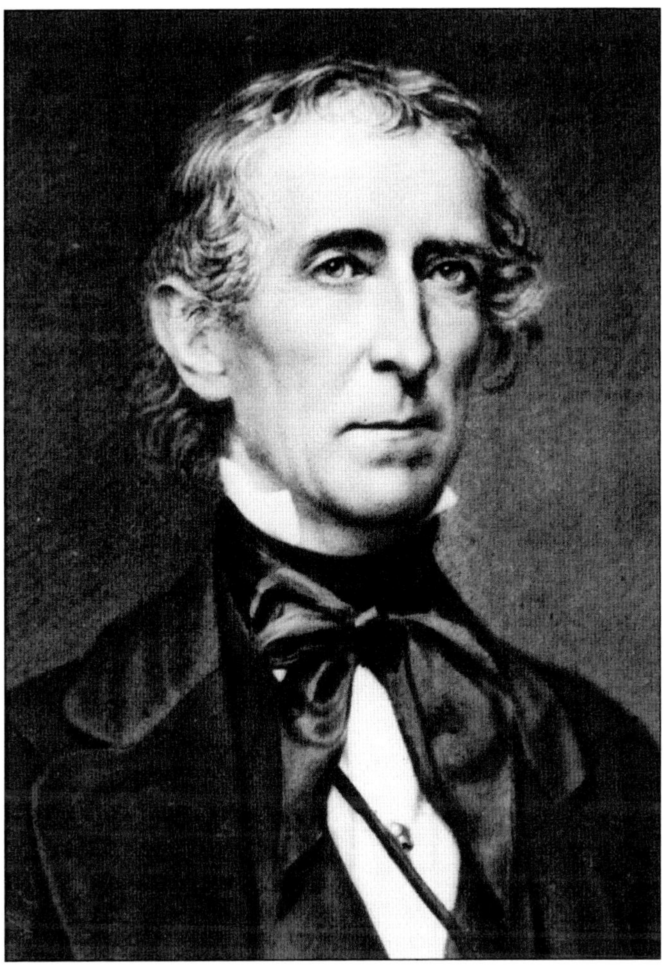

John Tyler, the nation's 10th president, was given little opportunity to advance his political agenda during his four years in the White House. Sworn into office following the death of the ninth president, William Henry Harrison, he quickly alienated himself with members of his own party. However, President Tyler, on his last day in office, signed into law the act granting Florida its statehood. (AC.)

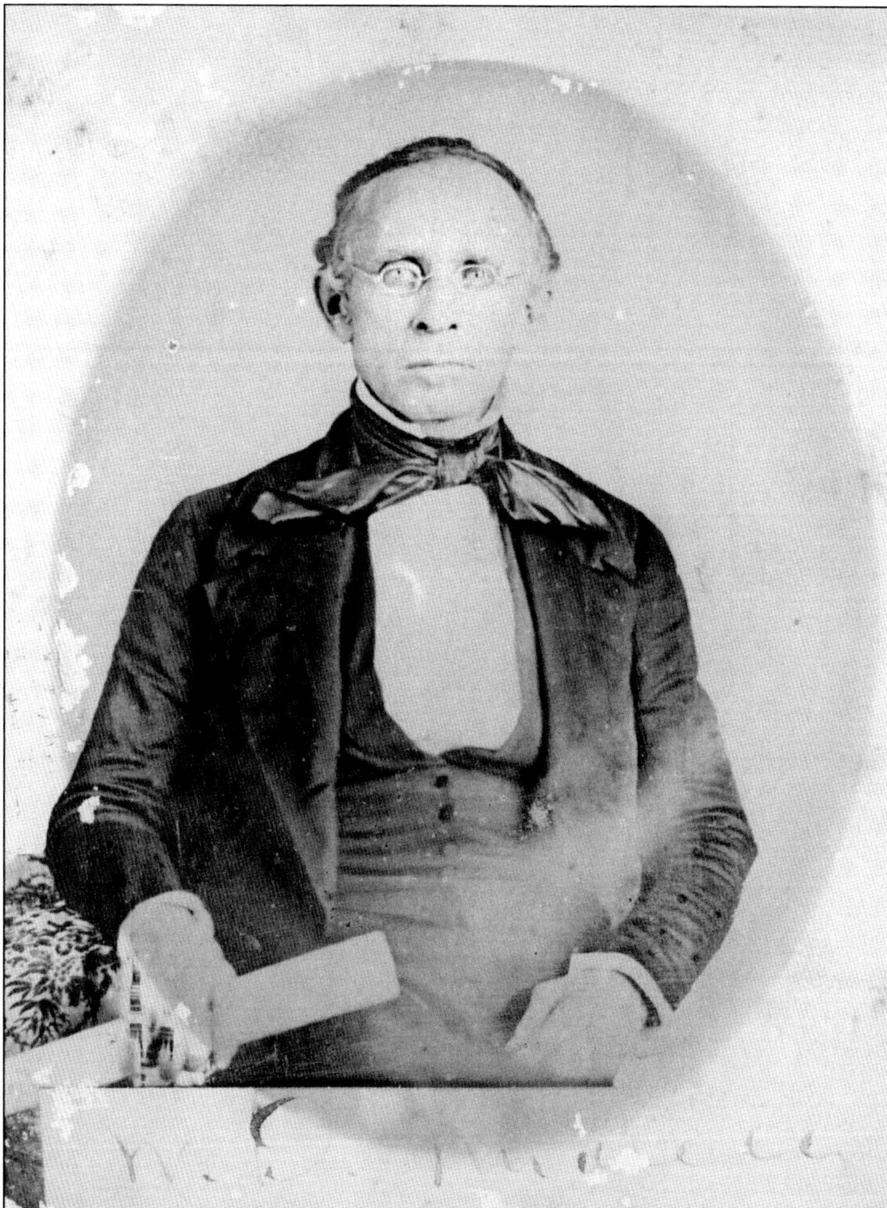

Democrat William Moseley, a native of North Carolina, defeated Whig Robert Call's attempt at a third term as governor, winning by a mere 600 votes. Call's unexpected defeat was due in large part to his outspoken support of President Harrison, a very unpopular figure for his nationalist beliefs. Moseley, a strong believer in a limited central government, quickly set the tone for the next two decades of state government. He was sworn in with as much celebration and pageantry as George Washington a generation earlier. The *St. Augustine News* correspondent described the inaugural event to his readers, saying, "You have no idea how hot it is!" During these first years of statehood, Florida's motto was "Let us alone." The relationship between the Moseley administration and the nation's capital was at times troubled. The state capitol was completed during his first year in office, and Moseley oversaw the state's role in the Mexican-American War, supporting the conflict in an effort to expand slavery. (SAF.)

Thomas Brown became the second elected governor of Florida, in the fall of 1849. He would be the only member of the Whig Party to be elected governor of the state. Brown was the inventor of the post office letterbox, the discoverer of the Lake Okeechobee area, and a prosperous hotel owner. (MFH.)

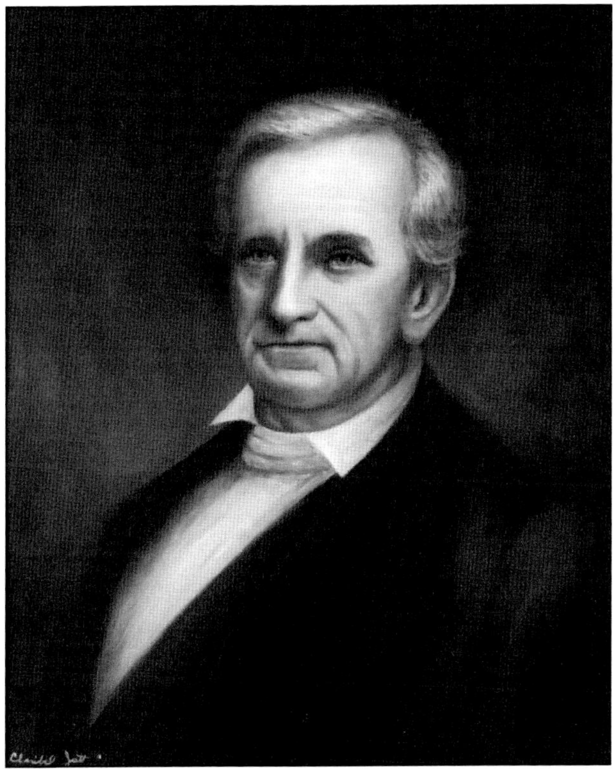

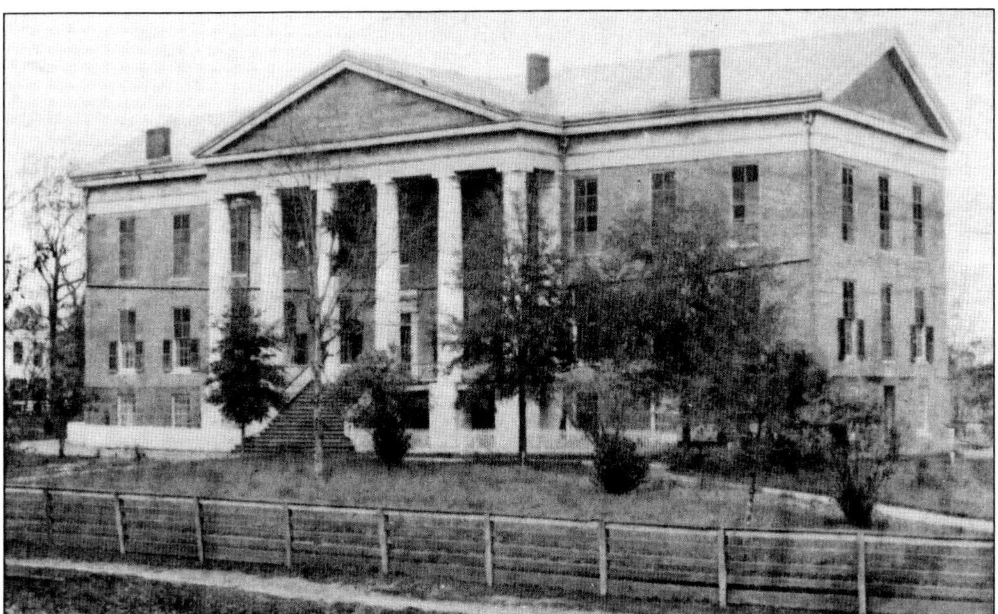

This is the earliest-known photograph of the state capitol. It shows the building as it appeared in 1845, when it was completed. In 1840, the location was congressional appropriated for the construction of the structure. However, Congress did not give Florida the $40,000 needed to finish construction until 1844, once it became clear that the territory would enter the Union as a state. (SAF.)

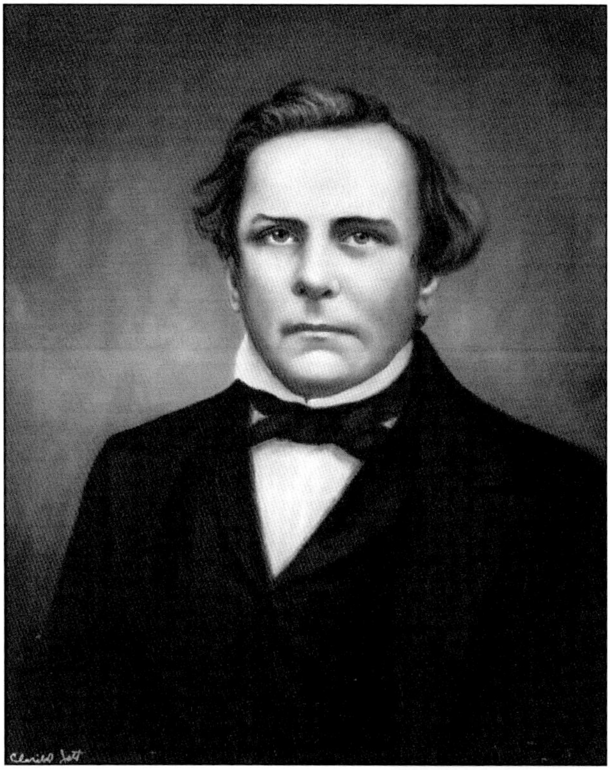

Gov. James Broome was perhaps the most independent man ever to serve in the state's highest office. Determined to chart his own course, he would be known as the "veto governor" due to his repeated use of the veto against the massive Whig majority in the legislature. A States' Rights Democrat, he was an ardent supporter of balanced government and fought hard to preserve the state's supreme court. (MFH.)

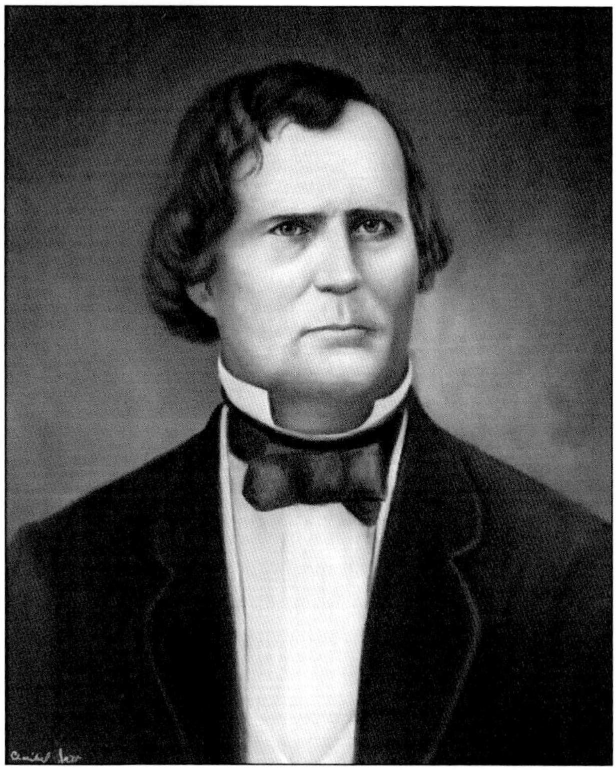

Madison Stark Perry, the fourth governor of Florida, was a South Carolina native who became one of the leading planters in Alachua County. Serving in the state senate before winning the Democratic Party nomination in 1856, Governor Perry helped Florida solve a boundary dispute with Georgia and expanded its railroad lines. Perry, a supporter of states' rights, seemed to sense the oncoming civil war and reestablished the state militia. (MFH.)

Three

Secession, Civil War, Reconstruction

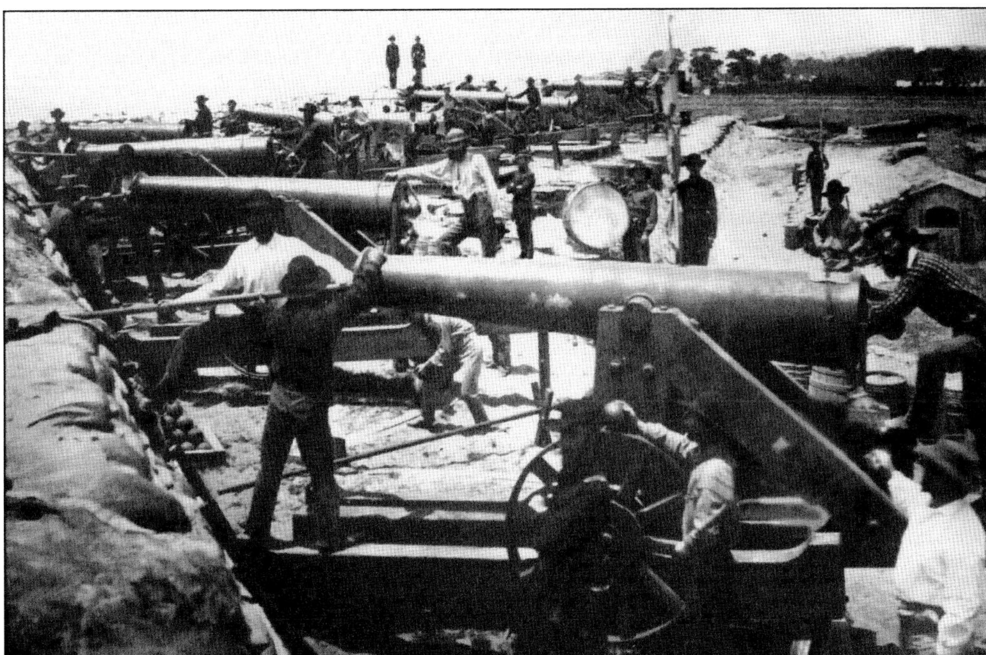

Shown here is the Confederate Battery at Pensacola Harbor, known as the "Water Battery." This photograph showcases the tragic conditions many Confederate soldiers found themselves in once hostilities commenced. The South had not produced ammunition or large weaponry for over 50 years, and soldiers had no proper uniforms and virtually no training. Florida was different from most Confederate states. Several existing military bases, like Fort Pickens, would remain in Union hands, aiding the federal blockade of the state. (AC.)

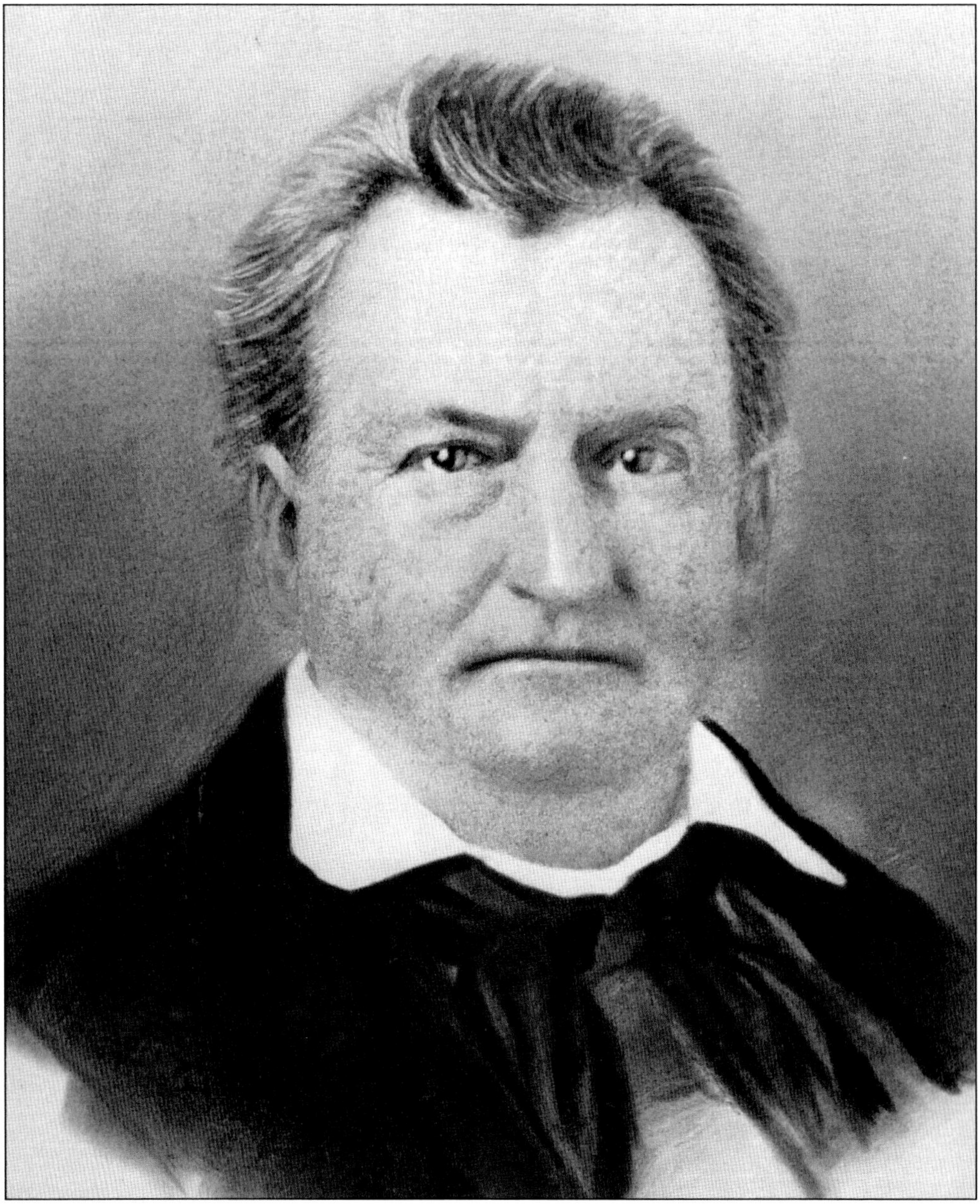

John Milton was the first of what would be three men to occupy the governorship of Florida in 1865. He came to Florida in 1846 to avoid capture for shooting another man in cold blood on the main street of Columbus, Georgia. The future governor and his victim were both in love with the same local girl. Milton served as both a presidential elector and a member of the Florida House of Representatives. As a strong supporter of states' rights, he was an early advocate for secession from the Union. During the Civil War, Gov. John Milton stressed the importance of Florida as a supplier of goods rather than of men. Milton, himself an owner of 50 slaves, was a secessionist Democrat and the state's Confederate wartime governor. Hearing the news that Gen. Robert E. Lee surrendered, Milton left a message for the Florida House of Representatives: "Yankees have developed a character so odious that death would be preferable to reunion with them." He then went to his Marianna plantation and killed himself. (SAF.)

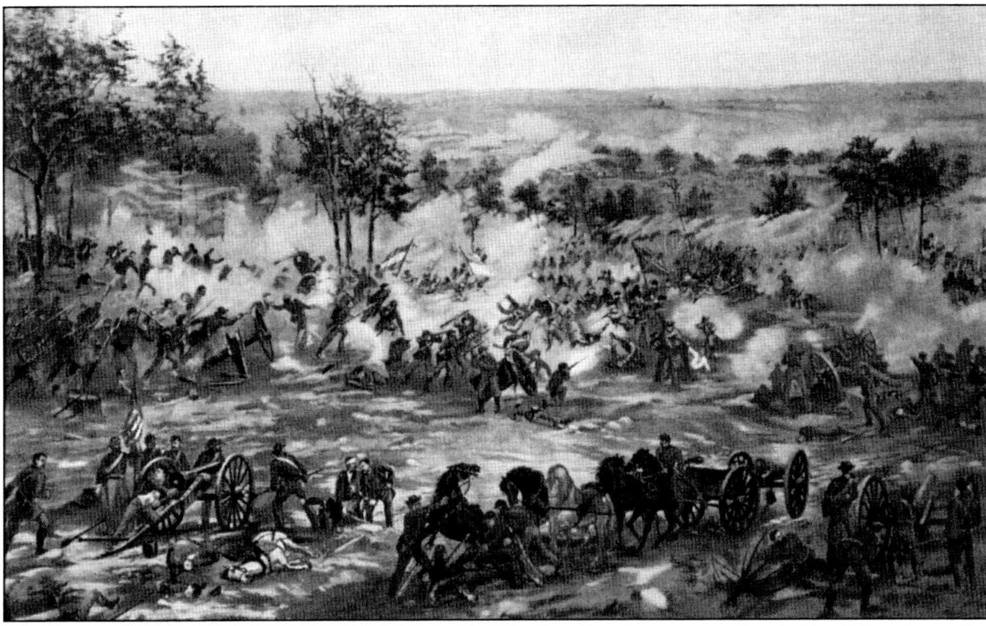

The Battle of Gettysburg was the bloodiest conflict in the American Civil War. The three-day battle resulted in casualties of nearly 51,000 soldiers. Nearly every state was represented on the Pennsylvania battlefield, and Florida fought alongside Alabama and Georgia brigades. In total, the state of Florida supplied three infantry regiments at the infamous battle. (AC.)

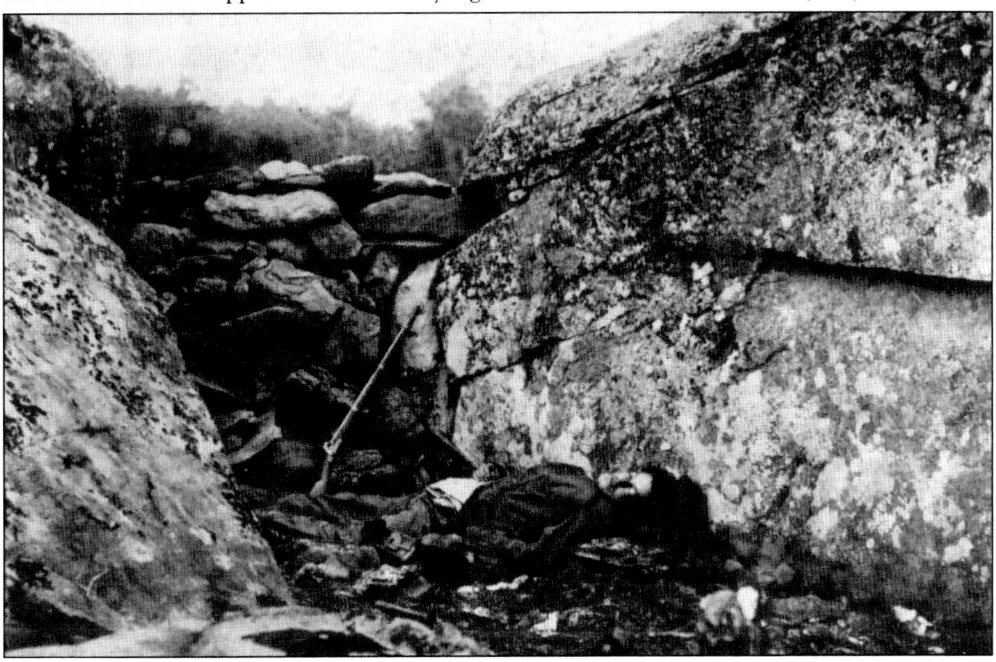

Shown here is a confederate sniper at Devil's Den, likely killed by the Union batteries on the first day of the conflict. The Battle of Gettysburg involved two future Florida governors; Gov. Francis Fleming served as a private in the 2nd Florida Regiment and received a battlefield promotion to first lieutenant. He would play a pivotal role alongside future governor Edward Perry's brigade in Pickett's Charge up Cemetery Ridge. (AC.)

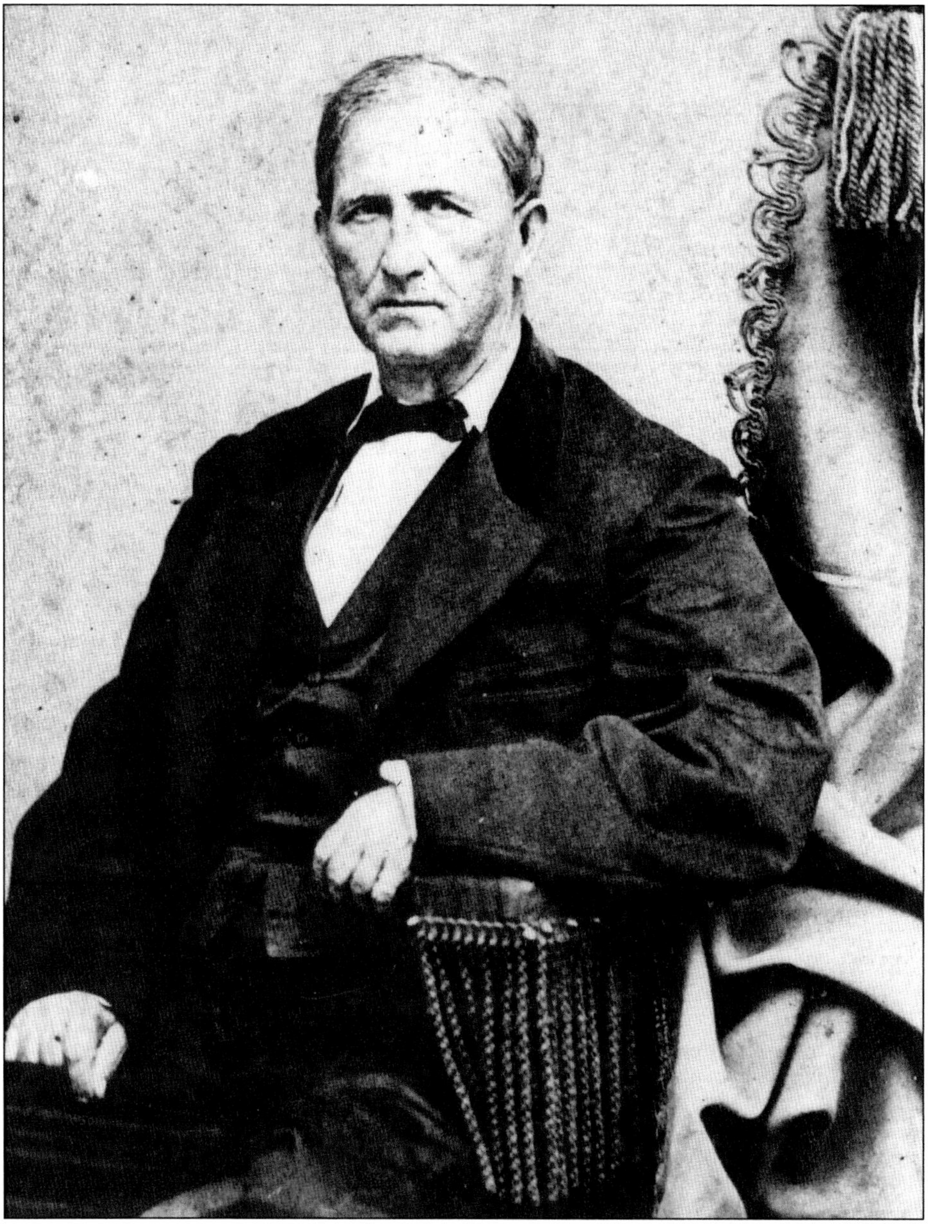

After John Milton committed suicide, Abraham K. Allison, the state senate president, assumed the office of governor. It was the second time in his life that happenstance had placed him in the office. Allison served briefly as acting governor from September to October 1853, while Governor Brown was out of the state and Governor-elect Broome was en route to the capital city. Allison did not, however, exercise any of the executive powers available to him, and it is for that reason alone he is not regarded as an official state governor during this period. Before serving as the last Confederate governor of Florida, for 49 days, he had a prolonged career of political firsts. He was elected the first mayor to Apalachicola, the first county judge of Franklin County, and a member of the territorial legislature. Allison resigned his office on May 19, 1865, and went into hiding as Federal troops occupied Tallahassee. He was captured by Union forces the following month and held for several months at Fort Pulaski. (SAF.)

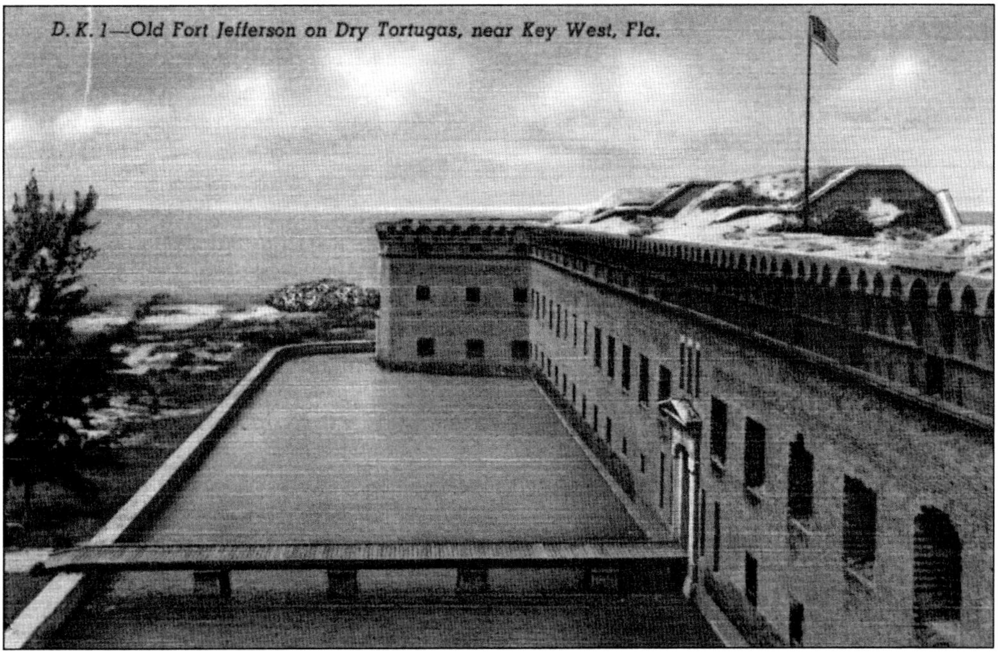

Seen here is Old Fort Jefferson, sometimes known as the old citadel on the Dry Tortugas. The massive fortress covered 47 acres and was originally used to suppress piracy in the Caribbean. During the Civil War, it was an important asset to the Union's control of the Florida Keys. After the war, it was a federal prison. Dr. Samuel Mudd was imprisoned there for supplying medical aid to presidential assassin John Wilkes Booth. (AC.)

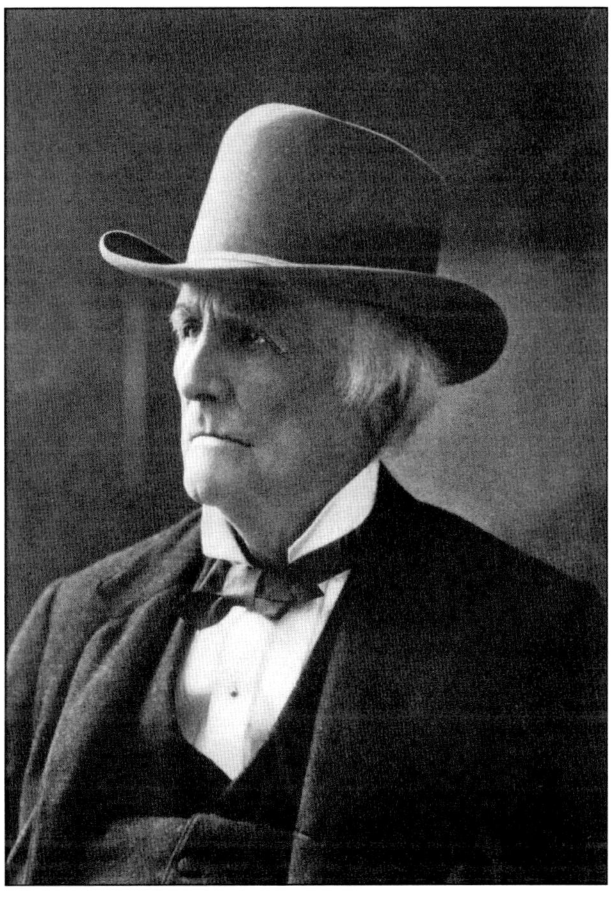

William Marvin served briefly as Florida's seventh governor. Marvin, a judge, was perhaps one of the best legal minds in Florida. He wrote a book on salvage laws and made a fortune prosecuting those who stole from shipwrecks off the Florida Keys. As the last federal judge south of Washington, DC, during the Civil War, Marvin was an obvious choice by Pres. Andrew Johnson for provincial governor. (SAF.)

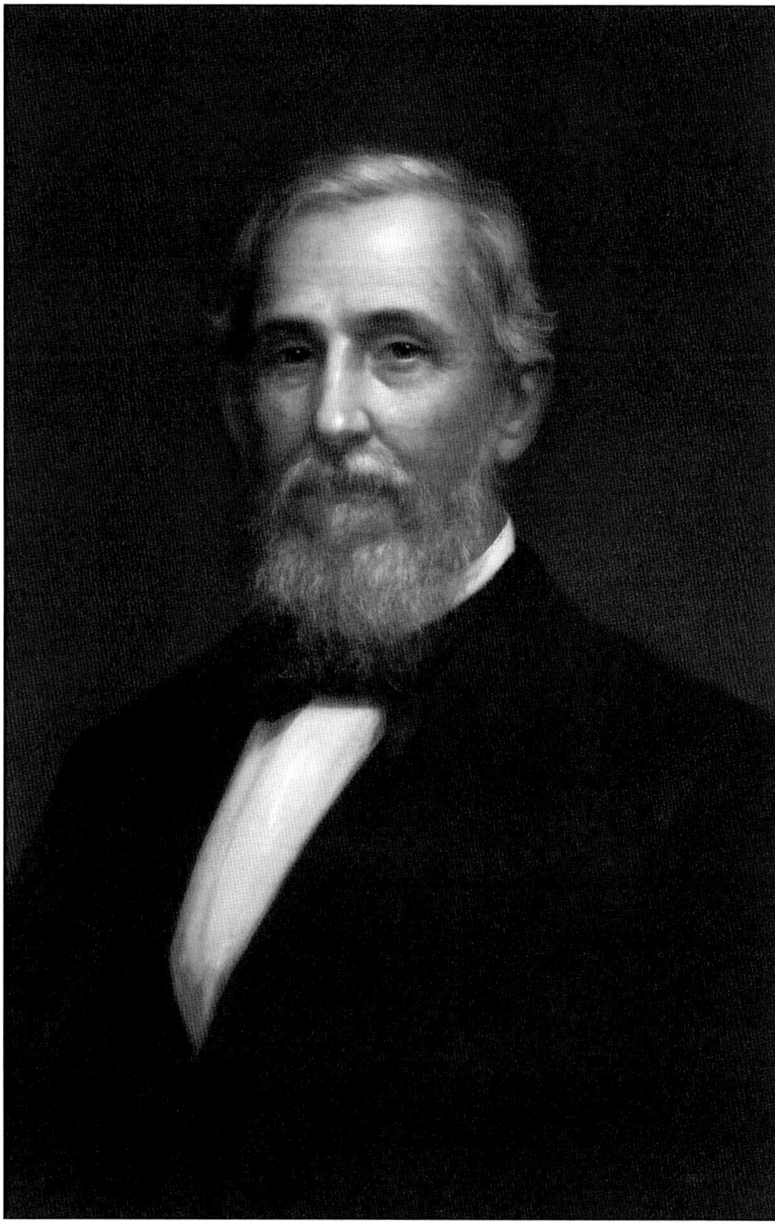

Gov. David Walker was elected during Florida's constitutional convention, along with countless other officials. The convention was designed to jump-start the state on the road to congressional reconstruction. Instead, the convention entrusted the government to a group of Southern sympathizers, alienating Florida from the US House of Representatives. Gov. Walker had to share executive power with federal military officials. The state Republican Party was strengthened as a direct result of Walker's leadership and his opposition to the 14th Amendment. Reconstruction would prove to be a difficult period for Florida. Walker's actions would lead to all of the states' congressional members being denied seating in the national capital. Even former governor Martin, now Florida's senator-elect, was not permitted into the chamber. The radical faction of the national Republican Party, which controlled Congress, also strengthened its new Florida Republicans, leading them to powerful gains in the state legislature. (MFH.)

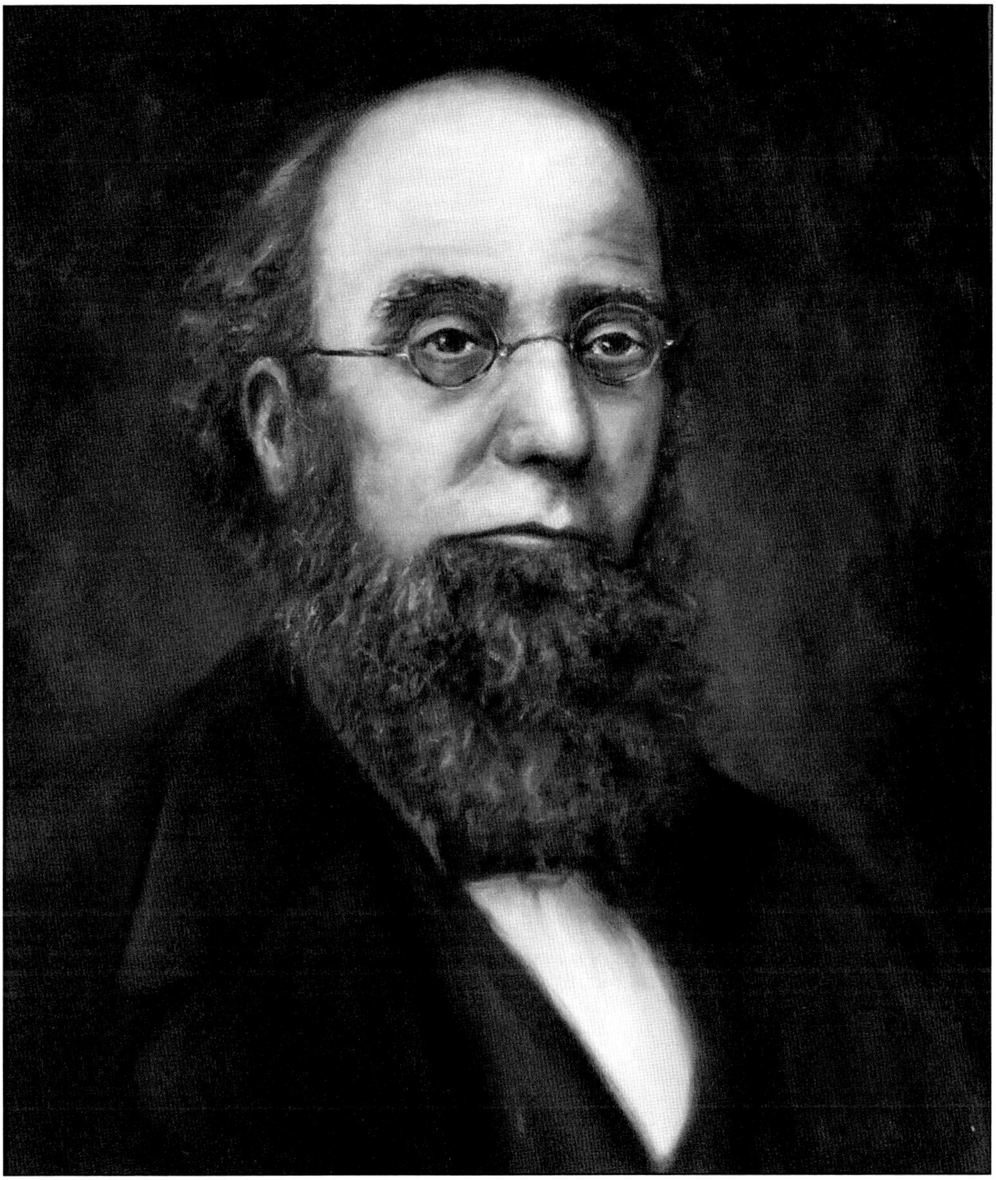

By outward appearance, Harrison Reed comes across more like a mild-mannered bank clerk than what he really was—the most controversial governor in the state's history. As copublisher of the *Wisconsin State Journal*, he moved to Washington, DC, where he was appointed by Pres. Abraham Lincoln as a tax commissioner in Florida to deal with seized Confederate property. While Reed worked as commissioner, Pres. Andrew Johnson appointed him the postal agent for Florida in 1865. With the state's new constitution in place, he was elected governor in 1868. His carpetbagger reputation and frosty relations with the legislature made him the target of four impeachment proceedings. In the governor's office for only a few months, Harrison tried to get elected to the US Senate, a task other governors have also attempted without success, in 1868. But, this action seemed to alienate him from many in the legislature, who backed other candidates for the appointment. From that moment, Reed's governorship was under siege. (MFH.)

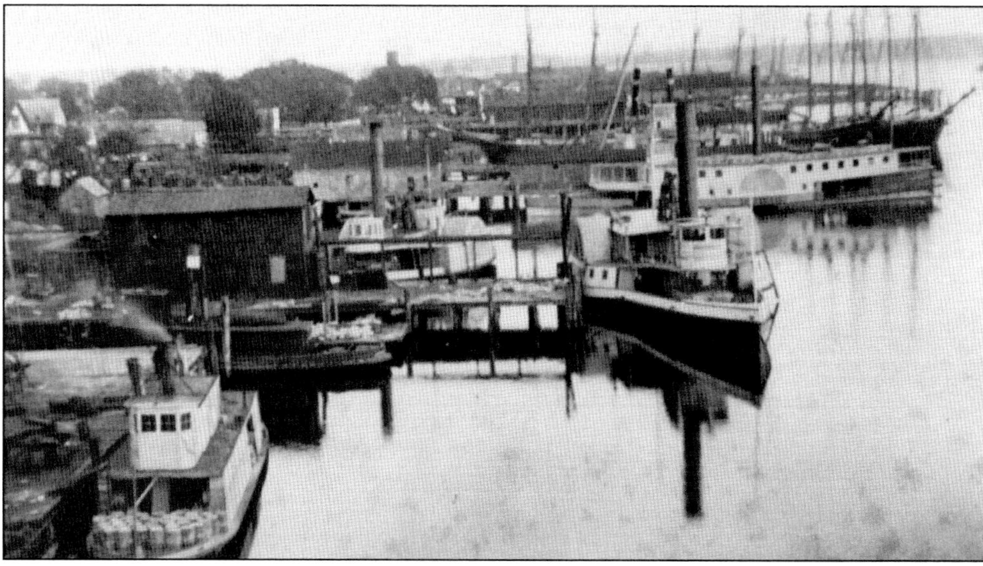

During the second attempt to impeach Reed, Lt. Gov. Samuel Day claimed to be acting governor from February 10 to May 4, 1872. While his impeachment was pending, Reed felt he was disqualified from holding office, so he went to his farm outside Jacksonville, pictured here at the time, to await events. The legislature adjourned without bringing him to trial, and Reed returned to Tallahassee and declared himself governor. Following his term, Reed went back to his farm along the St. Johns River and later served in Florida's House of Representatives as Duval County's representative. (JHS.)

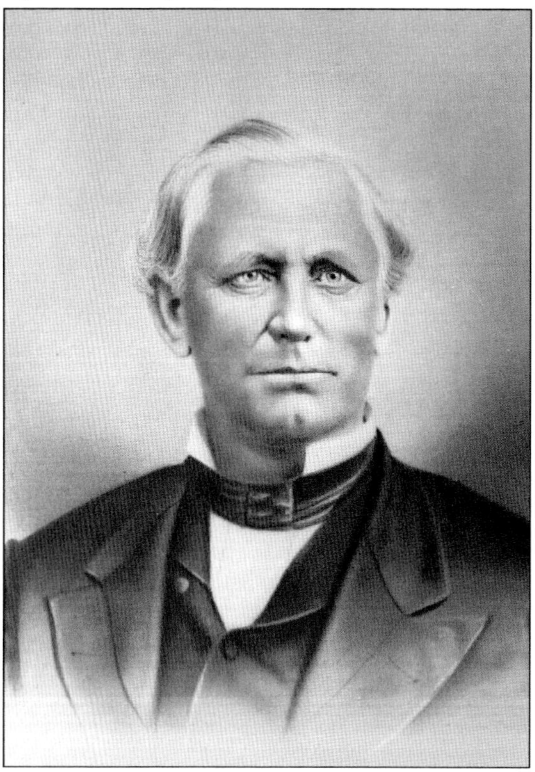

Ossian Bingley Hart was not only the 10th governor of Florida, but he was the first born in the state. A lawyer by profession, Hart was both a founding member of the St. Lucie County Board of Commissioners and a justice of the Florida Supreme Court. A staunch Republican by birth, he was one of the founders of the modern state Republican Party, and he was strongly against secession. (SAF.)

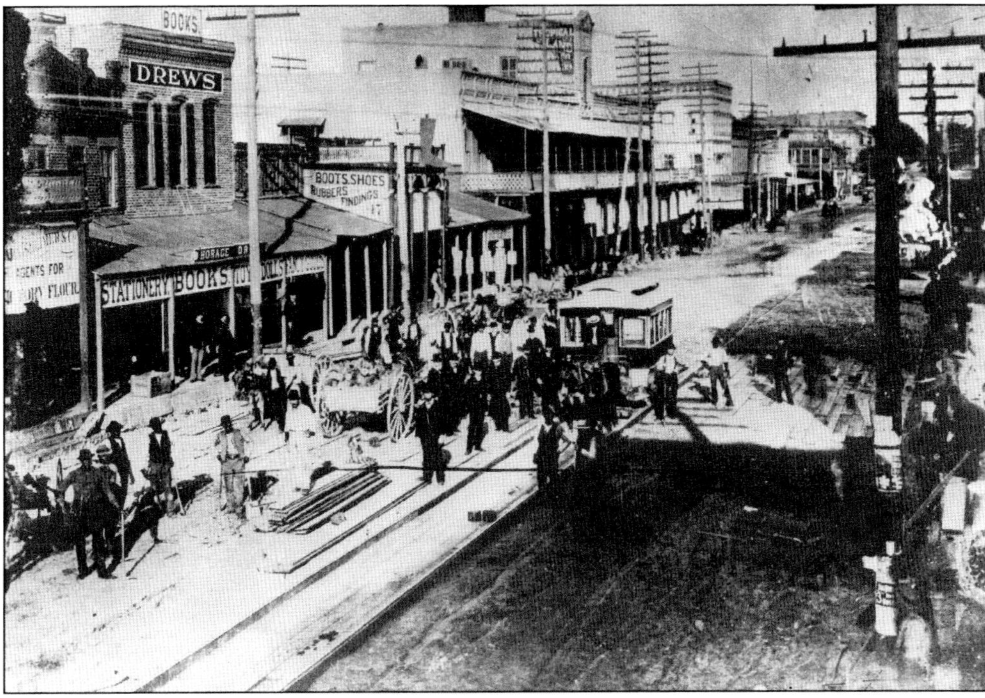

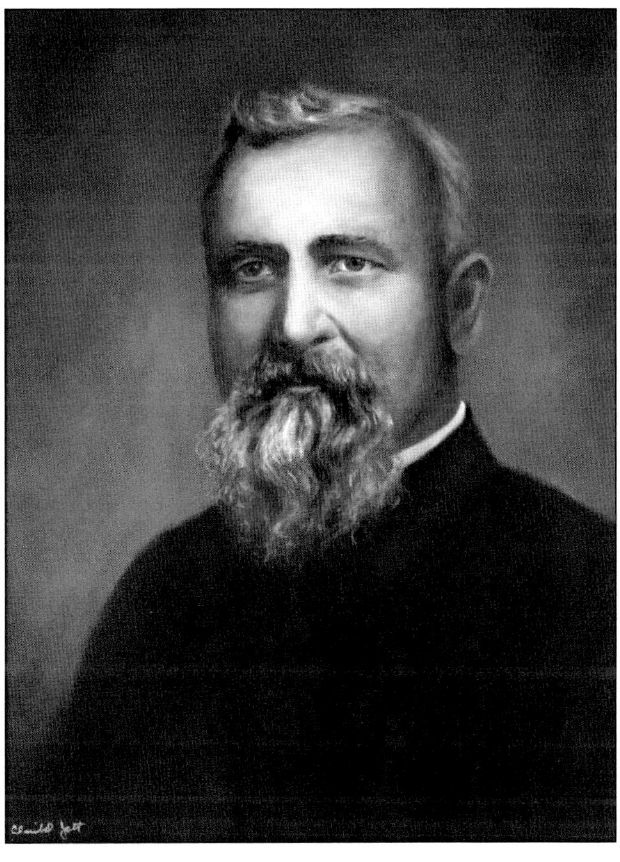

Governor Hart's father, Isaiah Hart, was one of Jacksonville's founders. Ossian was raised on his father's plantation along the St. Johns River. The gubernatorial campaign was tiring business for Hart, who was already in fragile health. By the time of his swearing-in ceremony, he was gravely ill with pneumonia. He spent a majority of his brief time in office at his home in Jacksonville, and it was there that he passed away in March 1874. (JHS.)

Marcellus Lovejoy Stearns was elected the state's fifth lieutenant governor in 1872. He became governor on March 18, 1874, when Gov. Ossian B. Hart died of pneumonia. Prior to his brief and largely dull tenure as lieutenant governor, the one-armed war veteran served as both a member and speaker of the Florida House of Representatives. (MFH.)

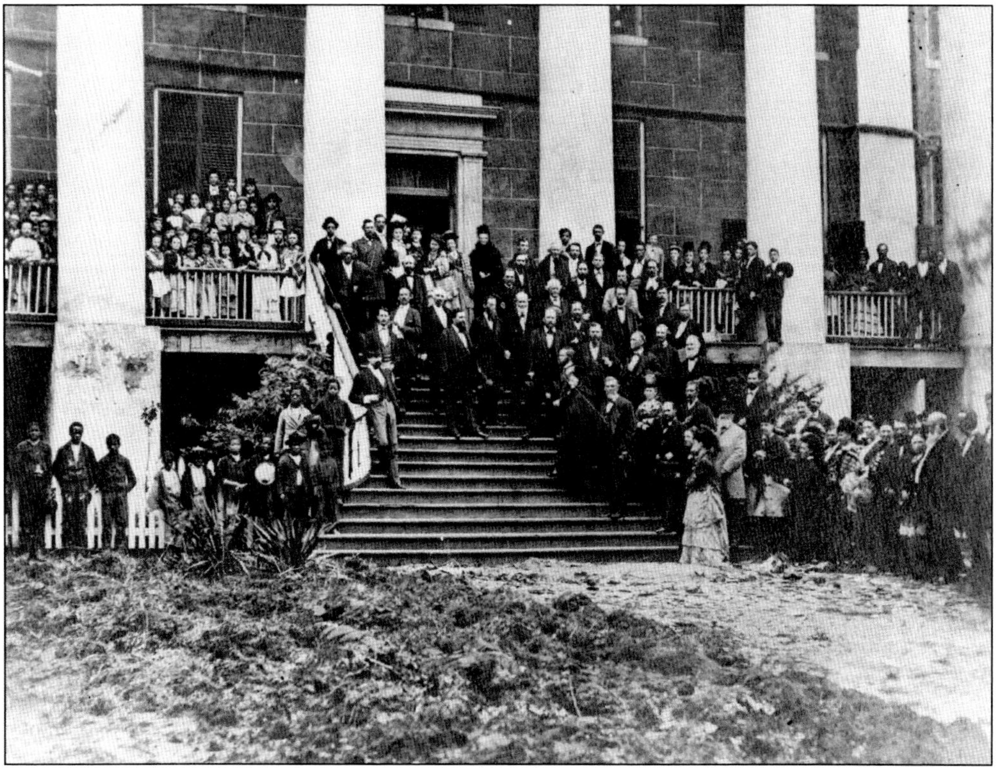

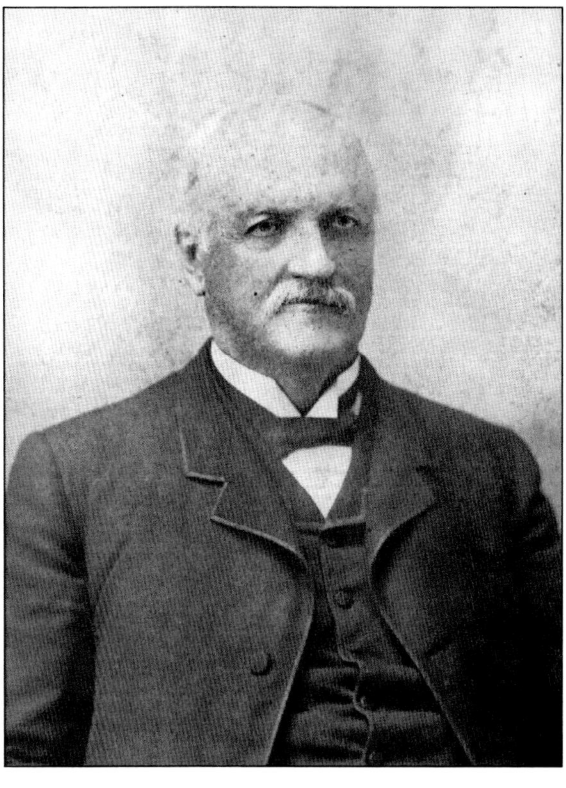

Governor Stearns (center landing, ninth step) poses with members of the legislature outside the capitol. Like the national election in 1876, the contest for governor in Florida was every bit as controversial and potentially dangerous. The state supreme court was ordered to decide the victor in the state's closest gubernatorial election. George Franklin Drew, the Democratic nominee, was certified the winner over Governor Stearns, the Republican nominee, by just 195 votes. (SAF.)

George Franklin Drew would soon be known as the first in a series of Bourbon Democrats. A former Republican, Drew would help restore Democratic dominance in Florida politics. A successful businessman and New York native, he established the state's largest sawmill, known as Ellaville, and in time, he would become a powerful political force in north Florida. (SAF.)

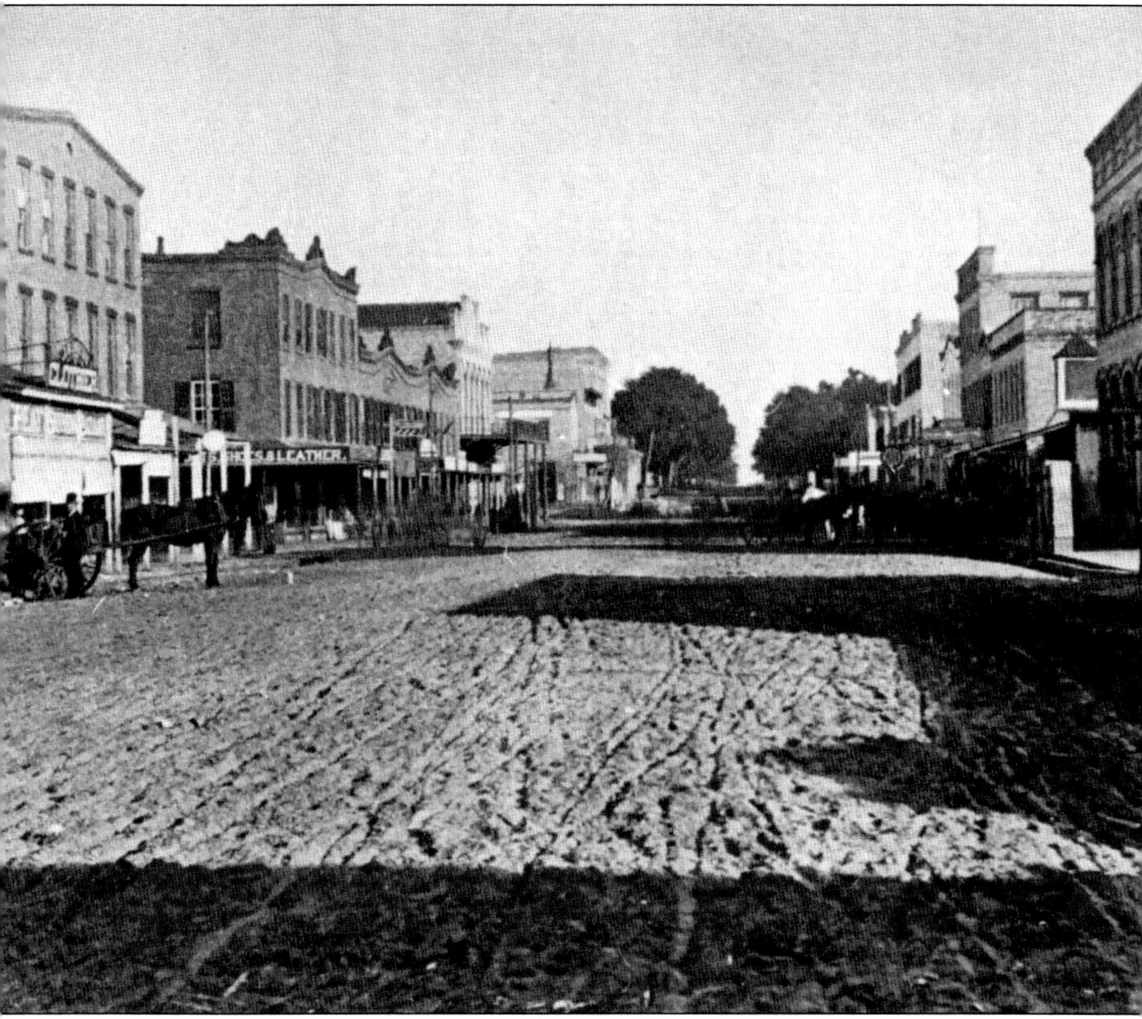

The city of Jacksonville is seen here shortly after George Franklin Drew's election to the governorship. No other city apart from Tallahassee would play a bigger role in Florida politics during the latter part of the 19th century than Jacksonville. It was a stepping-stone for several future governors, and its development was greatly aided by its association with them. (JHS.)

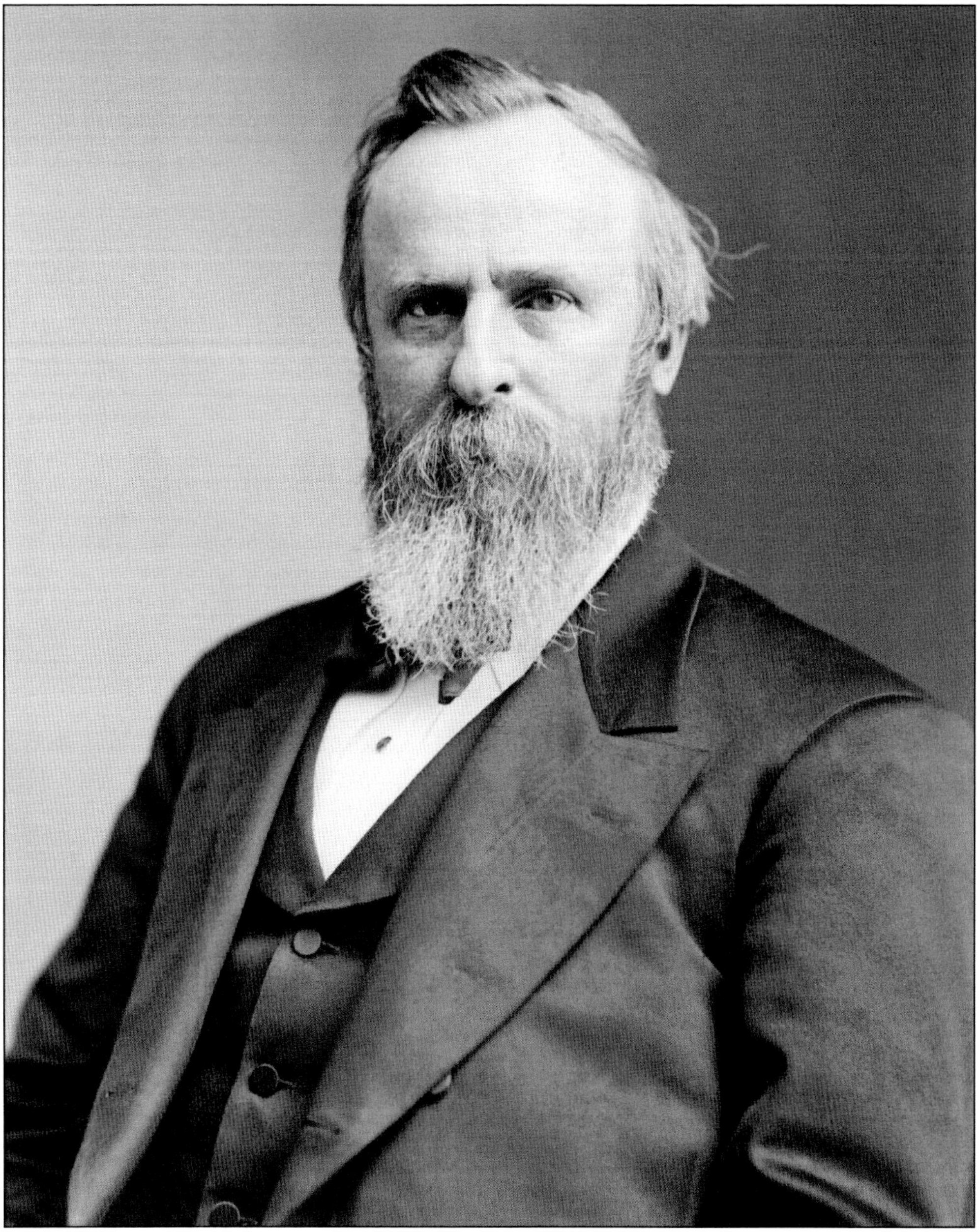

In the election of 1876, the Republican nominee, Rutherford B. Hayes, lost the popular vote on election night to Democrat Samuel Tilden. The electoral college vote was in doubt in Florida, Louisiana, Oregon, and South Carolina. A special election committee was established. After weeks of deliberation, it awarded the election to Hayes. With Democrats openly threatening a second civil war, secret meetings were held between the national chairmen of both parties. A deal was made: the Democrats would accept Hayes as president, and the Republicans would remove federal troops from the South. This incident caused the collapse of Reconstruction and led to 75 years of racial segregation and disfranchisement in the region. Florida's Republican Party overnight became obsolete, and the Northern carpetbaggers, a major political faction in state politics for a decade, quickly returned to the North. (AC.)

Four

One-Party Rule

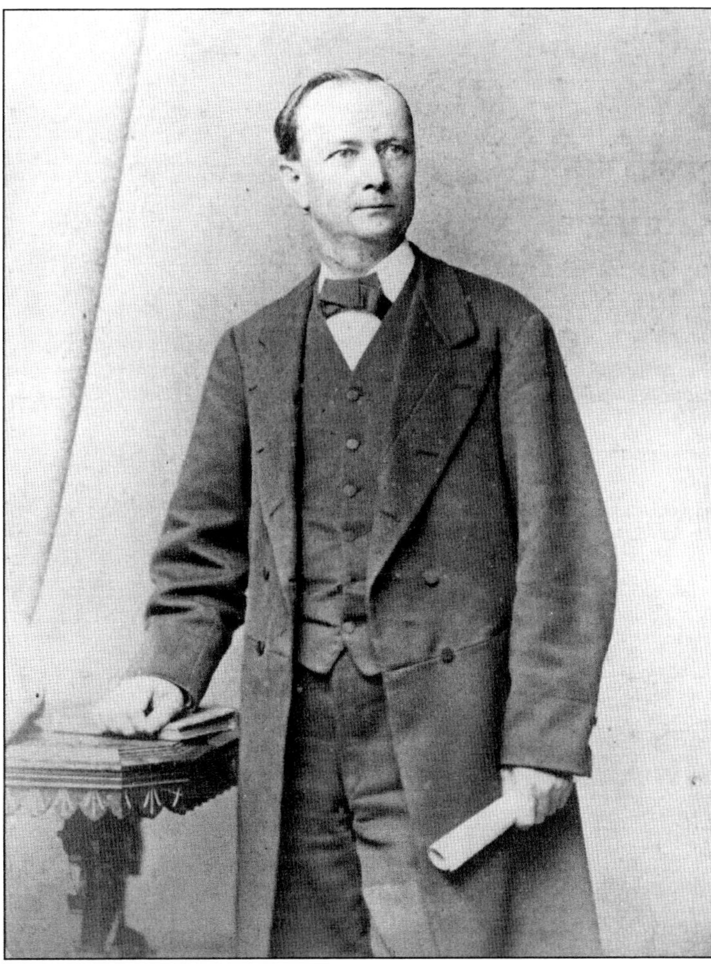

William Dunnington Bloxham was, as of 2015, the only individual elected to two nonconsecutive terms, serving as the state's 13th and 17th governor. One of the most accomplished men ever to win the governorship, he was Governor Drew's secretary of state and the comptroller under Governor Fleming. He was only the second Florida-born governor. In his second term, he became the first governor of the 20th century. (SAF.)

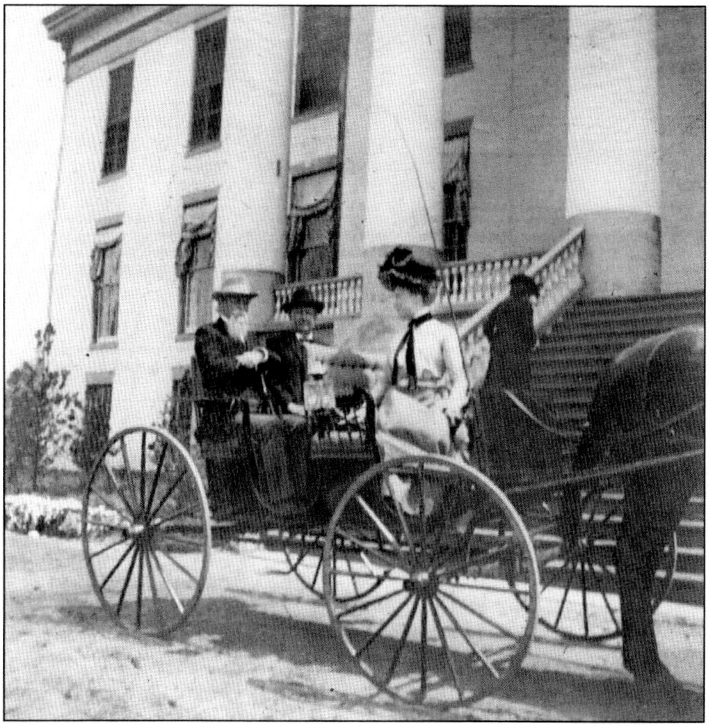

Governor Bloxham (right), seen here in the back seat of his carriage outside the state capitol, was a constant presence in the capital city. From his days as an active supporter of President Buchanan's 1856 campaign, to his state funeral in 1911, Bloxham could usually be found at the capitol. In 1872, Bloxham was defeated by Ossian B. Hart for the governorship. In 1880, he ran again, winning by a sizable margin. (SAF.)

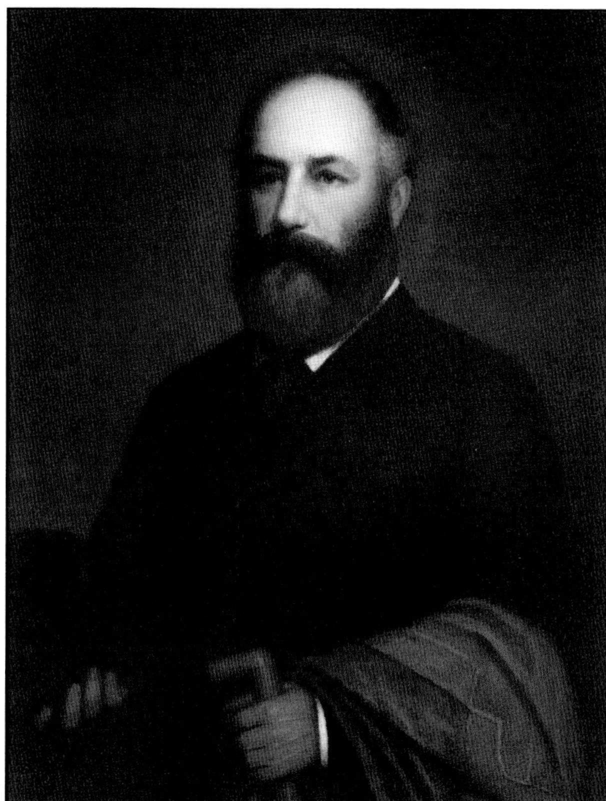

Gov. Edward Perry was a Northern-born lover of the South. Educated at Yale, he would become a local legend in Pensacola and fight with great distinction in the Civil War. Twice wounded in combat, Edward rapidly rose from private to brigadier general. During Perry's administration, Florida adopted a new constitution and established the state board of education to support public schools. (MFH.)

Francis Fleming was a man of conflicting qualities. A friend to Henry Flagler and a member of the Florida Yacht Club, he also was a humble and modest man. Fleming's family immigrated to Florida from Scotland in 1785, receiving land grants from the Spanish government. His paternal grandfather was a friend to Richard Keith Call. Fleming fought valiantly at Gettysburg and the Battle of Natural Bridge. During his term as governor, Fleming established a state board of health, with the goal of containing yellow fever, and he reformed the tax structure. He also began the tradition of having an official portrait painted and hung in the Florida state capitol. His portrait is shown below. At heart, Florida's 15th governor was a historian, doing much to reestablish the Florida Historical Society, becoming its president in 1906. (Both, SAF.)

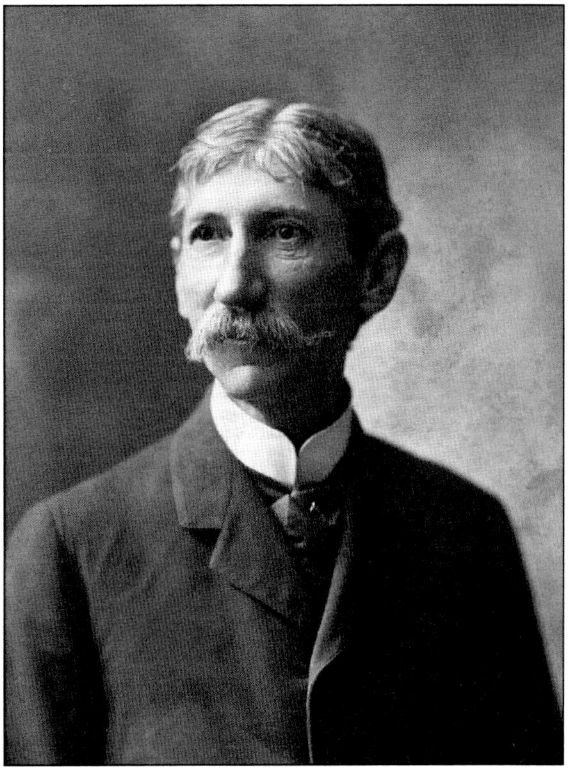

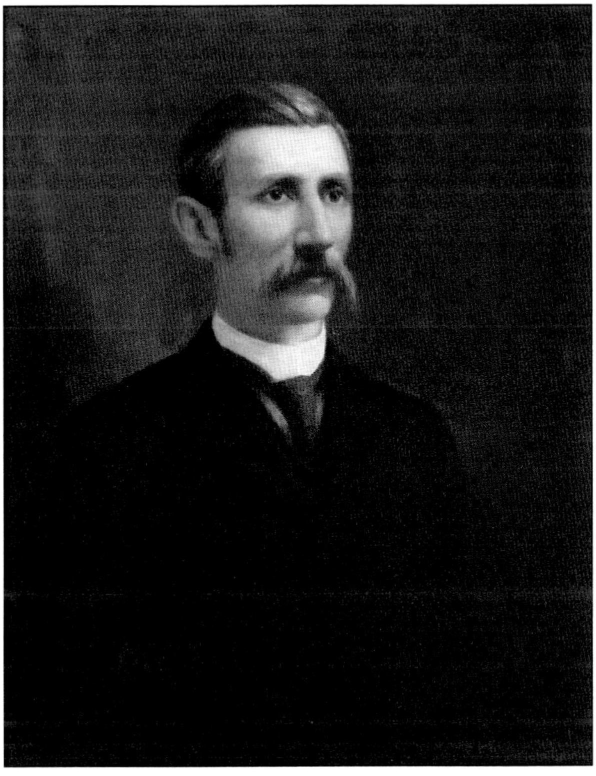

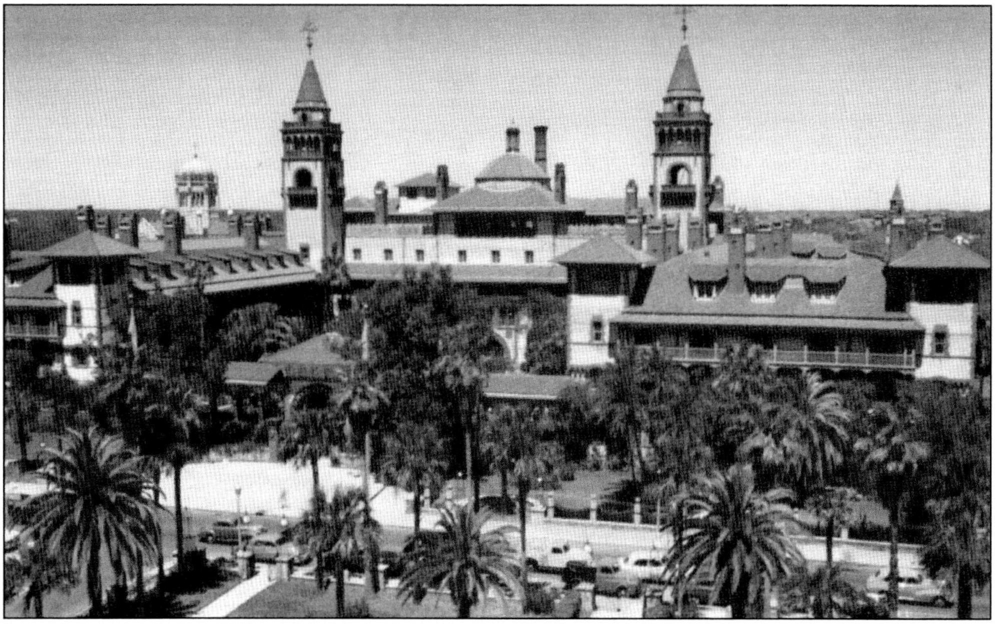

Hotel Ponce De Leon (above) and the Florida East Coast Railway (below) were the Crown Jewels of Henry Flagler's Florida-based empire. Completed in early 1888, it was regarded as the nation's finest hotel. The millionaire developer and Standard Oil founder influenced state lawmaking by a mix of persuasion and aggressive tactics. His good will was greatly sought after, and the shadow of his disappointment could haunt a political career for years. The Tiffany-furnished, Edison-powered structure effectively turned St. Augustine into a tourist hub for the wealthy. Governor Mitchell's political career was permanently weakened when he crossed paths with Henry Flagler, who was wanted in Texas for violations of antitrust laws. Mitchell, a former state supreme court justice, approved the request to transfer Flagler back to Texas. However, when political pressure was placed on Henry Mitchell, he reluctantly changed his mind. (Both, AC.)

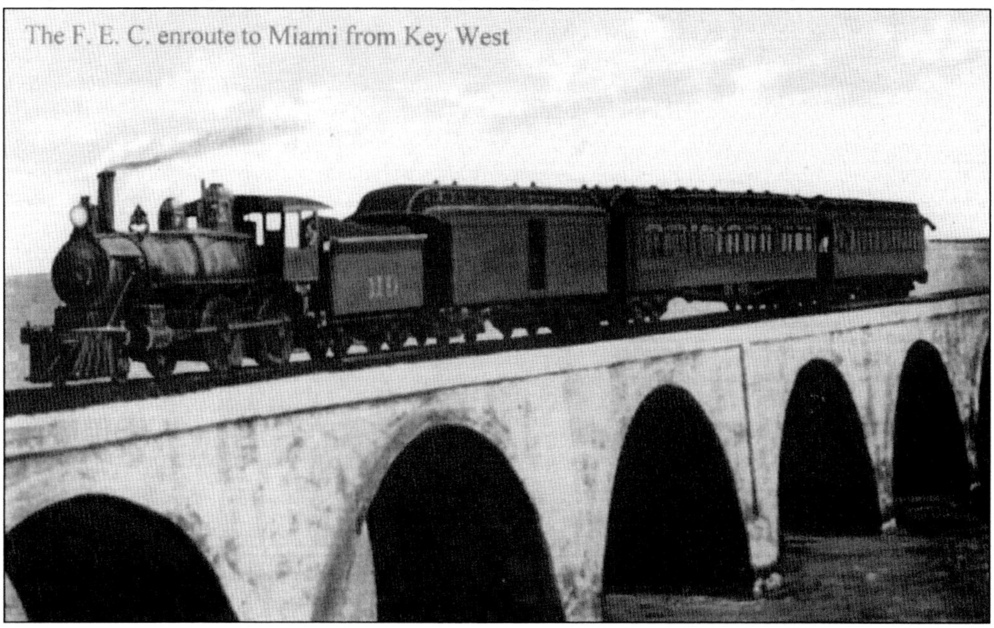

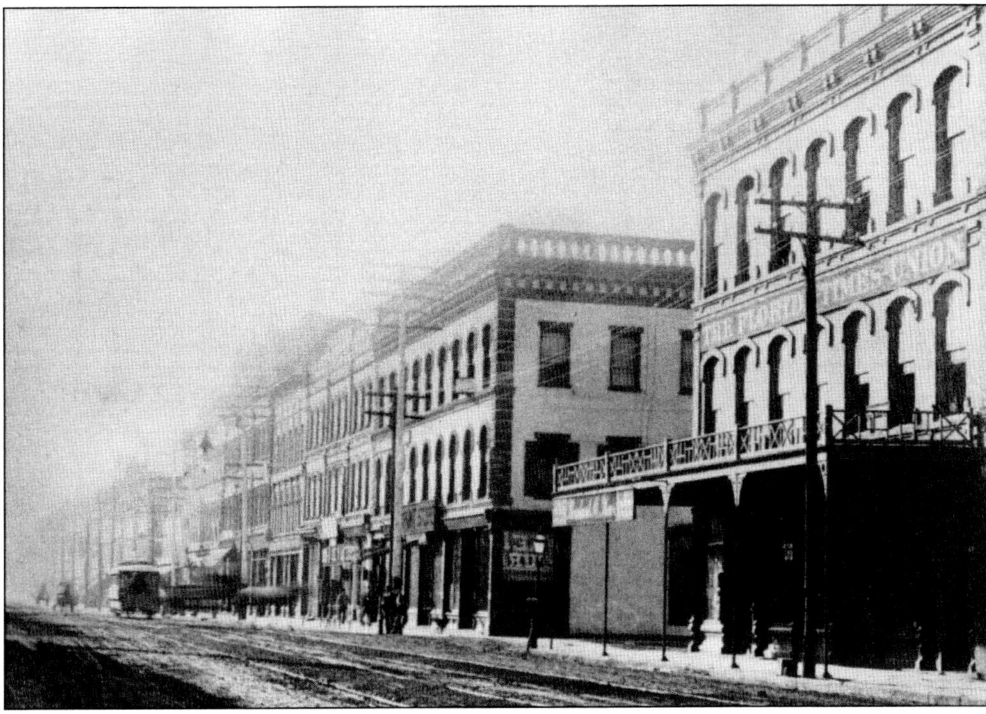

In 1887, future governor Napoleon Broward, then a steamboat pilot on the St. Johns River, was appointed by Governor Perry to replace the county's tragically incompetent sheriff. During Jacksonville's great yellow fever epidemic of 1888, Broward was the only public official who did not leave the city. He opened his office to health officials and effectively ran the city while it was cut off from the rest of the nation. (JHS.)

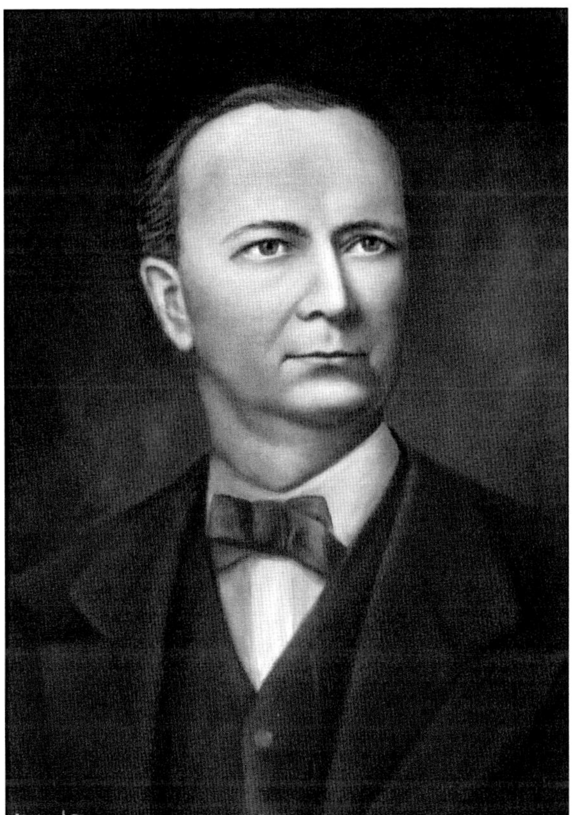

Following the end of his first term as governor, Bloxham declined a presidential appointment to serve as minister to Bolivia. He would, however, accept the post of US Surveyor General before becoming state comptroller. Upon entering the governorship a second time, Bloxham was confronted with the looming outbreak of the Spanish-American War. An active supporter of the conflict, Bloxham relished his position as Florida's wartime governor. (MFH.)

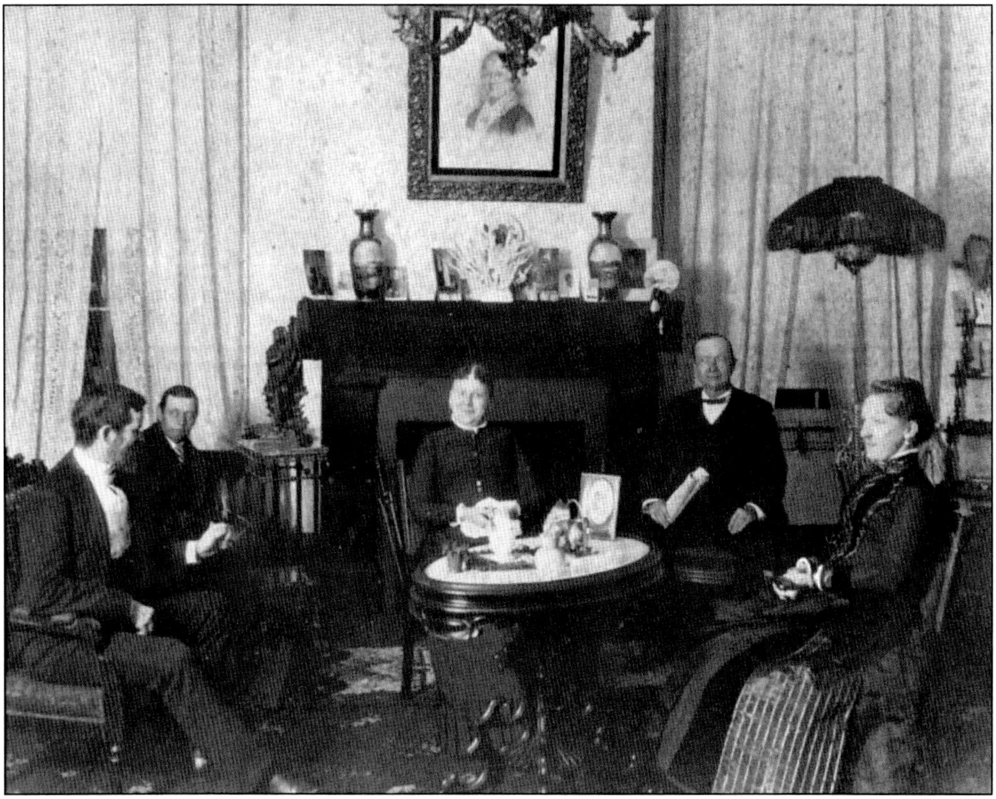

The governor and his family relax in the sitting room of the Bloxham house. During Bloxham's two terms as governor, the state's chief executive was still required to find his own housing. The usual selection of a hotel or boardinghouse as the official residence made state social functions almost impossible to perform. (SAF.)

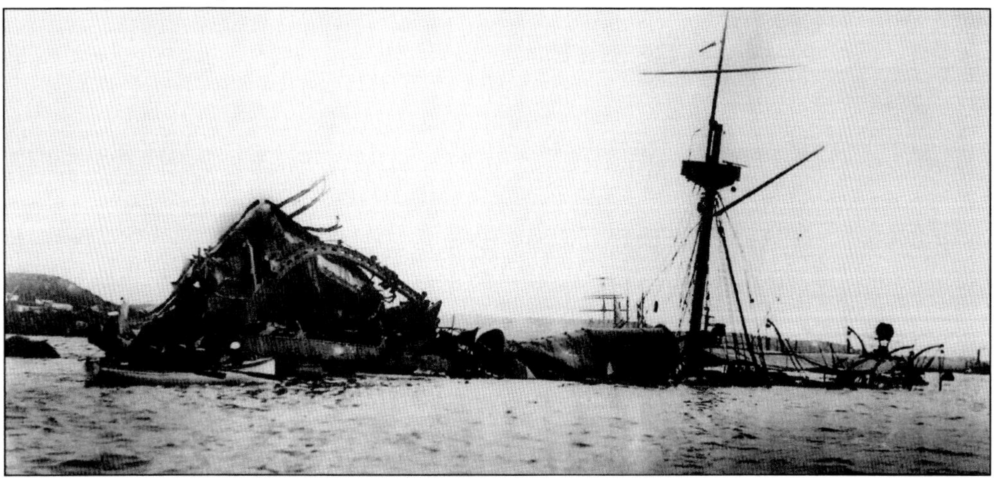

The USS *Maine* lies half-exposed in Havana Harbor. When this member of the legendary Great White Fleet suddenly exploded in 1898, it propelled the United States into war with Spain. Perhaps no other state played more of a role in the conflict than Florida. Invasion forces used Tampa as a base of operations. Several future governors fought valiantly in this much-romanticized struggle. (AC.)

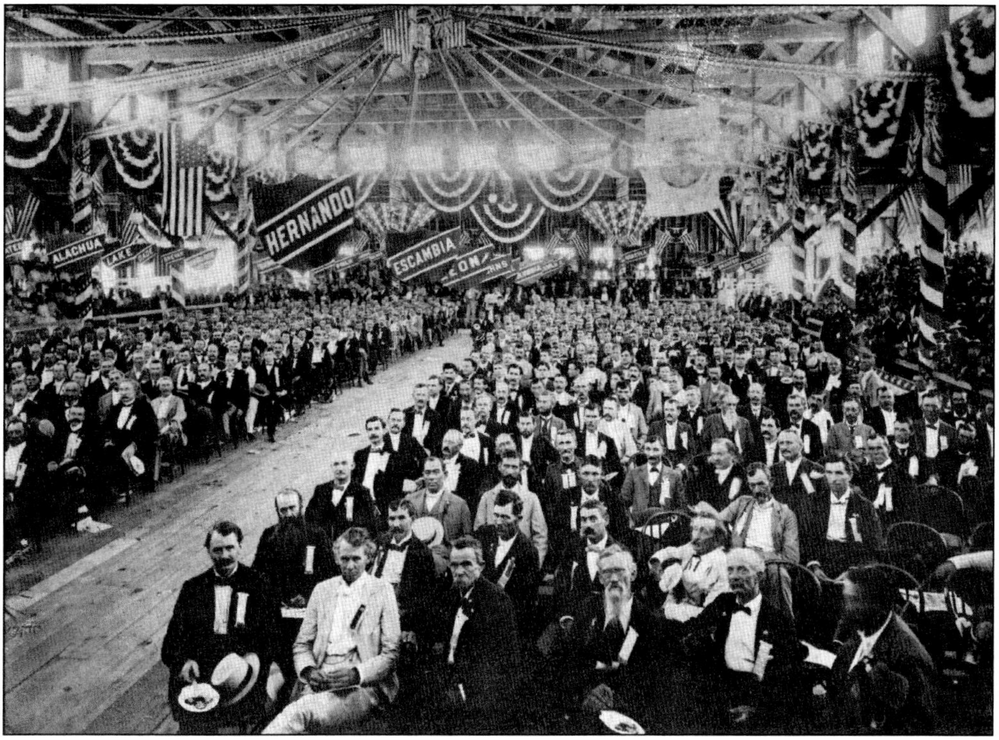

In the first row, from left to right, soon-to-be governor-elect William Jennings, Sen. Patrick Houston, George Saxon, Raymond Cay, Gov. W.D. Bloxham, and Clay Crawford await the final ballot results in the last statewide convention of the Florida Democratic party. From the end of Reconstruction until the 1920s, there was virtually no Republican presence in the state. Between 1889 and 1901, Democratic statewide candidates were nominated during these conventions. (SAF.)

Governor Jennings (second from the left) and his cabinet are pictured outside the new capitol building. They were the first elected officials to occupy the newly enlarged structure. The governor's office now included a public suite and offices for his secretary and stenographer. State Comptroller Croom had the largest staff in the building, with eight clerks, a bookkeeper, and a stenographer. (SAF.)

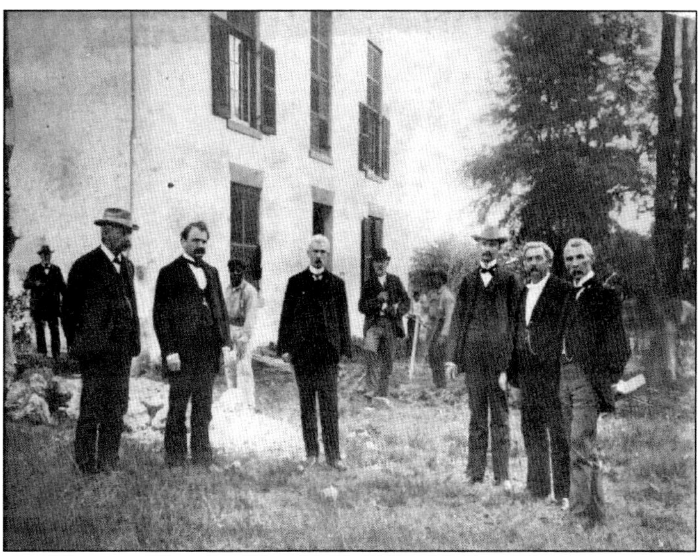

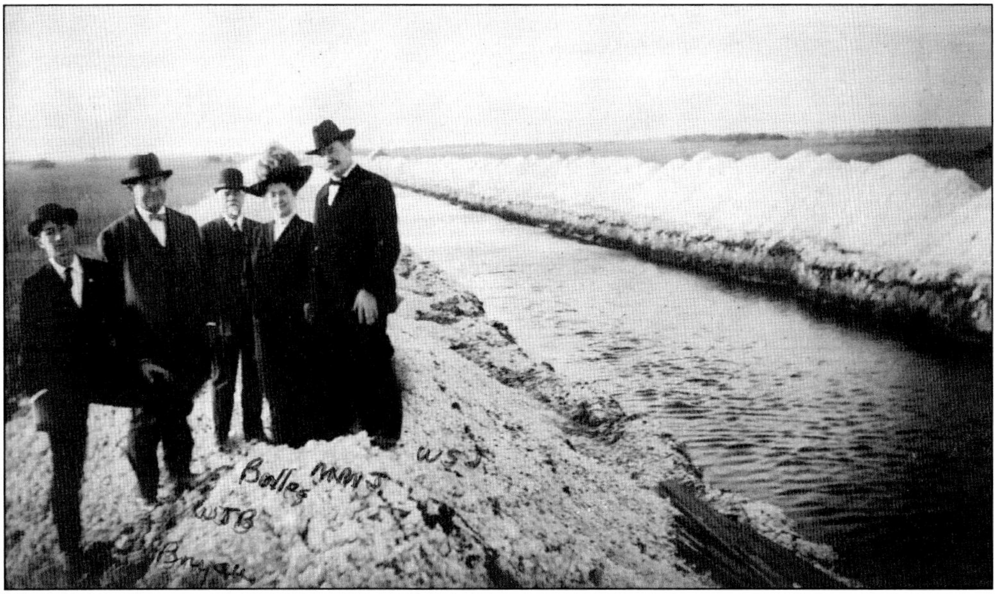

William S. Jennings (identified far right) observes the Everglades drainage with a small group that includes his first cousin William Jennings Bryan (identified second from left), a congressman and a Democratic presidential nominee. In December 1902, Governor Jennings was nearly assassinated by an escaped inmate of the Georgia insane asylum. A Mr. Dickinson, the governor's private secretary and a member of the Florida cabinet, threw the man on the floor after he pulled a pistol on the governor. (SAF.)

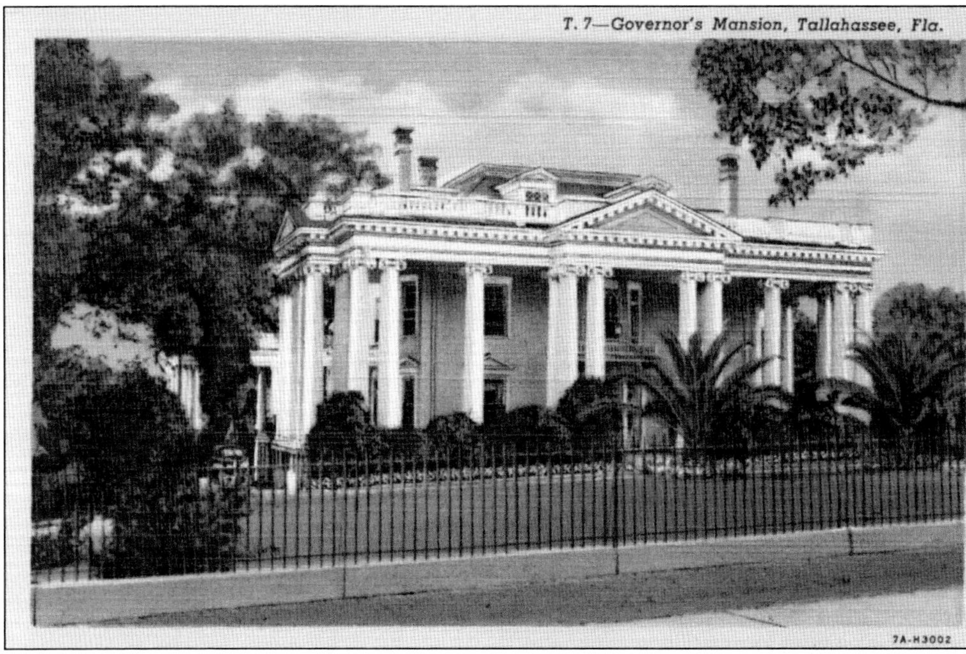

Napoleon Bonaparte Broward was known as the fighting governor of Florida and the state's version of Teddy Roosevelt. In 1907, Broward and his large family were the first residents of the new executive mansion. The Browards had spent the first few years of the governor's term living in a converted church, the only structure big enough to accommodate them. (AC.)

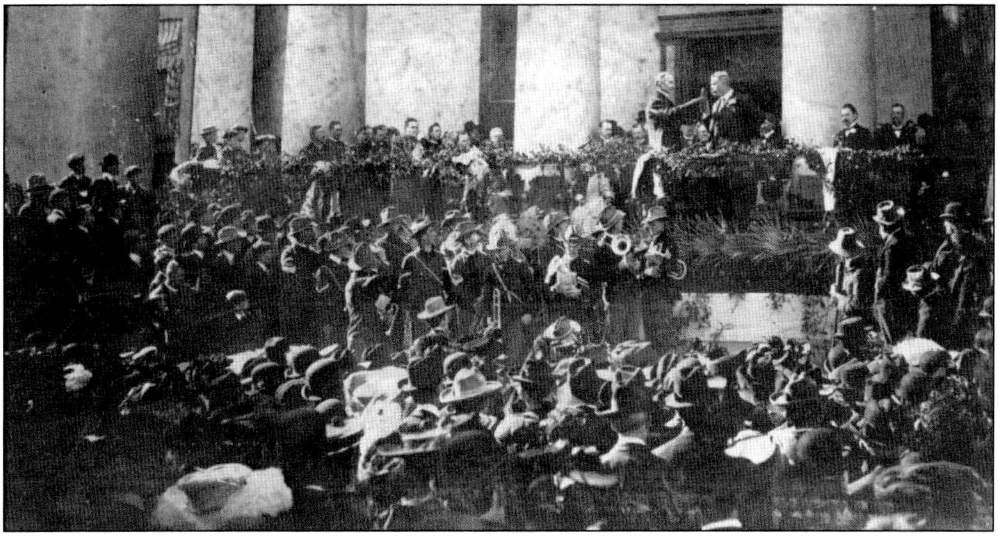

Napoleon Bonaparte Broward takes the oath of office on the state's historic capitol's west portico. During Broward's single term, Florida would experience and benefit from a wealth of progressive legislation, the drainage of nearly 17 million acres of Everglades lands, the ending of child labor, speed limits for automobiles, and a pure-food law. His administration was also an active champion of both education and mental health. (SAF.)

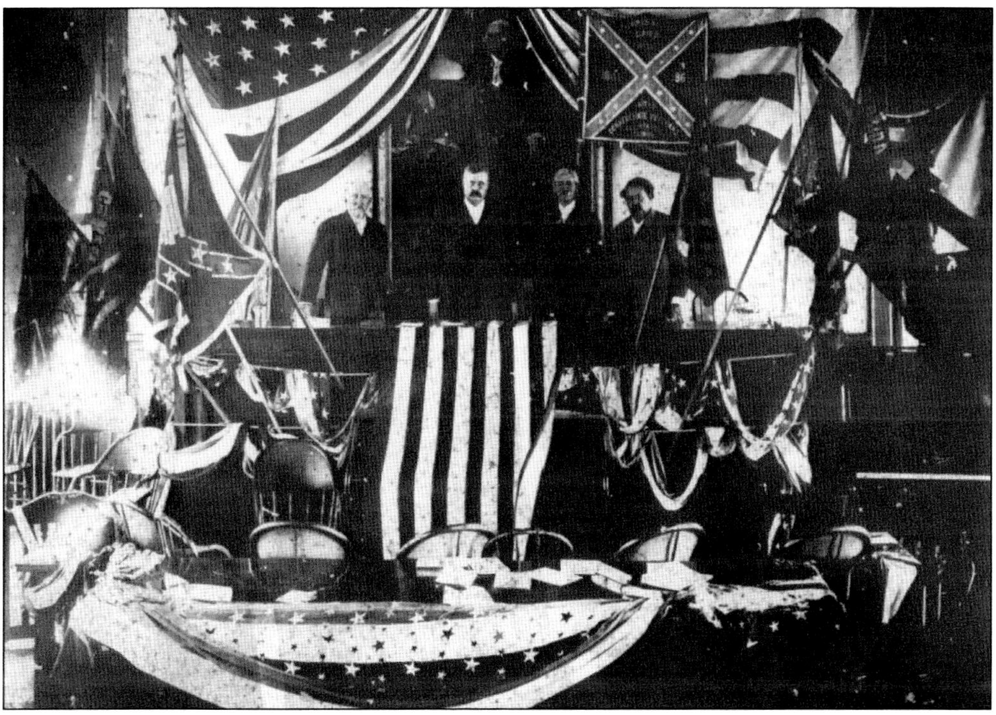

Broward won the governorship in 1904, and his single term in that office became known as the Broward Era. His platform was progressive in its desires to preserve public lands and regulate the railroads, while a bit conservative in his championing the drainage of the Everglades. During Broward's brief and meaningful life, Florida would benefit from his great example and furious loyalty. (JHS.)

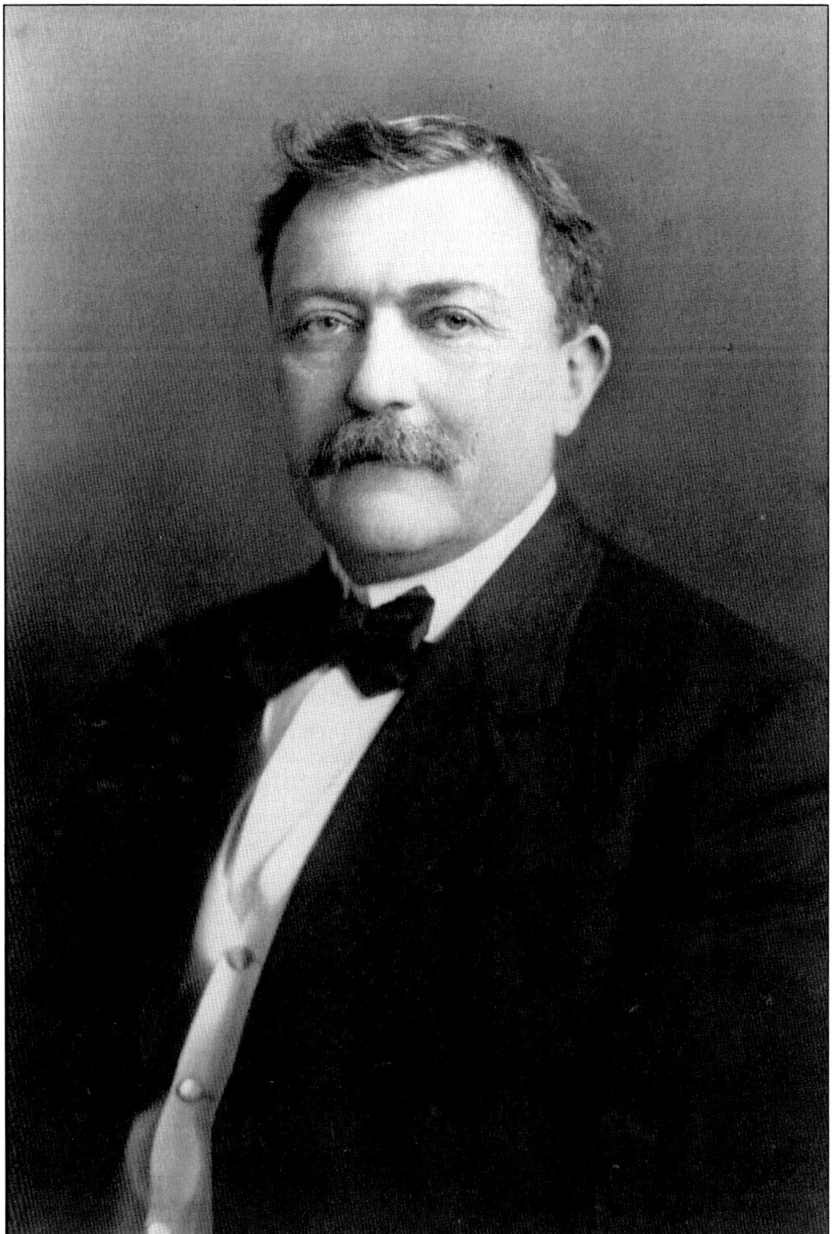

On a cold, wet day in 1909, the house chamber served as the location for the oath taking of Albert Gilchrist. The crowded location was called into service after the original site was soaked to the brim by a heavy rain. Florida's good-natured bachelor governor-elect would have been content taking the oath on the roof of a moving train, so evident was his enthusiasm. A native of South Carolina, he was a descendent of both George Washington and James Madison. In time, Gilchrist would be a civil engineer, orange grower, real-estate dealer, and brigadier general of the Florida militia. He would resign from that military position in 1898 to enlist as a private in the US volunteer infantry and serve in Cuba during the Spanish-American War. Like Napoleon Bonaparte Broward and Teddy Roosevelt, this conflict would be the key event in his life, propelling him to political, financial, and personal triumphs. (SAF.)

Repeatedly elected to the Florida House, Gilchrist served as that body's speaker in 1905 while secretly planning a race for the governorship. Gilchrist traveled extensively across the South as both speaker and governor, promoting the Sunshine State. Although he personally detested the executive mansion, he did reluctantly live there during legislative sessions. (Michael Croom.)

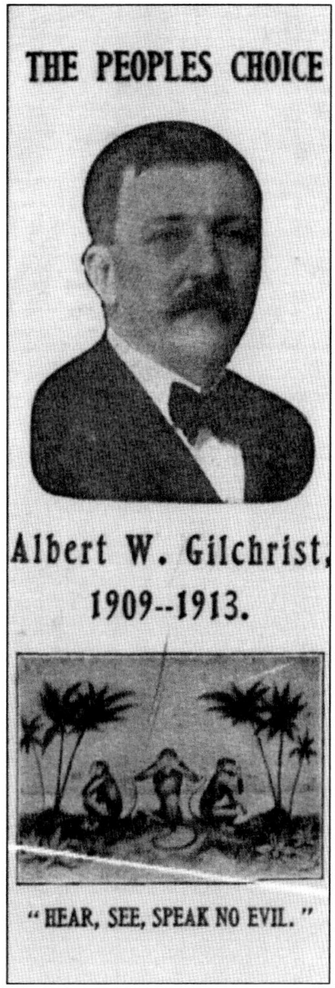

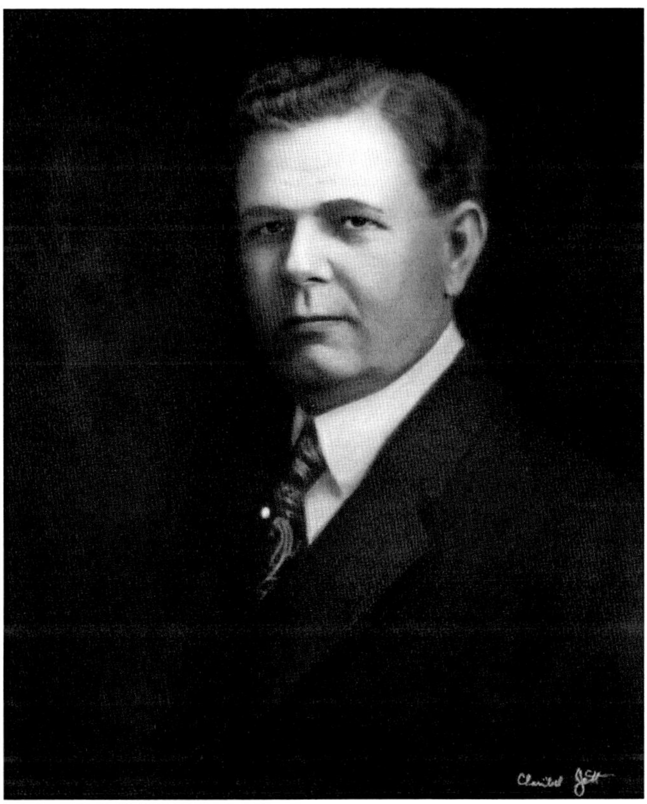

In his short life of just 60 years, Park Trammell held nearly every elected office possible in the state of Florida. The state's 21st governor had also served as mayor of Lakeland, member of the Florida House of Representatives, state senator for Polk County and senate president, Florida attorney general, and after his term as governor, a US senator until his death in 1936. (MFH.)

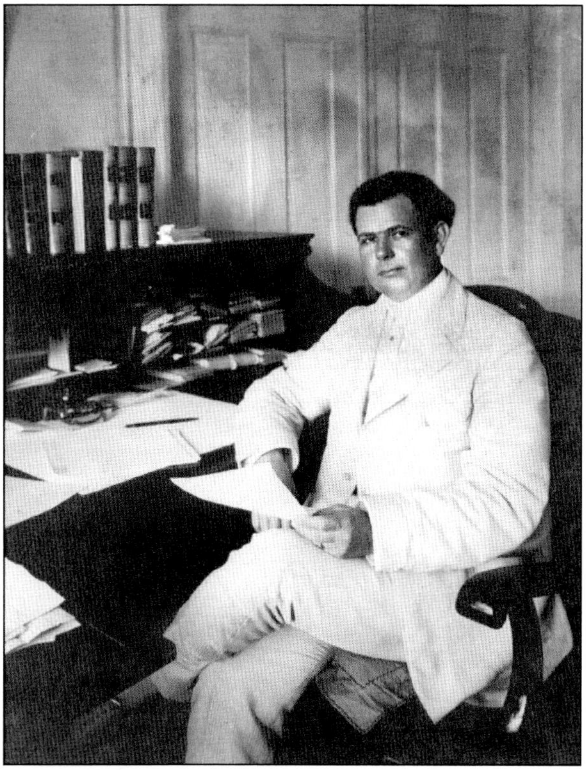

Governor Trammell pauses for a photograph in his office at the old capitol. During his term, Trammell proved to be an industrious yet hardly courageous leader. He advocated a state tax commission and endorsed legislation to manage money used during elections. He oversaw the creation of a labor commission and stricter statutes on railroads. Yet, these progressive reforms have usually been overshadowed by his support of racial segregation. (SAF.)

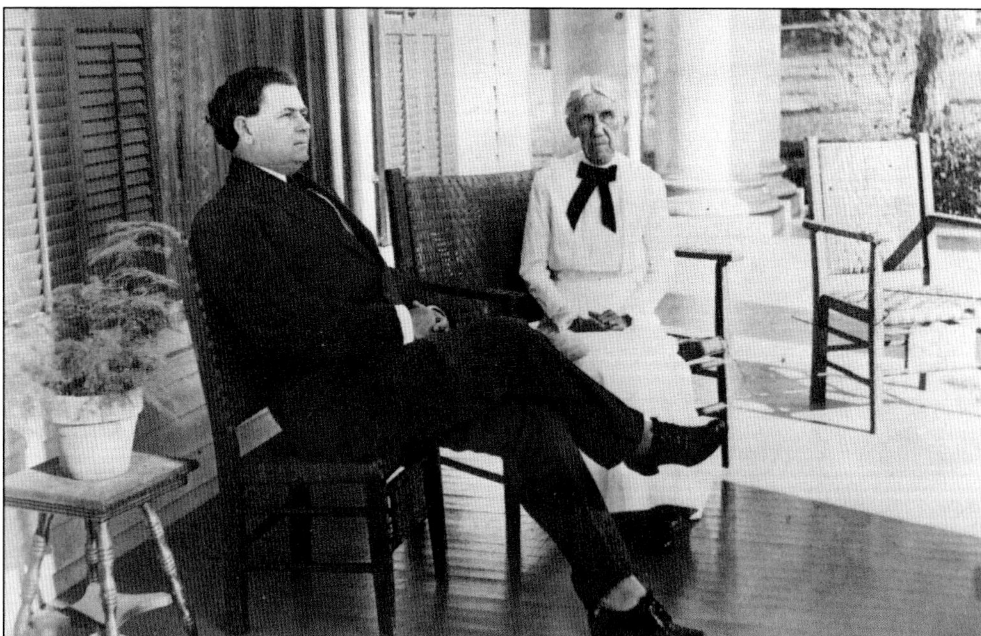

Family would prove to be an important influence on Governor Trammell. Elected at only 36, he would frequently be visited by his mother and grandmother. This photograph of the governor sitting on the front porch of the mansion was later used as a campaign advertisement when he ran for the senate. (SAF.)

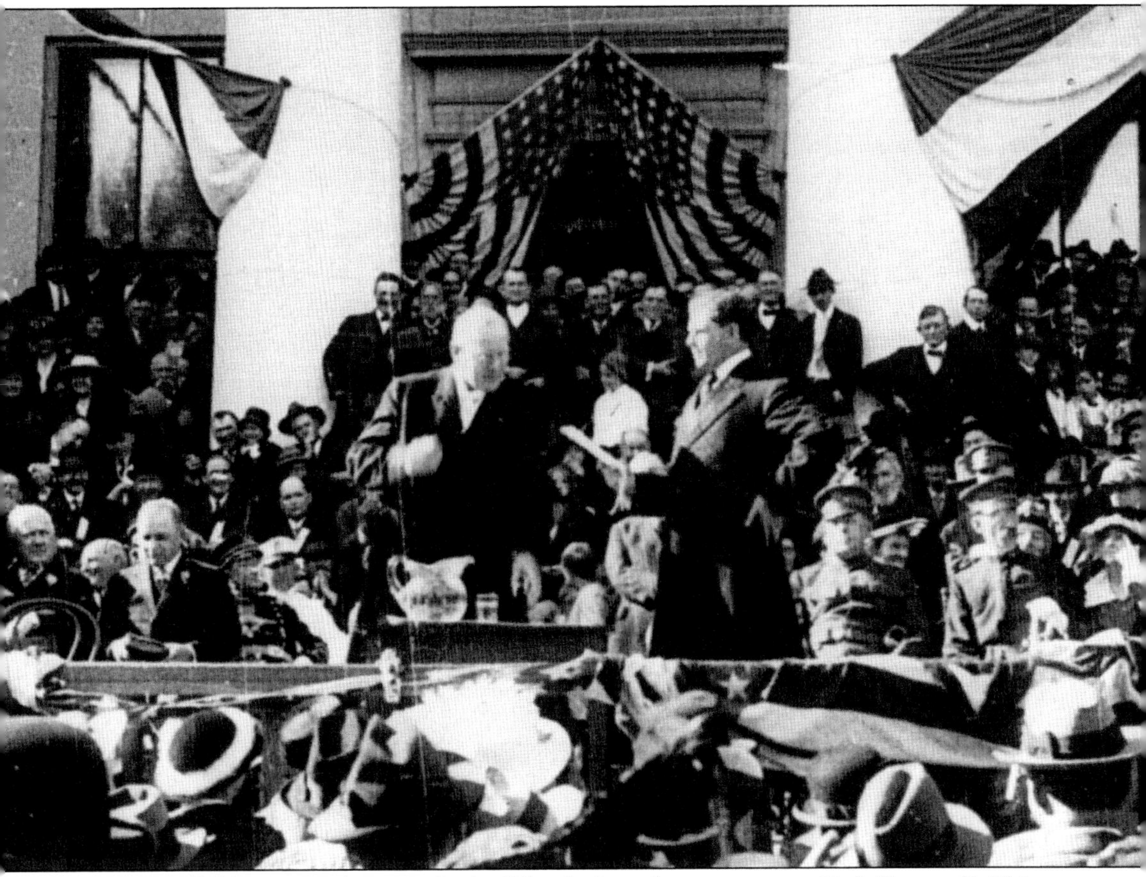

Sidney Catts (left) receives the great Seal of Florida from former governor Park Trammell. This was the first inauguration recorded on film, and Catts, a former pastor, made sure that it was an eventful ceremony. His inaugural address laid out an agenda that was both anti-Catholic and prejudiced, claiming that Pope Benedict XV was secretly trying to take over Florida. The state's sole Prohibition Party governor had originally run for the Democratic nomination in 1916. Catts won the nomination, but, following a mandated recount, it was revealed that he finished second. After that, he received the nomination of the Prohibition Party and won the three-party general race with only 43 percent of the popular vote. Though he ran as a radical, once in office, he proved to be a typical member of the spoils system. He appointed members of his family to important positions and governed as a traditional chief executive. (SAF.)

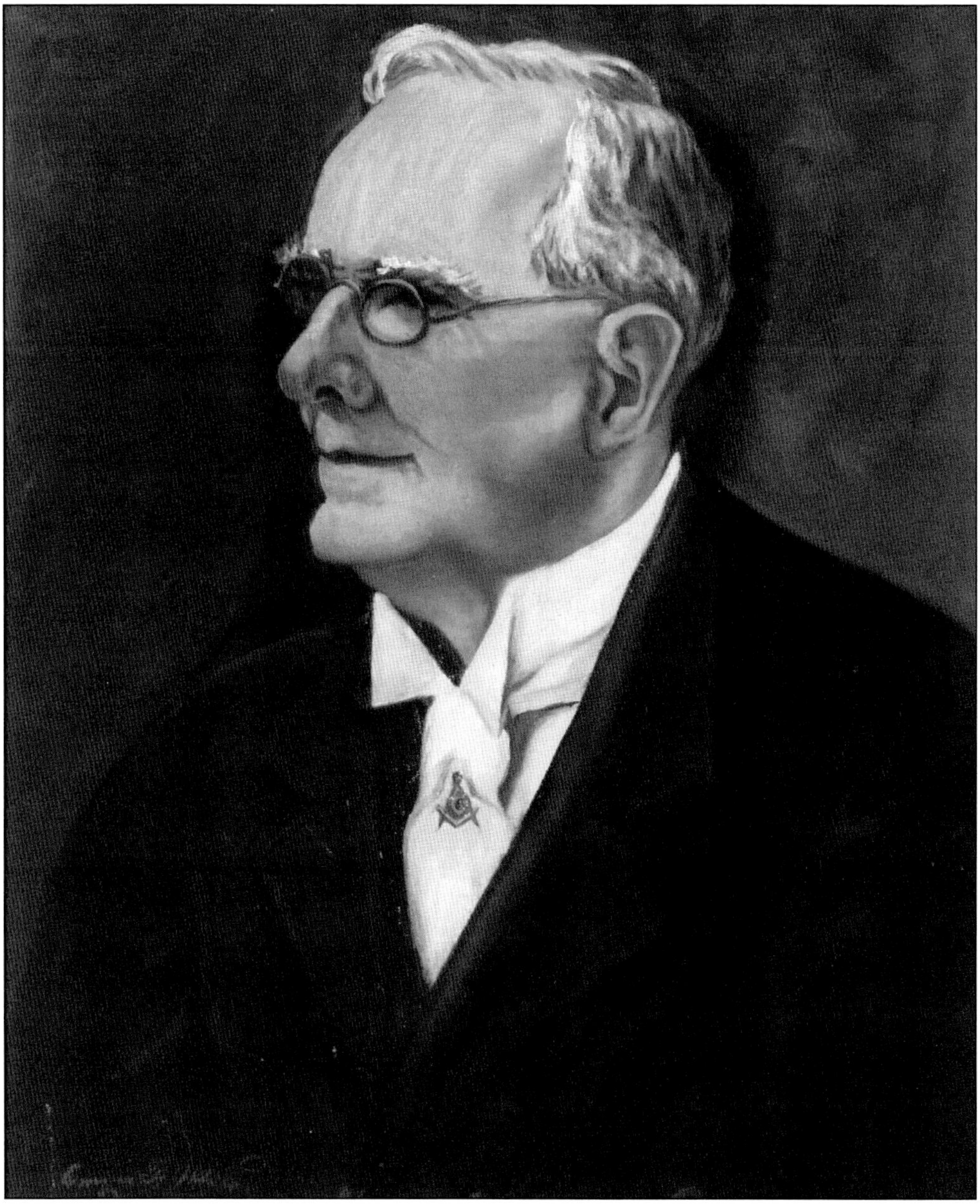

Legend has it that what sparked Catts's interest in the governorship was his discovery that, once elected, the governor can live in the executive mansion rent-free. His campaign was historic for its use of both an automobile and a loudspeaker, which he used to travel extensively to rural areas. It was in this race that a form of campaigning now referred to as "barnstorming" was born. Catts's major opponent in the Democratic primary was state comptroller William Knotts, who, following his close primary defeat, contested it in court. Knowing that the courts would back Knotts against him, Catts took to the roads in his Model T. Turning the race into a populist revolt against the corrupt establishment of state government, he actively courted and received support of the state Prohibition Party, which quickly nominated him. Despite losing the Democratic nomination, he beat Knotts in a landslide. The new governor did not attend his own inaugural ball, over fears that the punch would be spiked. (MFH.)

Five

LAND BOOM AND BUST

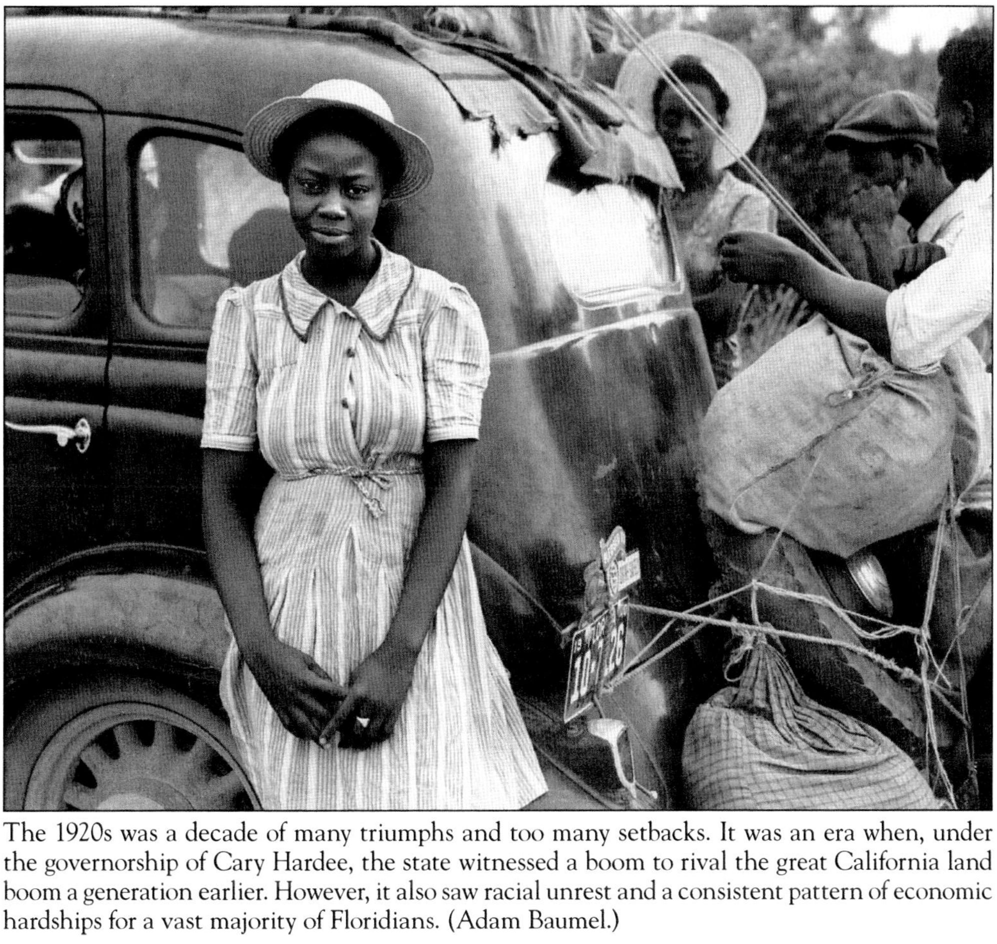

The 1920s was a decade of many triumphs and too many setbacks. It was an era when, under the governorship of Cary Hardee, the state witnessed a boom to rival the great California land boom a generation earlier. However, it also saw racial unrest and a consistent pattern of economic hardships for a vast majority of Floridians. (Adam Baumel.)

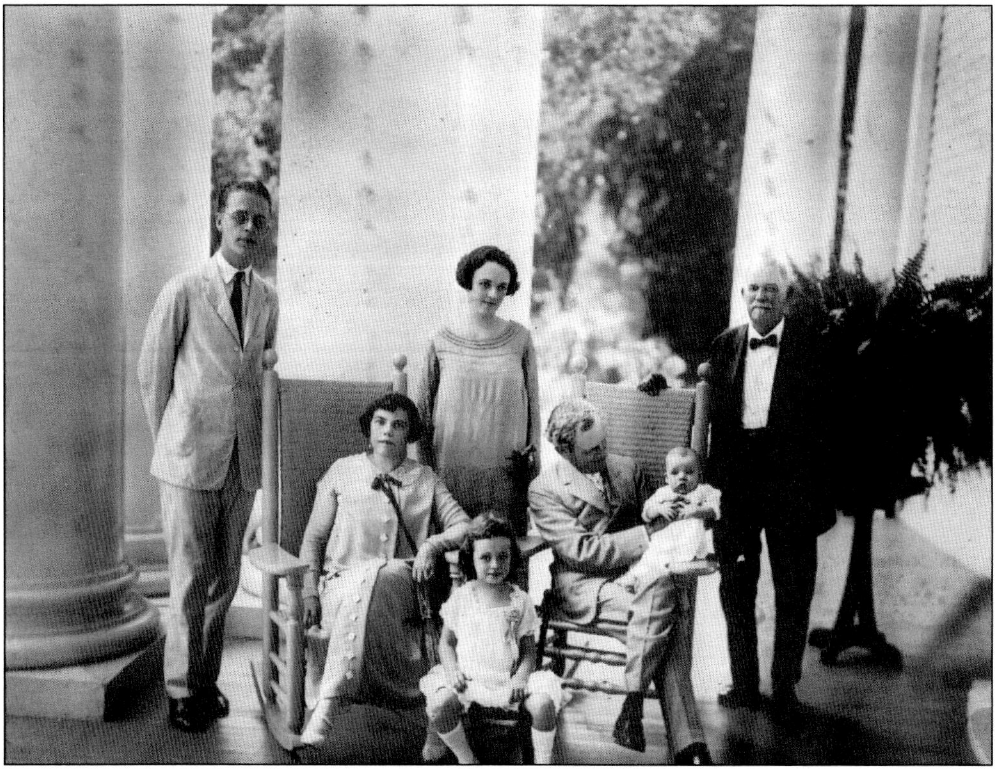

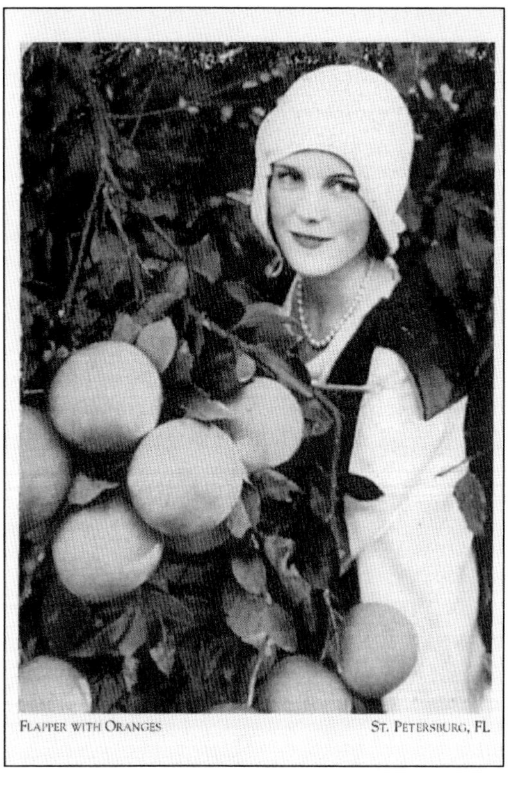

Gov. Cary A. Hardee and his family pose on the executive mansion porch. Cary Augustus Hardee, the fourth of ten children, was born just outside of Perry, Florida. A rural schoolmaster in his youth, he studied for the bar by night, eventually becoming a widely successful attorney. In 1902, he was a founding partner of the First National Bank of Live Oak, and in 1907, he was named its president. He later served as president of the State Bank of Branford. While serving as Florida's 23rd governor, Hardee simultaneously remained president of the national bank. (SAF.)

The early 1920s was an exciting period in the state's history. Not only did national trends of the Jazz Age make their way to Florida, a skillfully created publicity campaign made Miami Beach seem like paradise on Earth. Soon, images of Florida could be seen on billboards in New York's Times Square. Outside money poured into the state for land development, and property prices rose swiftly. (Adam Baumel.)

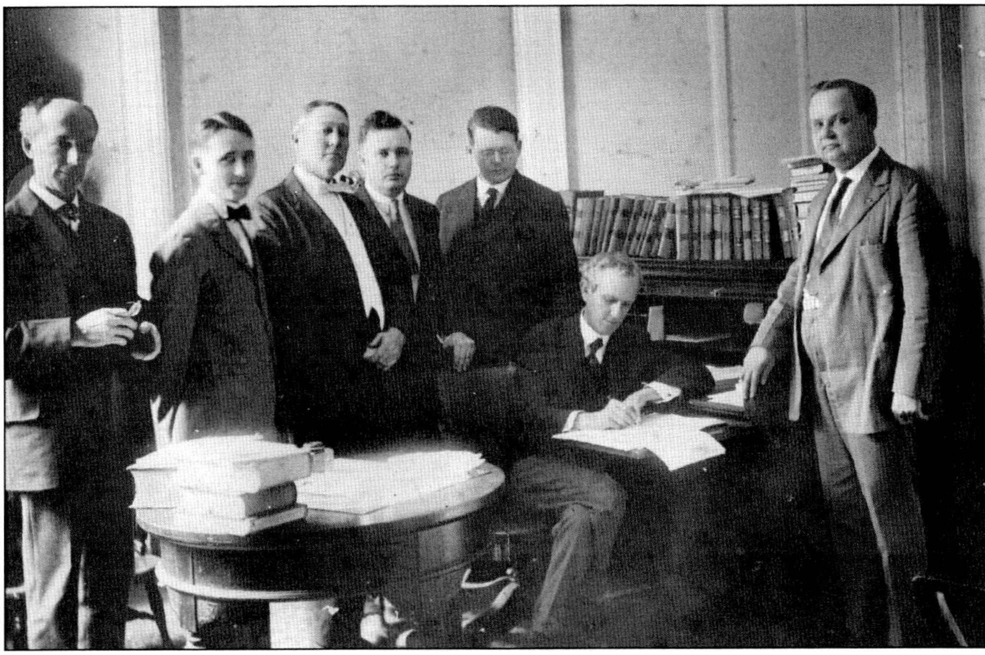

The chief accomplishments of Hardee's tenure were the eradication of cattle ticks in rural Florida, a prohibition on state income and inheritance taxes, and a constitutional amendment reapportioning the legislature. The state also created nine new counties, including Hardee County. Here, Governor Hardee signs the county act into law. (SAF.)

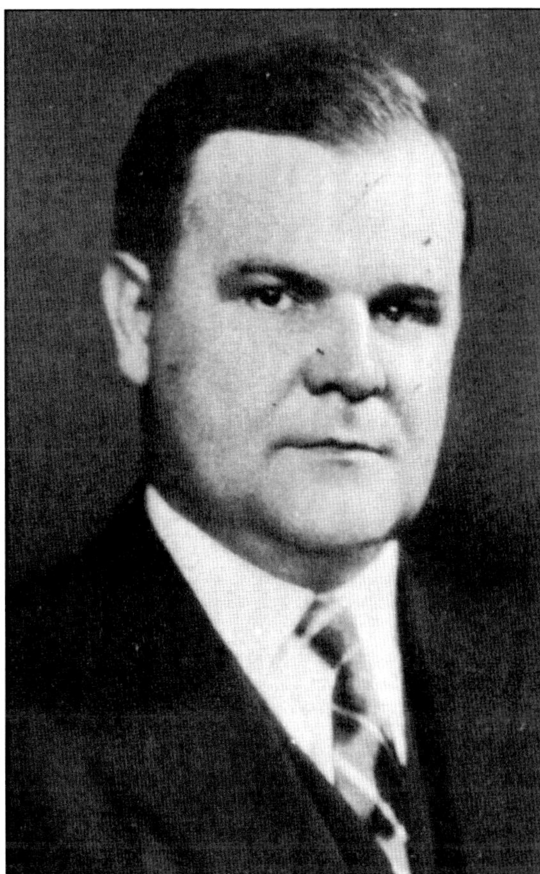

At a young age, John Martin seemed destined for great things. His determination and drive served him well throughout his life. Yet, events would overwhelm him once he reached the governorship. Economic development in Florida went bust, and a severe hurricane left thousands dead in south Florida. However, the progressive initiatives Martin enacted helped see Florida through this unprecedented rough patch. (JHS.)

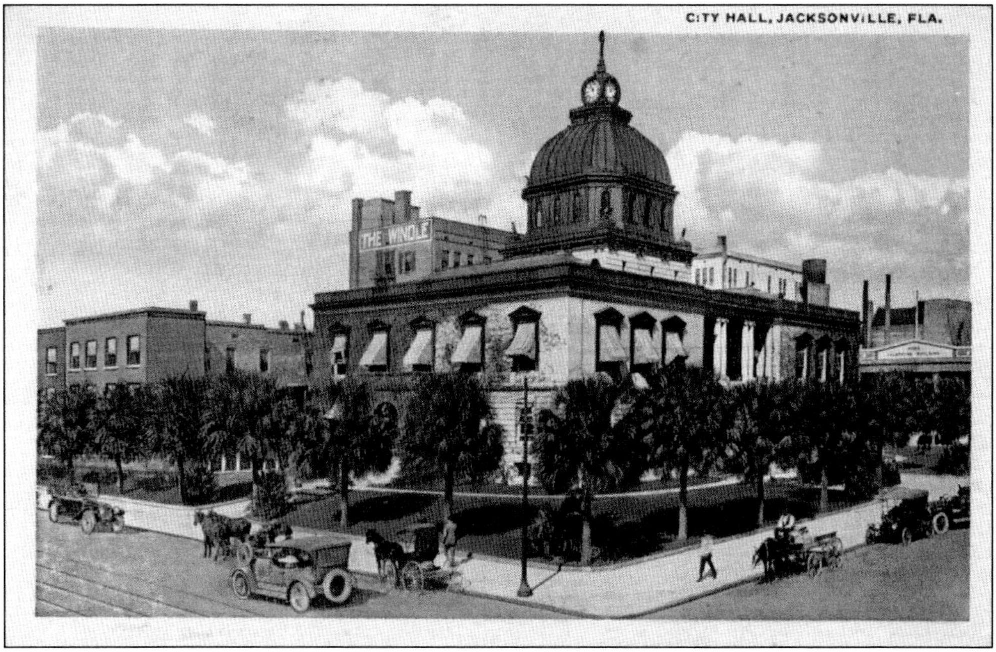

This postcard shows Jacksonville's old city hall building in 1918, when John Martin served as mayor. He served as Jacksonville's 32nd mayor from 1917 to 1923. While the city had yet to develop the office into a separate executive branch with governing power over the city council, Mayor Martin was still a dominant force in the booming metropolis. (AC.)

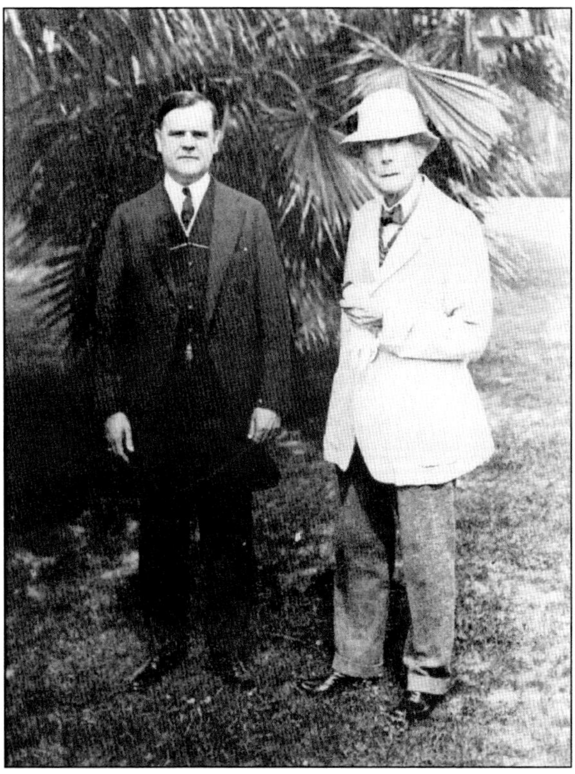

John Martin (left) poses with legendary oilman and Florida resident John D. Rockefeller. Martin, a great supporter of big business, did much during his single term to promote Florida. The sudden economic slump due to the land bust was seen as such a threat to Florida's other industries that Martin led a delegation of potential developers to New York on an all-inclusive sales pitch. (SAF.)

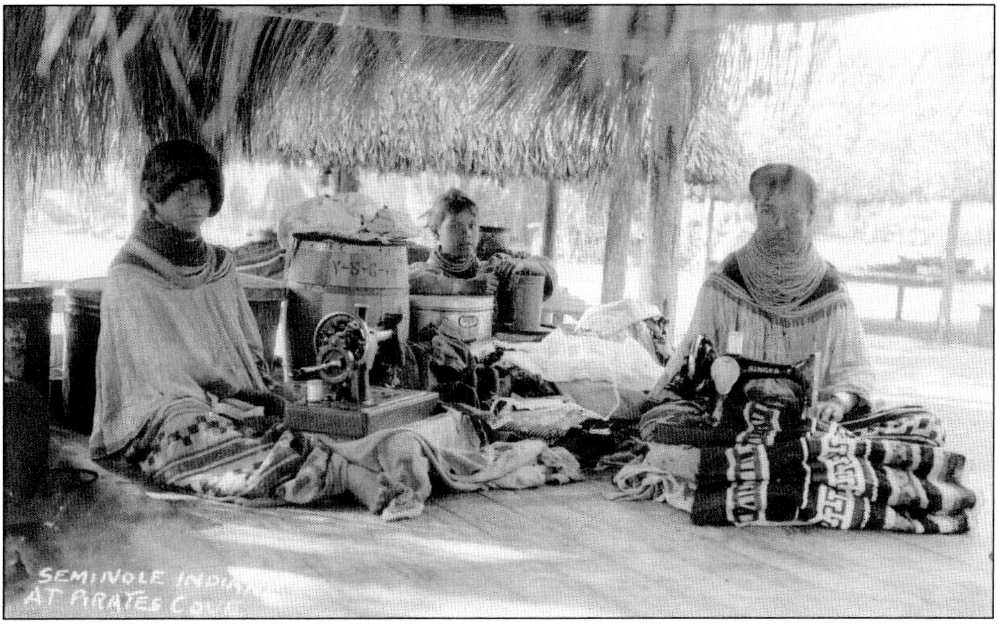

The first territorial governor, William Pope Duval, was both an advocate and a friend to the Florida Seminoles. But, the Seminoles were ignored by subsequent governors. Under the Martin administration, and with the continued construction of Tamiami Trail, the Seminoles were finally regarded with a measure of respect. Martin made news in the state for meeting with tribe leaders; in time, this led toward greater Seminole advocacy. (Michael Croom.)

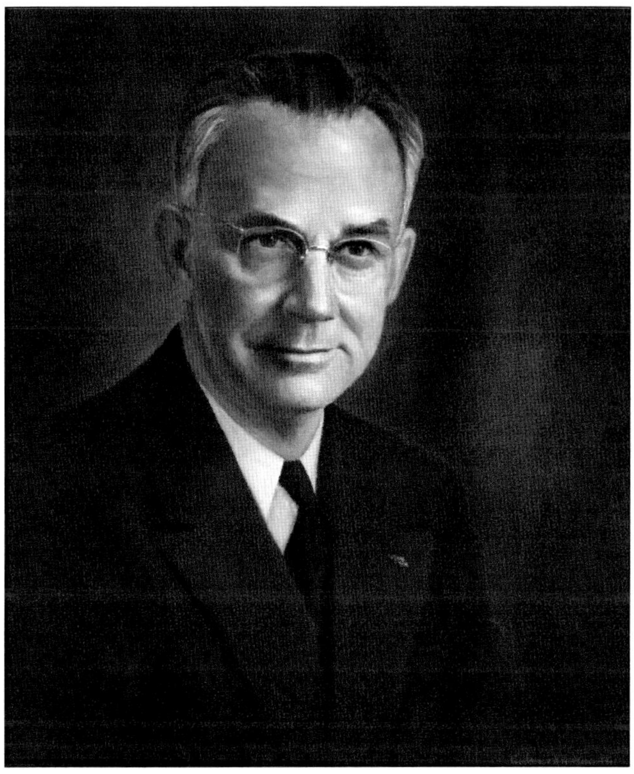

In hindsight, the state is incredibly fortunate that a man like Doyle E. Carlton was governor during some of its most difficult periods. In four years, Carlton faced four major natural disasters, the final collapse of Florida's land boom, an infestation of the Mediterranean fruit fly (crippling the state's citrus business), and the national Great Depression. (MFH.)

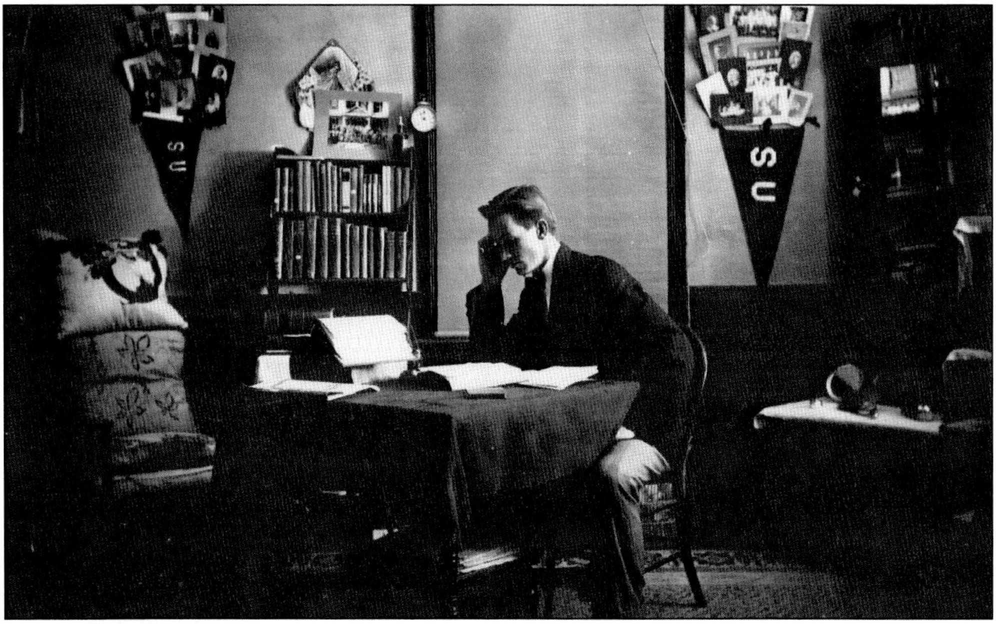

Future governor Doyle Carlton is seen here as a student at Stetson University, where he received his bachelor's degree prior to studying law at Columbia University. The best word to describe the state's 25th governor is "fearless." The moral governor, whom critics called self-righteous, once vetoed a gambling bill despite being offered $100,000 from the state's organized crime to sign it into law. (SAF.)

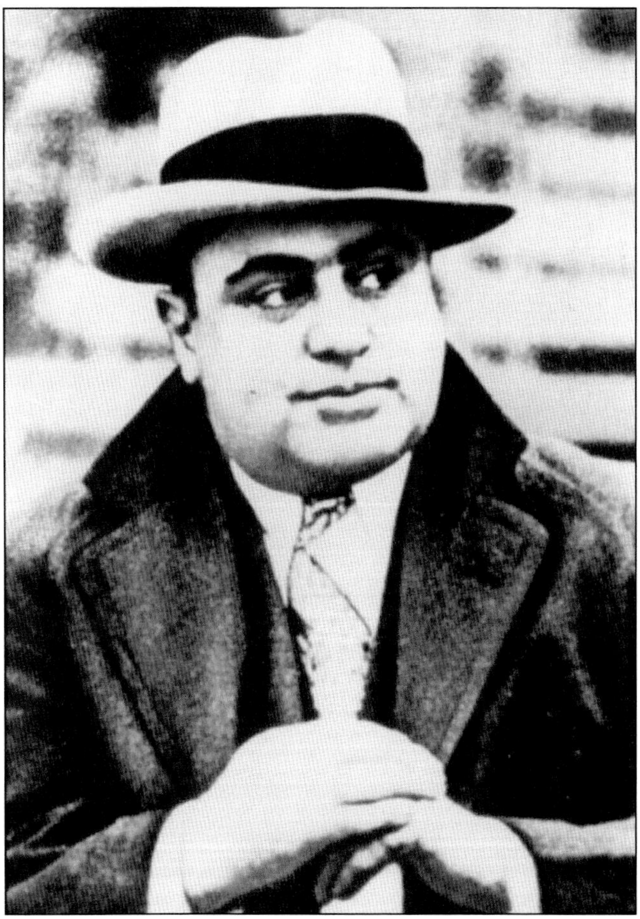

Governor Carlton made a powerful enemy in Florida resident and notorious mafia boss Al Capone (pictured). Carlton's public demand that Capone sell his Miami Beach home and leave the state caused the mobster to threaten the governor's life. The threat was apparently so credible that Pres. Herbert Hoover sent special FBI agents to the governor's mansion to beef up security. (Adam Baumel.)

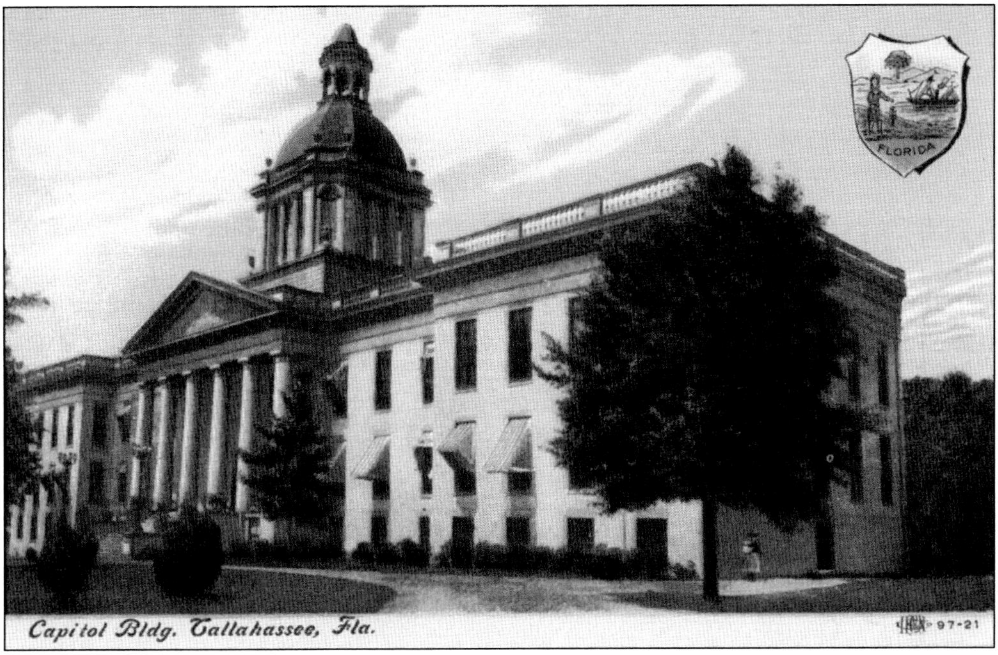

In 1921, the legislature authorized new wings to the east and west of the capitol's main structure. Jacksonville-based architect Henry Klutho was given the prestigious assignment. The first additions were completed in 1923. In 1936 and 1947, chambers for the house and senate were placed onto the existing wings, completing the expansions. (Walt Young.)

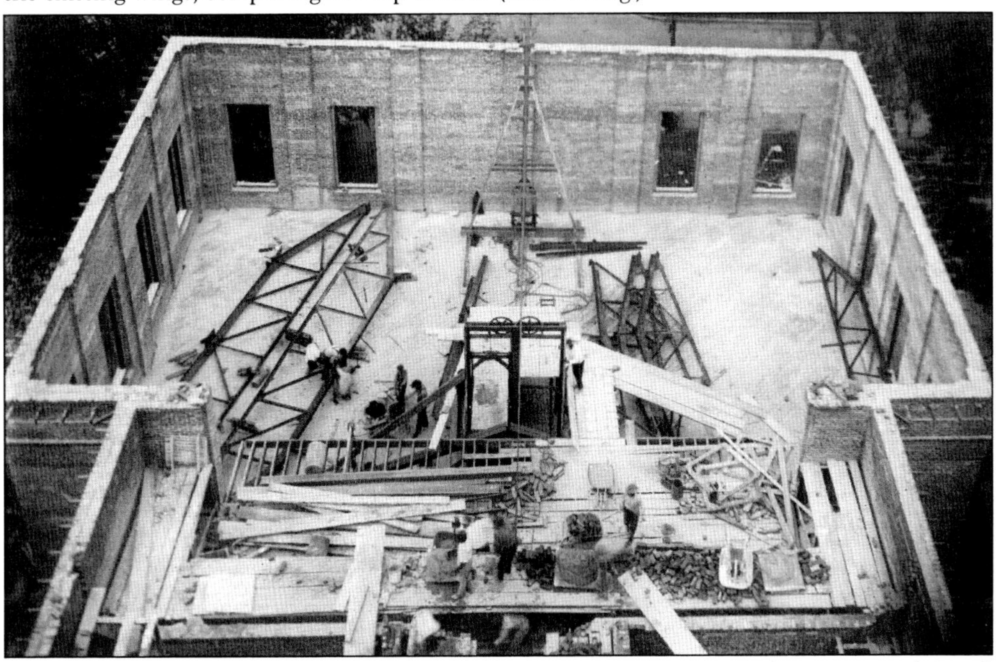

The construction of the capitol's additions would prove both long and controversial for all involved. Henry Klutho, the designer of many public buildings in Florida, was criticized for the quality of the finished product. His masterpiece, the original executive mansion, was at the same time starting to deteriorate, causing many to question his methods. (SAF.)

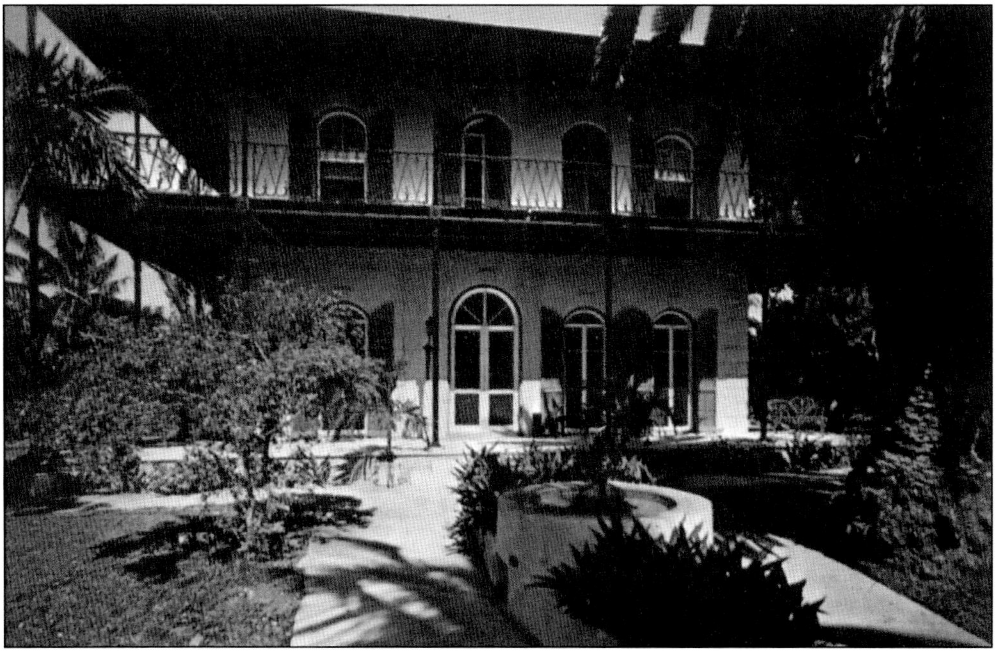

The Hemingway House is located at 907 Whitehead Street, across from the Key West lighthouse. Built in 1851, the home had a quarried basement, making it the only house in the Keys to have a basement. Ernest Hemingway lived here from 1931 until his death in 1961. It was in this house that Hemingway wrote some of his best work, including the classic *The Snows of Kilimanjaro.* (AC.)

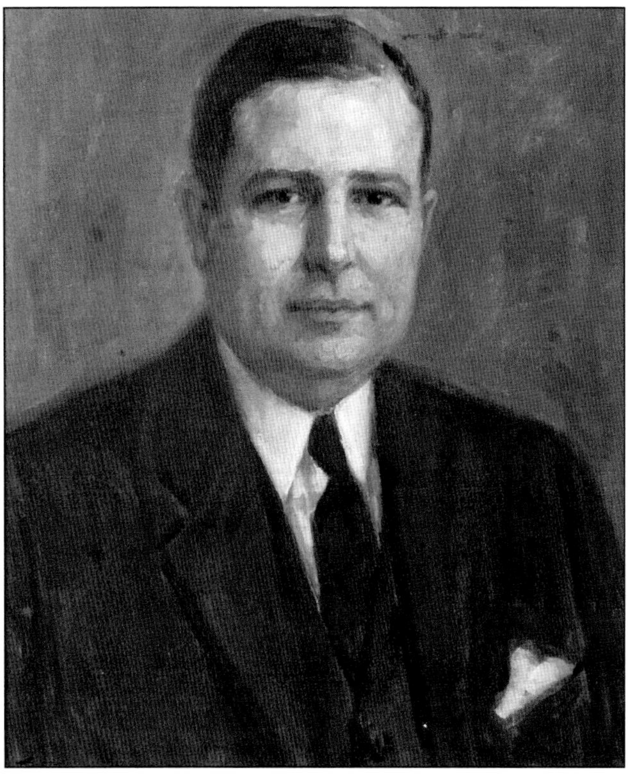

David Sholtz, the 26th governor of Florida, was a native New Yorker of Jewish descent. He was known as the New Deal Governor. His excellent working relationship with President Roosevelt helped shield the state from a lasting and crumbling depression. Winning the Democratic Party nomination against two popular former governors, Sholtz surprised everyone with his historic victory in 1932. (MFH.)

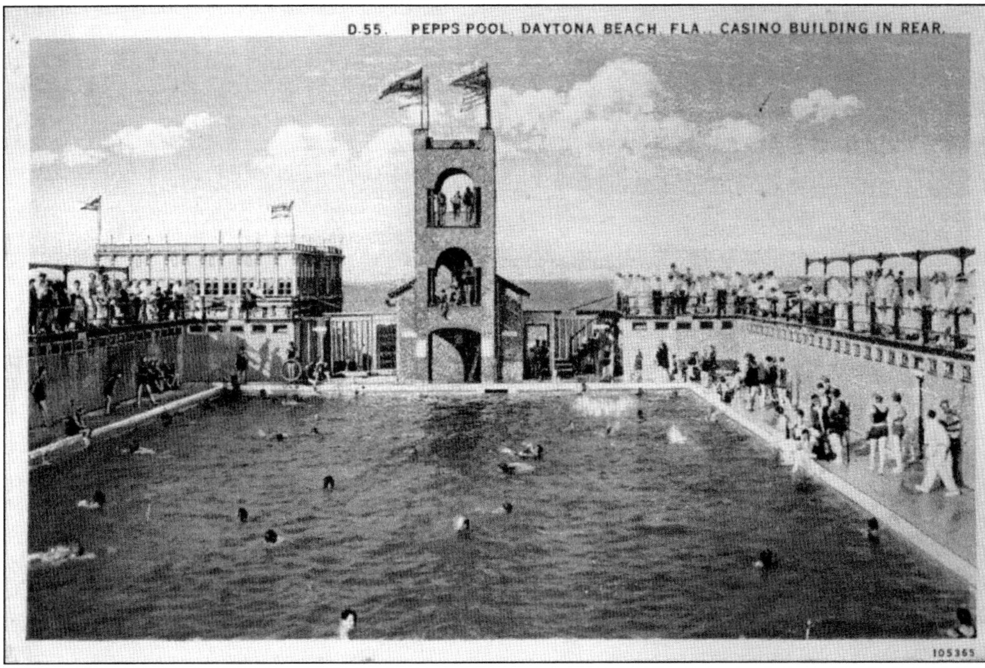

Daytona Beach's Pepps Pool, owned and operated by Harry Pepper, was located on Ocean Avenue, not far from Main Street. It was a popular location for many of the city's most prominent members. During the 1920s and 1930s, Daytona government was known for its cronyism. The seaside casino, visible at left, was a much-used location for deal making, which Sholtz was praised for avoiding. (AC.)

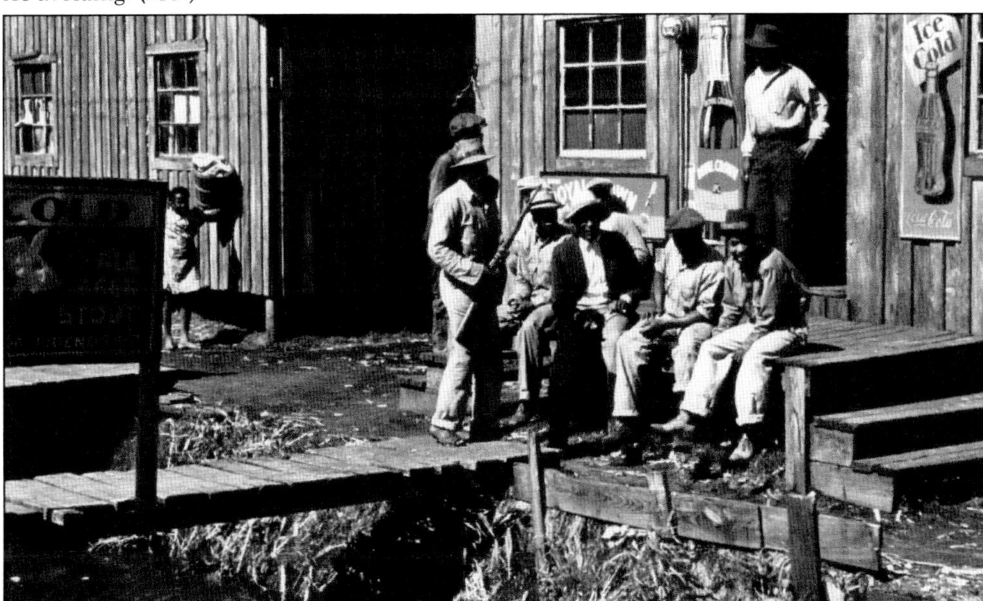

The Great Depression was merely the last in a series of disastrous financial and environmental events that affected the state during the later 1920s. South Florida was devastated by two historically severe hurricanes, and a Mediterranean fruit fly outbreak rocked the citrus industry to its core. During the depression, one in four Floridians lived on some kind of governmental relief. (Adam Bamuel.)

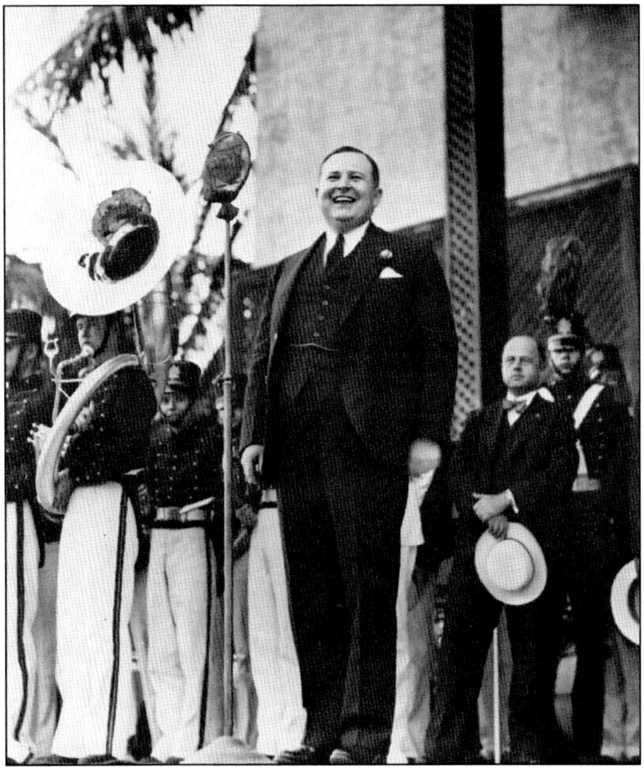

David Sholtz saw to it that Roosevelt's New Deal was promoted throughout the state. Soon, nearly 50,000 Floridians were working in programs like the Civilian Conservation Corps (CCC). Young men from all over Florida lived in work camps and sent their paychecks home to their families. The CCC Museum at Highlands Hammock State Park honors the work done by these young men. (SAF.)

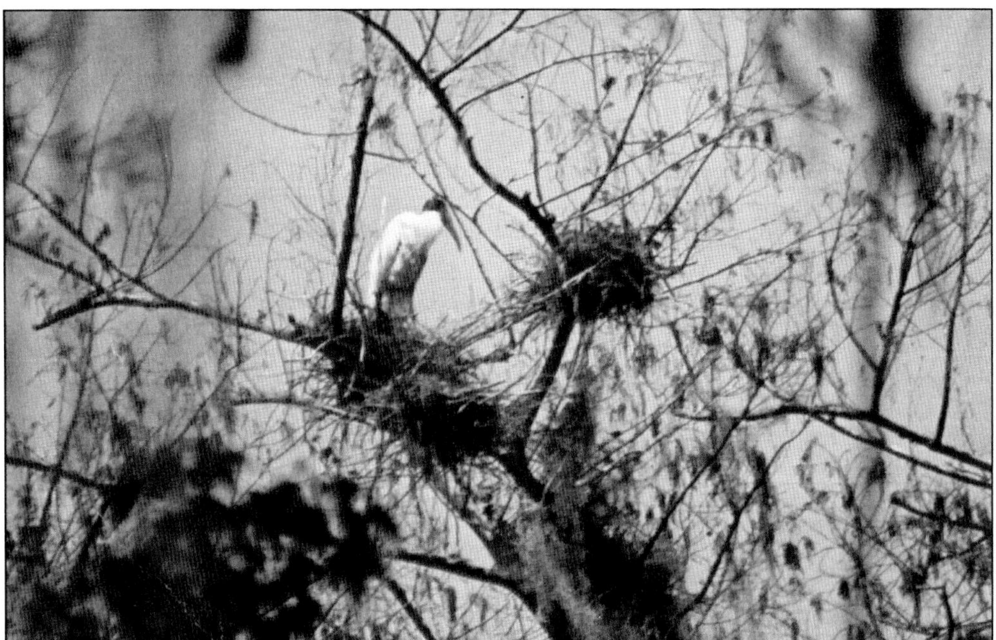

In 1935, Sholtz signed a bill into law that created the Florida Park Service. As a renowned supporter of the state's board of forestry, the governor actively sought to protect threatened species, like the Florida wood stork, pictured here nesting in the Everglades. Efforts to turn the Everglades into a national park were supported by Sholtz. (AC.)

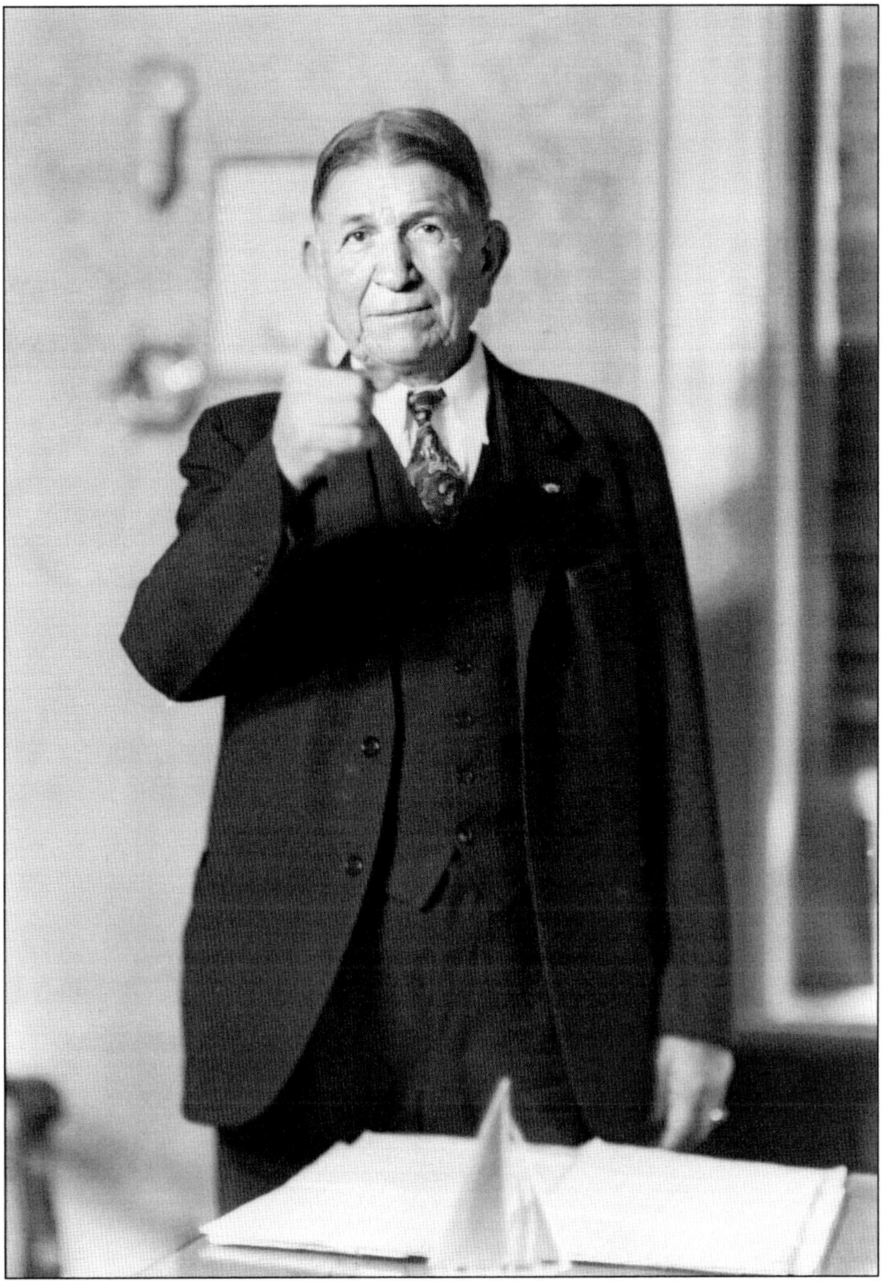

Gov. Frederick Preston Cone points a finger at the camera, displaying the no-nonsense, homespun nature of the state's 27th chief executive. Cone practiced law in Lake City following his graduation from Jasper Normal College. He served as Lake City mayor for three terms and represented the district in the Florida Senate from 1907 to 1913. Cone was the president of the state senate in 1911 and served as the chairman of the Democratic National Convention in 1932. In 1937, at the age of 65, he became the oldest Floridian in the 20th century elected to the governorship. With the Great Depression still limiting economic opportunity, Cone, unlike his predecessor Sholtz, proved to be no New Dealer. He had frosty relations with the White House, and important conservation measures begun under Sholtz effectively ended with Cone. (SAF.)

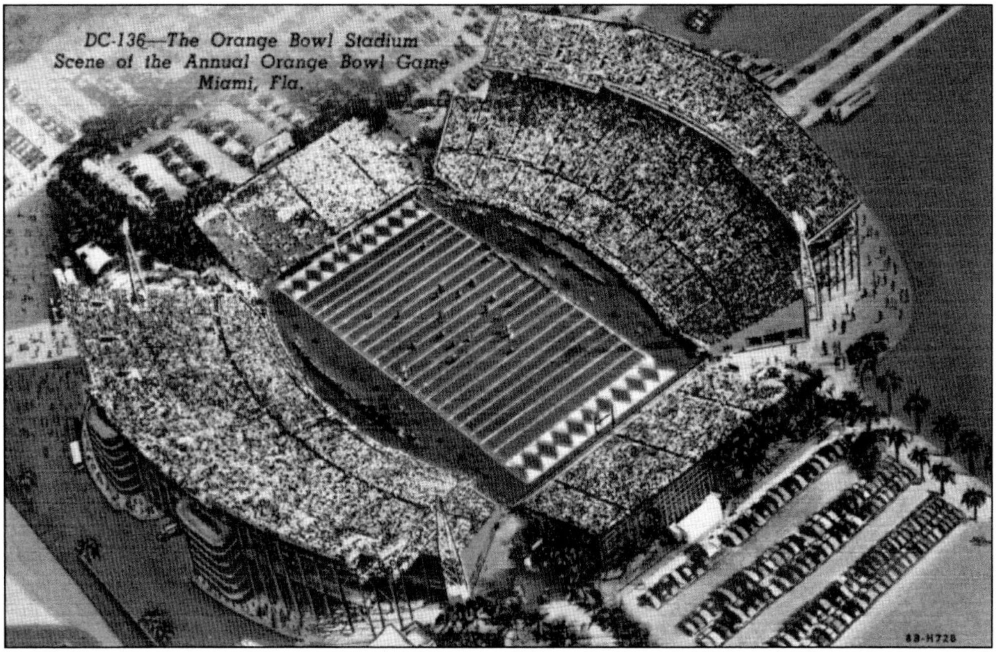

Known as Burdine Stadium when it opened in 1937, the Miami Orange Bowl became a landmark as the home stadium for the Miami Hurricanes and Miami Dolphins. The Orange Bowl was the site of the NCAA's longest college football home winning streak, and it was home to the Miami Dolphins and its 1972 perfect season. (AC.)

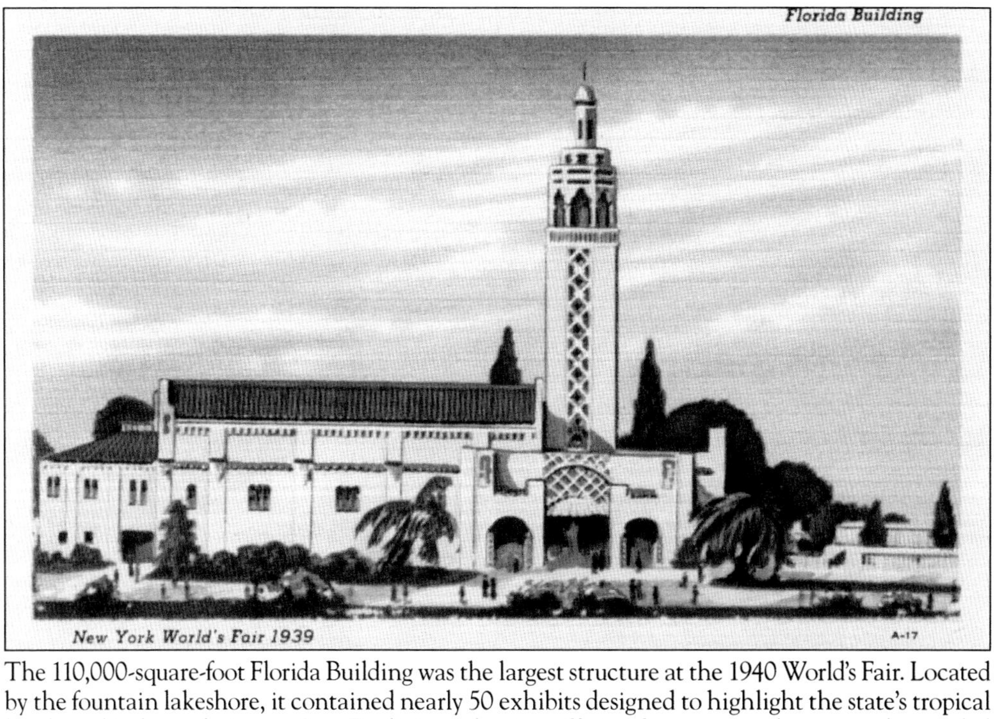

The 110,000-square-foot Florida Building was the largest structure at the 1940 World's Fair. Located by the fountain lakeshore, it contained nearly 50 exhibits designed to highlight the state's tropical locale and industrial virtues. Gov. Fred Cone, despite suffering from a severe heart attack, traveled to the opening of the exhibit and took great pride in its success. (AC.)

Six

War and Postwar Years

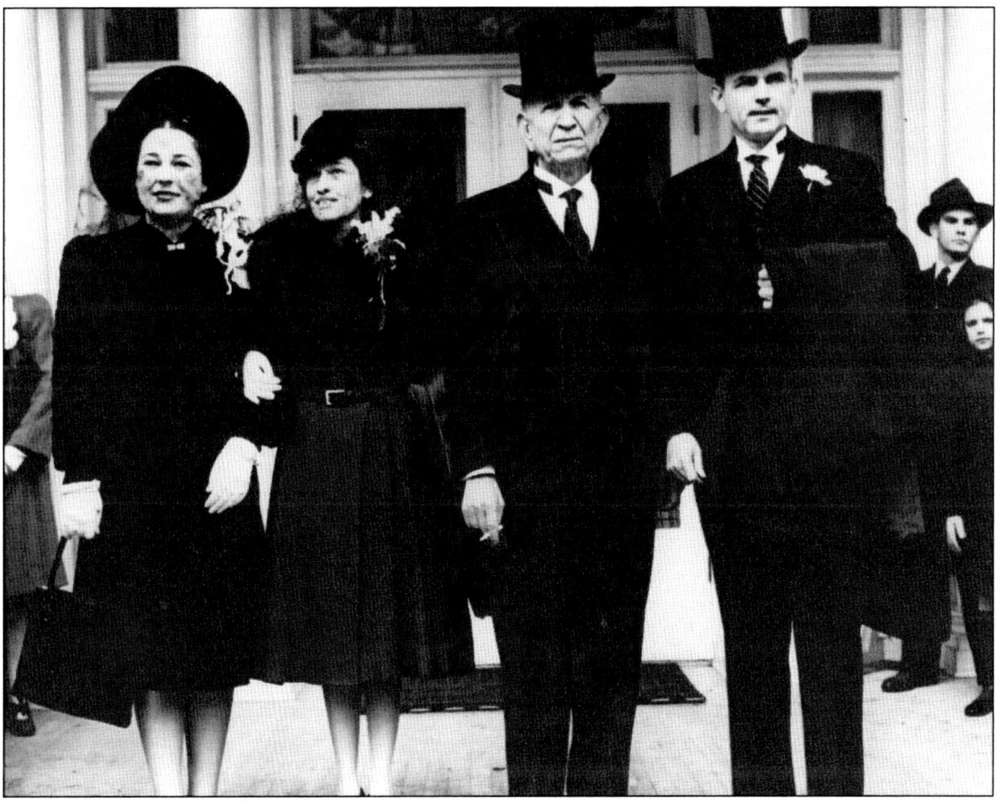

Governor Cone (second from right) leaves the mansion with future governor Spessard Lindsey Holland, on their way to the capitol for Holland's swearing-in. Cone, nearly 70, was in weak health when he left office. Holland, a young man dedicated to the state, came into office under a cloud of war. This transition was seen as a changing of the guard. Never again was the governorship so insulated from national politics. (SAF.)

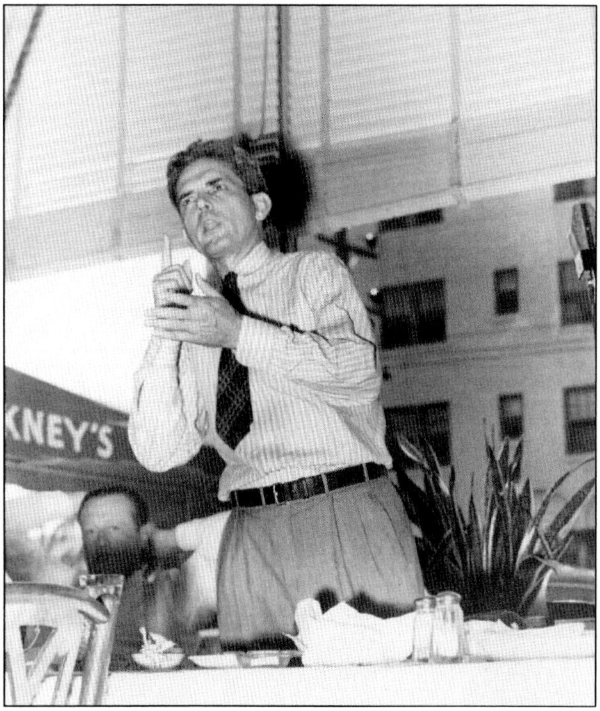

Son of a schoolteacher and a citrus grower, Holland proved that, with hard work and kindness, a person could achieve greatness. Florida's World War II governor was a qualified Rhodes Scholar who had abandoned his scholarship to fight in World War I. He was a county judge and state senator before entering the 1940 governor's race. (SAF.)

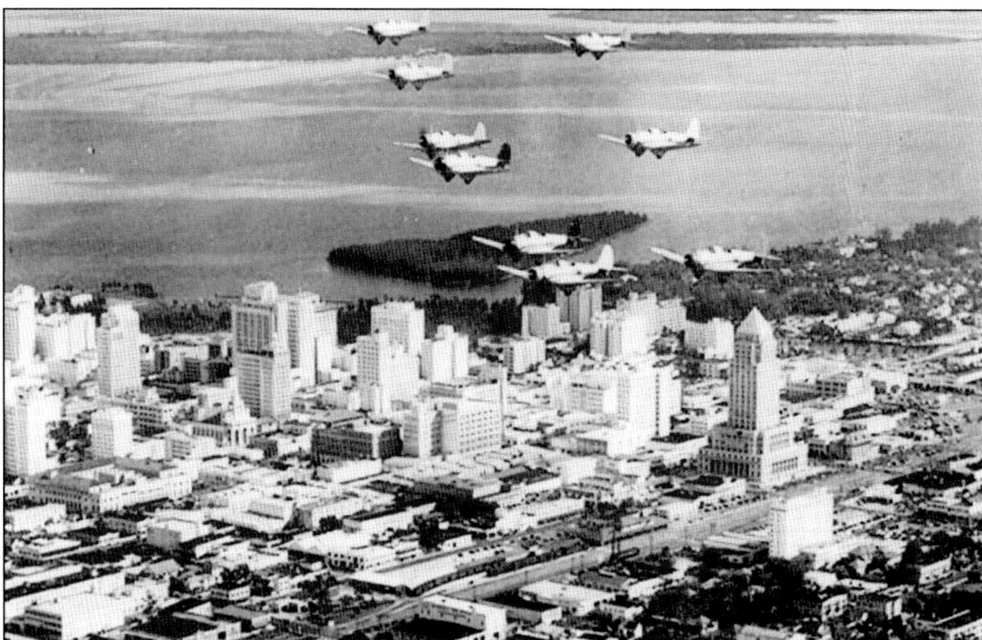

Navy dive-bombers fly over Miami in 1943. More than 250,000 Floridians served in the war effort, and its ship production was so extensive that the state won an Army-Navy award in 1944 for ship production. Due to the state's warm climate, it became the home base for 170 military training locations. The capital city of Tallahassee leased Dale Mabry Field to the Army Air Corps in 1941, and it housed more than 7,000 airmen throughout the war, including members of the British, French, and Chinese Air Forces. (AC.)

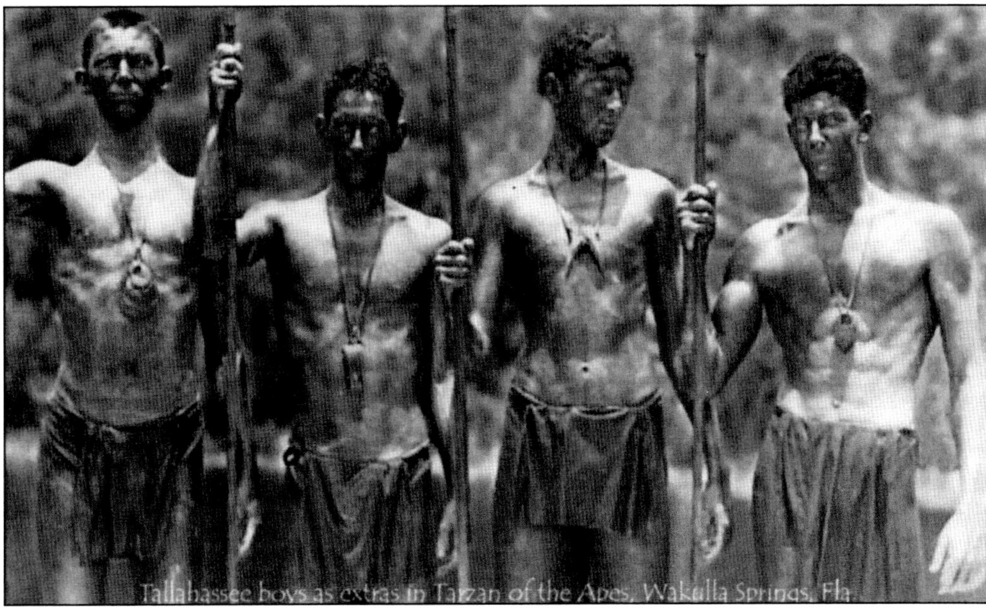

Painted extras pose on location in Wakulla Springs State Park during the filming of *Tarzan's New York Adventure*. Due to its moderate climate, friendly state government, and commerce-driven economy, Florida has always been a popular filming location. During the early part of the 20th century, Jacksonville was the movie capital of the world. Today, the governor's office has its own commission to attract new film and television productions to Florida. (Dottie Young.)

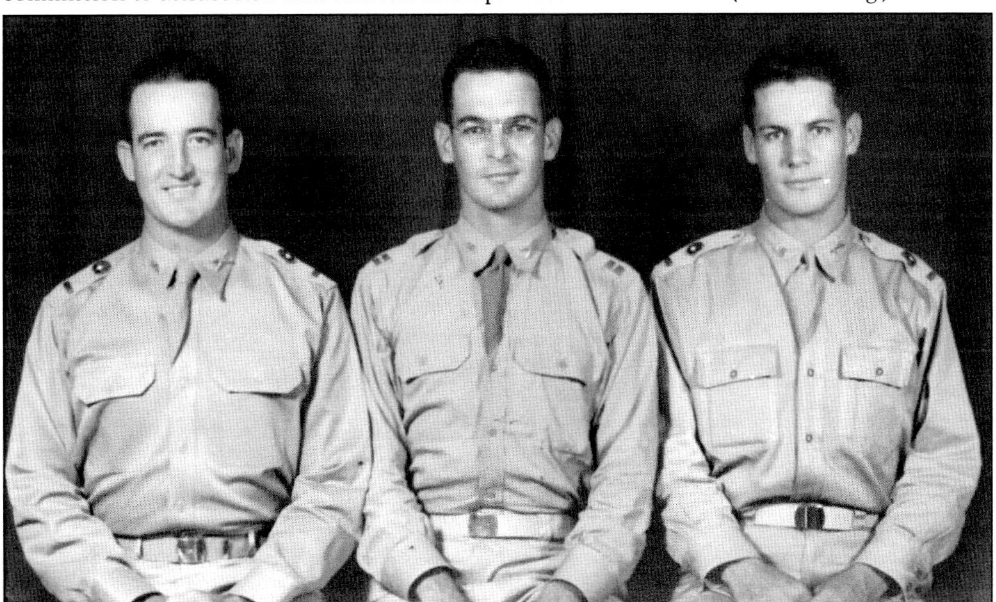

Several future governors fought in World War II. Fuller Warren was a gunnery officer, and Wayne Mixson was a member of the lighter-than-air squad. Claude Kirk was a US Marine, and Leroy Collins was a member of the Naval Reserves. Perhaps the governor with the most distinguished service record was Daniel McCarty (center), pictured here with his brothers. Stationed in both North Africa and France, McCarty was promoted to the rank of colonel after the Battle of the Bulge and awarded the Bronze Star Medal, the Purple Heart, and the Legion of Merit. (SLC.)

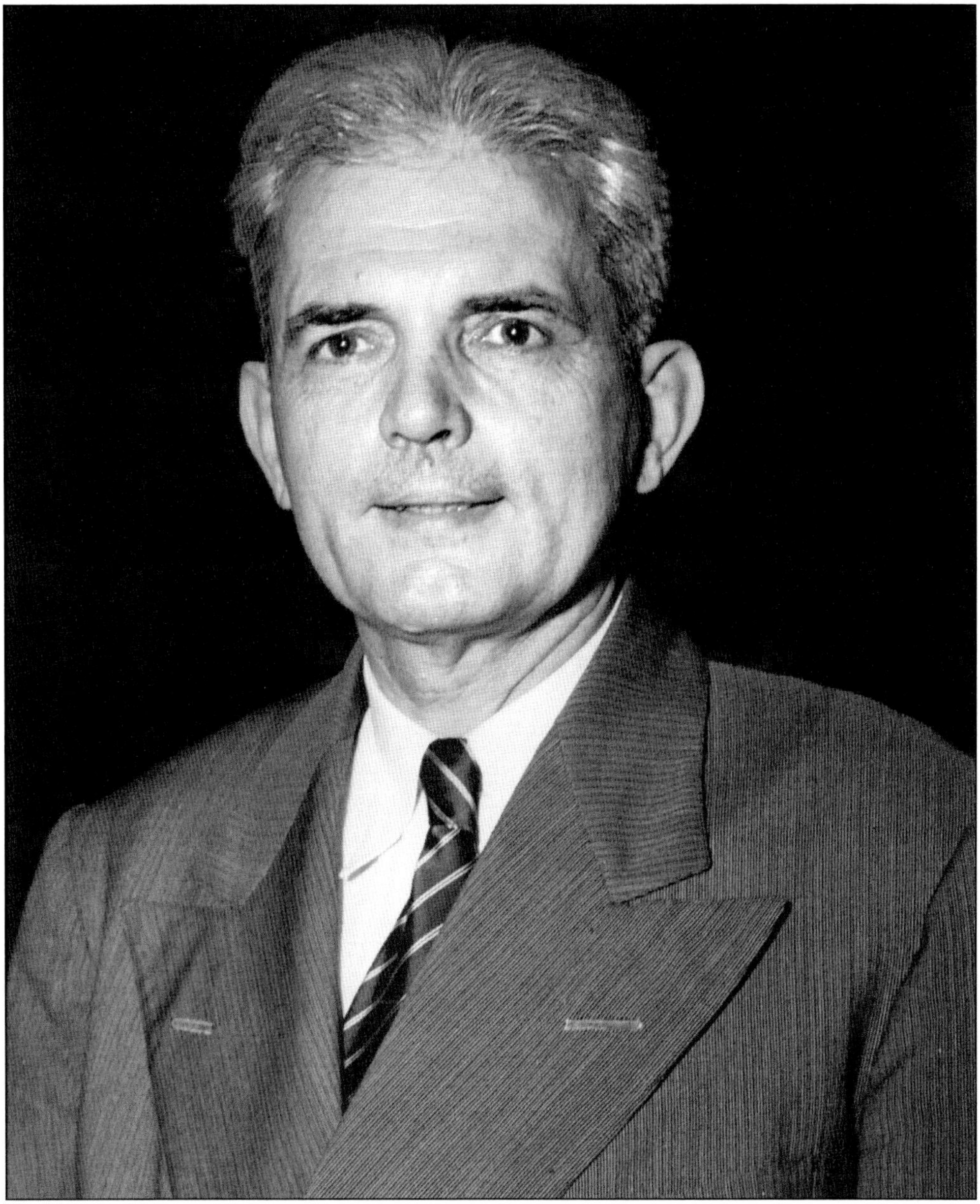

Spessard Holland avoided the fate of many Florida governors. He ran for and won a seat in the US Senate. Serving there until shortly before his death in 1970, he played a major role in state government for the next 25 years. At times, the conservative Holland had difficult relations with some of the more liberal Florida governors. His relationship with Dan McCarty was described as cold or thorny, and Leroy Collins openly disliked Holland's senate record. Claude Kirk was Holland's Republican challenger in 1964 as a way to gain exposure for his gubernatorial race two years later. Holland was a passionate supporter and kind mentor to future governor and US senator Lawton Chiles. Following his decision to not seek another term in 1970, Holland provided Chiles with much advice and guidance, as the unknown state senator challenged former governor Farris Bryant for the party nomination. Despite remaining neutral during the primary race, Holland was delighted when Chiles won his seat. (SAF.)

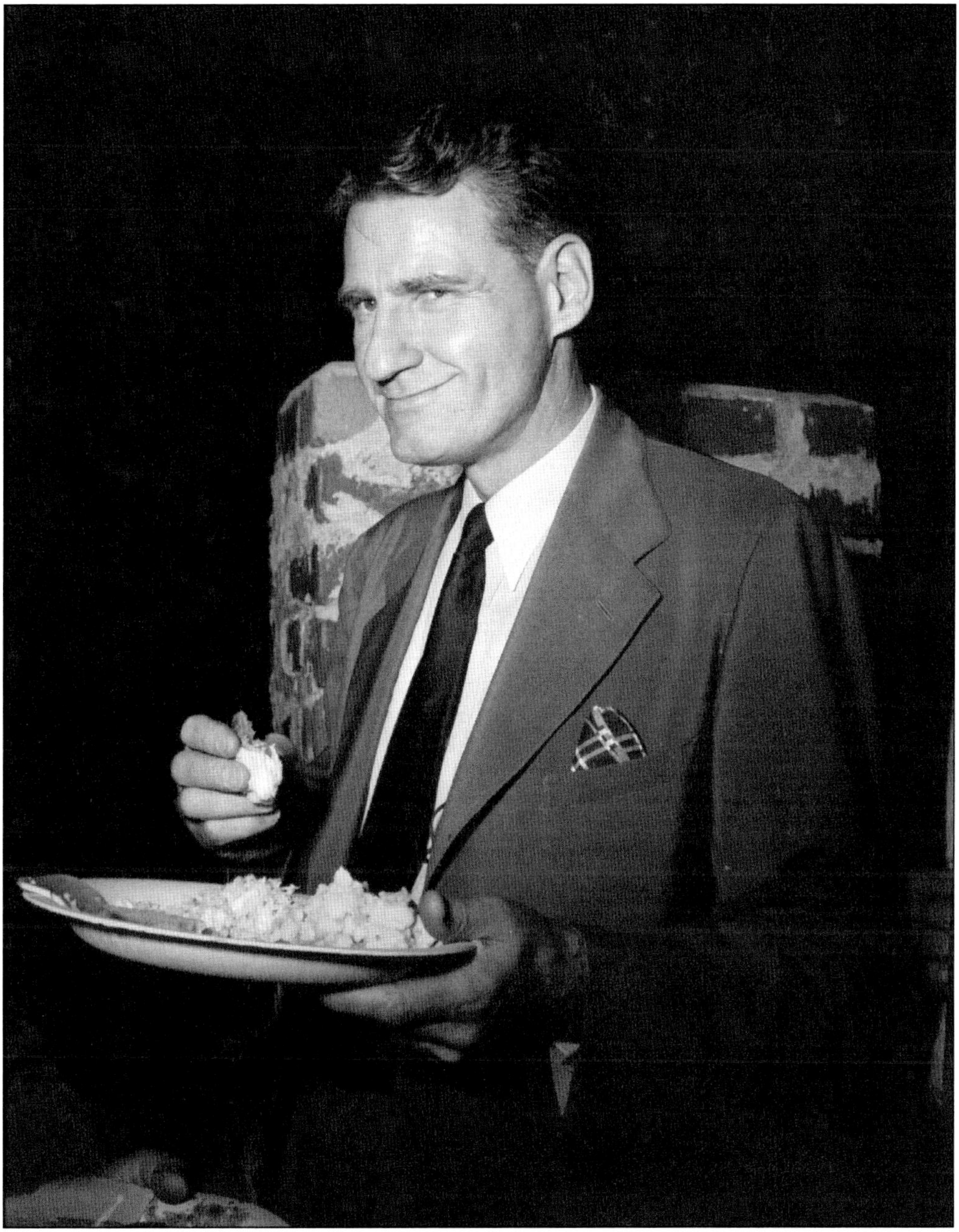

Millard Fillmore Caldwell, Florida's 29th governor, was a typical Southern gentleman with a gift for crowd-pleasing and winning elections. He served as Santa Rosa County's prosecuting attorney, a member of the Florida House of Representatives, and a member of the US House of Representatives before winning the 1944 Democratic gubernatorial nomination. Perhaps one of the most interesting aspects of Caldwell's term in office was his actions following the Japanese surrender that ended World War II. Upon hearing the news that the war was over, the governor issued a proclamation urging bars and other alcohol-selling establishments to close in order to prevent a frenzy of drunken celebration in the streets. He was the first governor to occupy the new capitol complex and was instrumental in funding education. (SAF.)

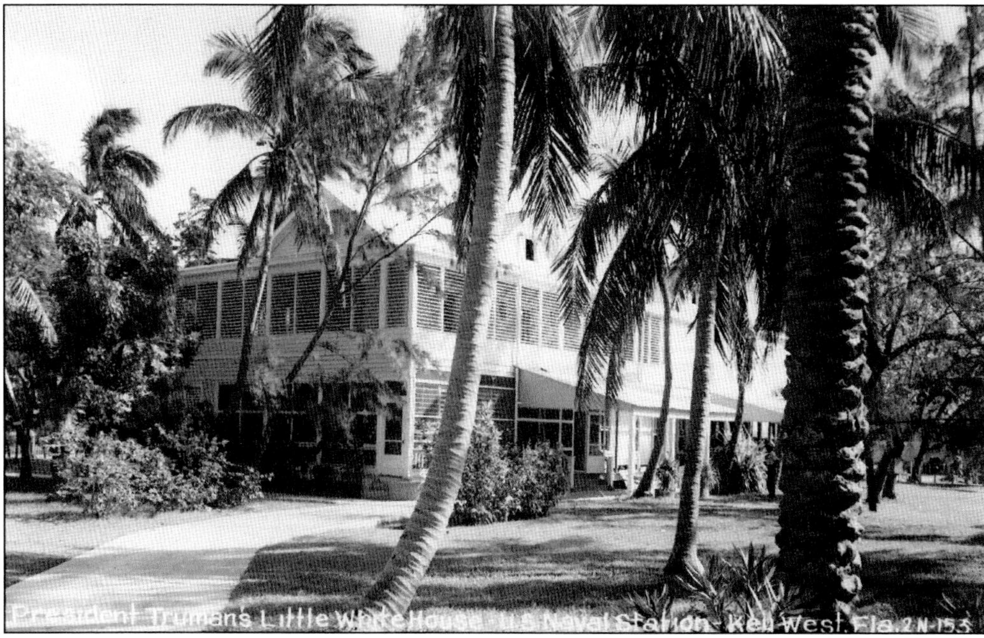

During his time in office, Pres. Harry Truman, like many of his predecessors, chose to make Florida the location for his summer White House. In total, Truman stayed for over 175 days during 11 visits at the Key West bungalow, which was once the residence of Thomas Edison. The "Little White House" served as a vacation site for Presidents Taft, Carter, and Clinton. (AC.)

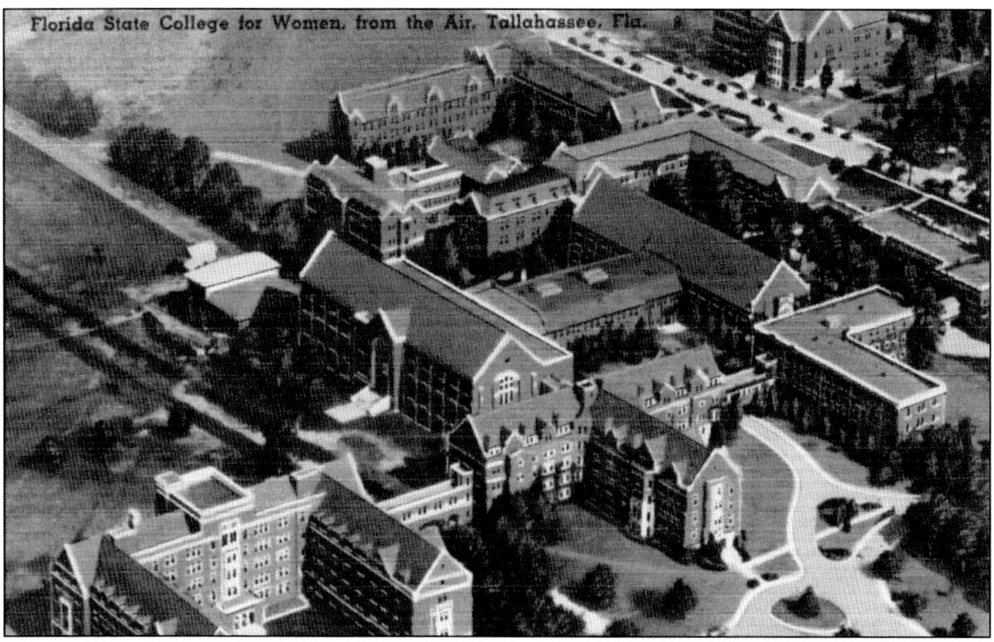

From 1905 until 1947, Florida State University was the Florida State College for Women. The collegiate Gothic redbrick buildings have become as important a historic landmark in Tallahassee as the state capitol building. By 1933, the Florida State College for Women had grown to be the third-largest women's college in the United States. (AC.)

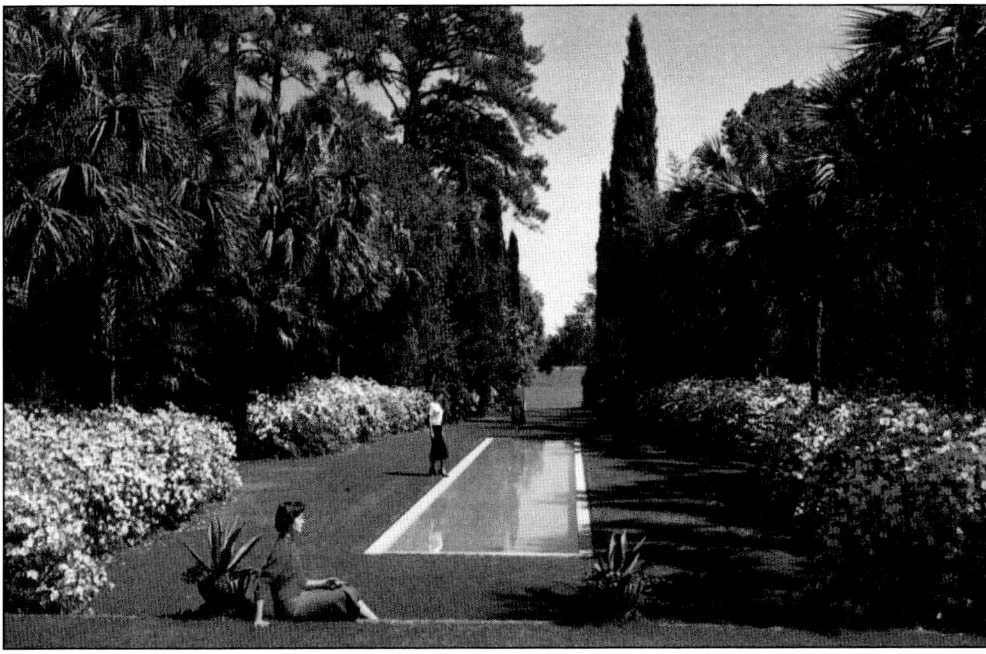

The reflection pool of Alfred B. Maclay Gardens, a state park and historic site entered in the National Register of Historic Places, was donated to the citizens of Florida in 1953. The 307 acres were placed by the governor's office under the supervision of the Florida Department of Environmental Protection. (AC.)

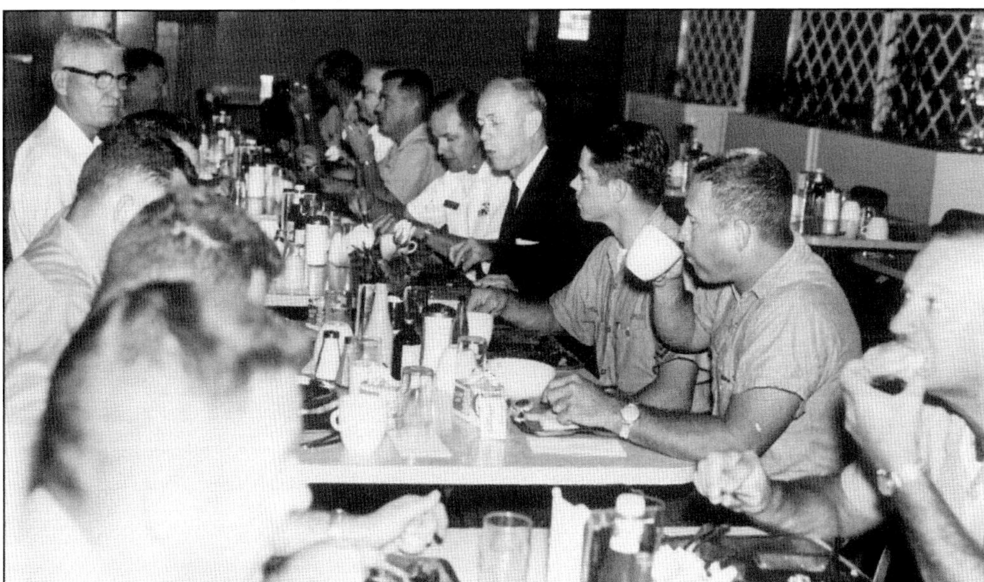

Governors Caldwell (left, wearing glasses) and Bryant (right, in jacket and tie) are seen here at Guantanamo Bay, Cuba, shortly after the Cuban Missile Crisis. Following his term of office, Caldwell continued to serve in a variety of different positions. President Truman appointed Caldwell the administrator of the Federal Civil Defense Administration in 1950, and he later served as both justice and chief justice of the state supreme court. In 1967, he administered the oath of office to Claude Kirk. (SAF.)

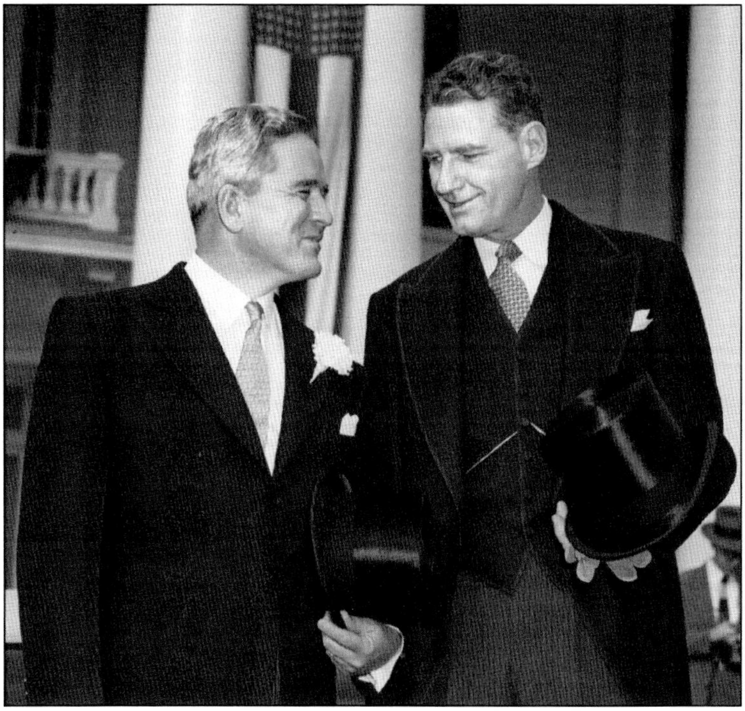

Millard Caldwell wanted Dan McCarty to be his successor, giving Fuller Warren only token support following his Democratic primary victory. On inauguration day, as they were leaving the executive mansion for the capitol, Governor Caldwell (right) reported to Warren (left) with much relish that the state was virtually bankrupt. Financial matters would dog the Warren administration. (SAF.)

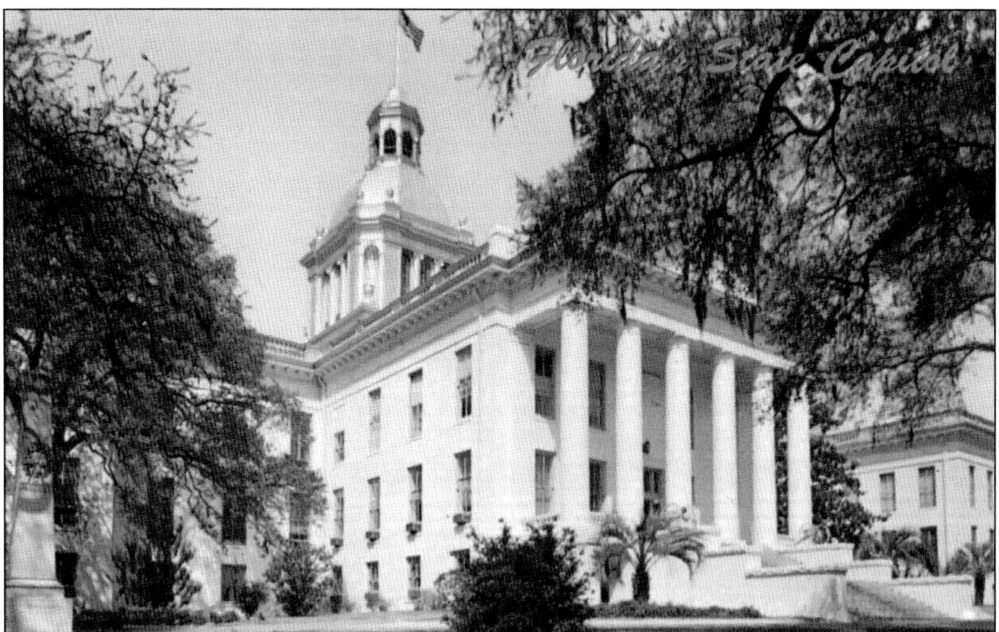

The old capitol is seen here with the addition of north and south wings, including an enlarged governor's suite. Lawmakers' only office space was their chamber desks. Before the 1968 constitution, the legislature met only biennially, and its members were deemed unworthy of private offices. The additions were poorly constructed, with the basement floors at different levels. As a result, talk began about constructing a new capitol. (Walt Young.)

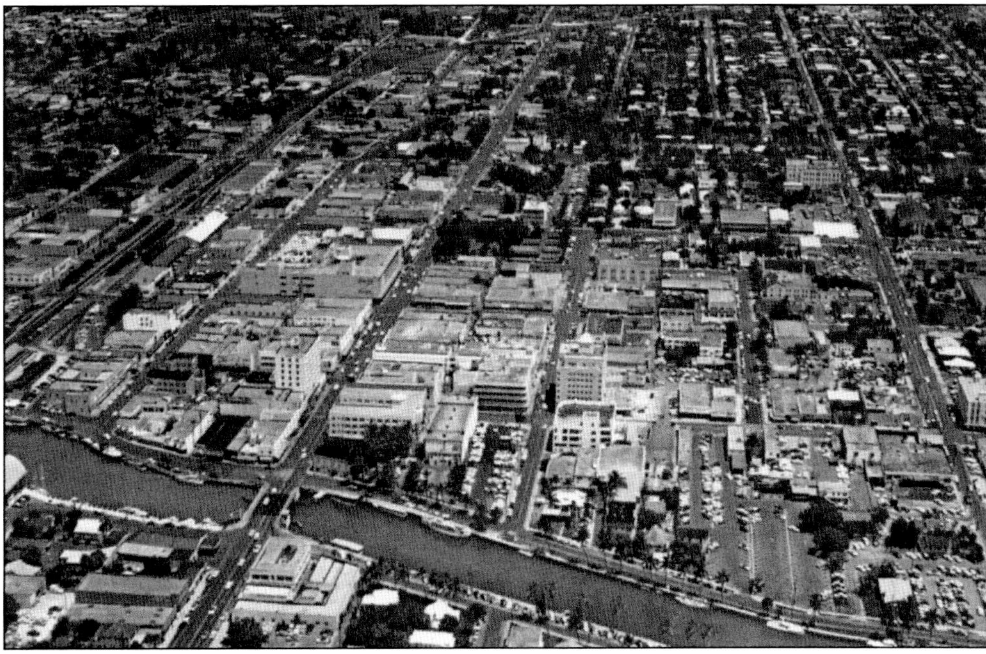

These aerial photographs of Fort Lauderdale (above) and Miami Beach (below) show how development changed postwar South Florida. A few decades earlier, in 1900, the state was home to only half a million citizens. Many veterans who trained in Florida during the war were now becoming permanent citizens in peacetime. Miami Beach's Lake Pancoast, which was largely underdeveloped in the early years of the century and had experienced a rough patch following the great 1926 Miami hurricane, was now becoming a major global tourist location. Fort Lauderdale was given the name "the Venice of America" and has been a popular spring break destination for 60 years. (Both, AC.)

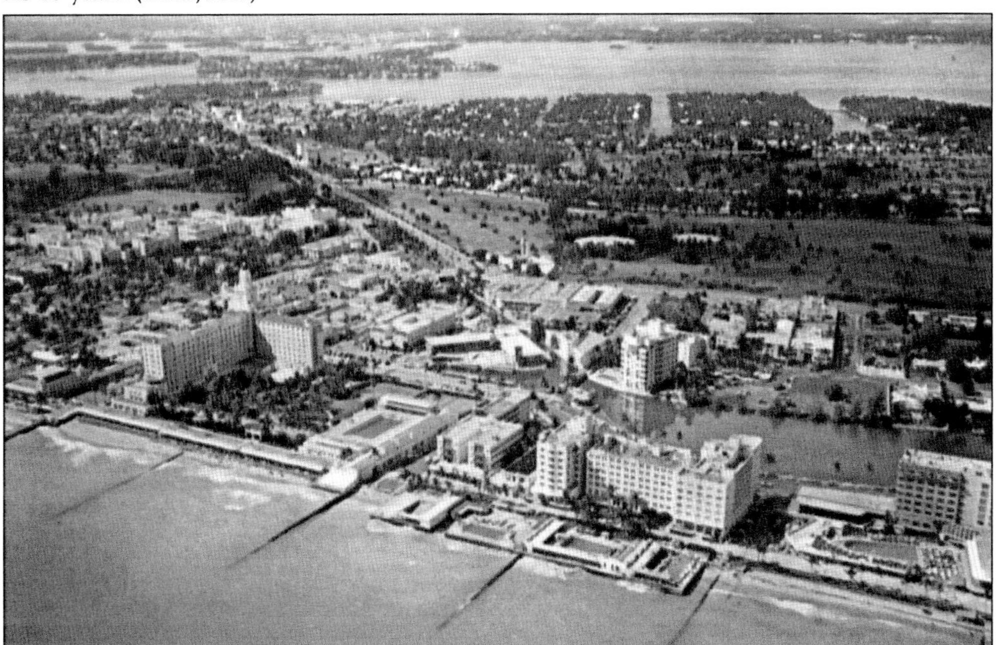

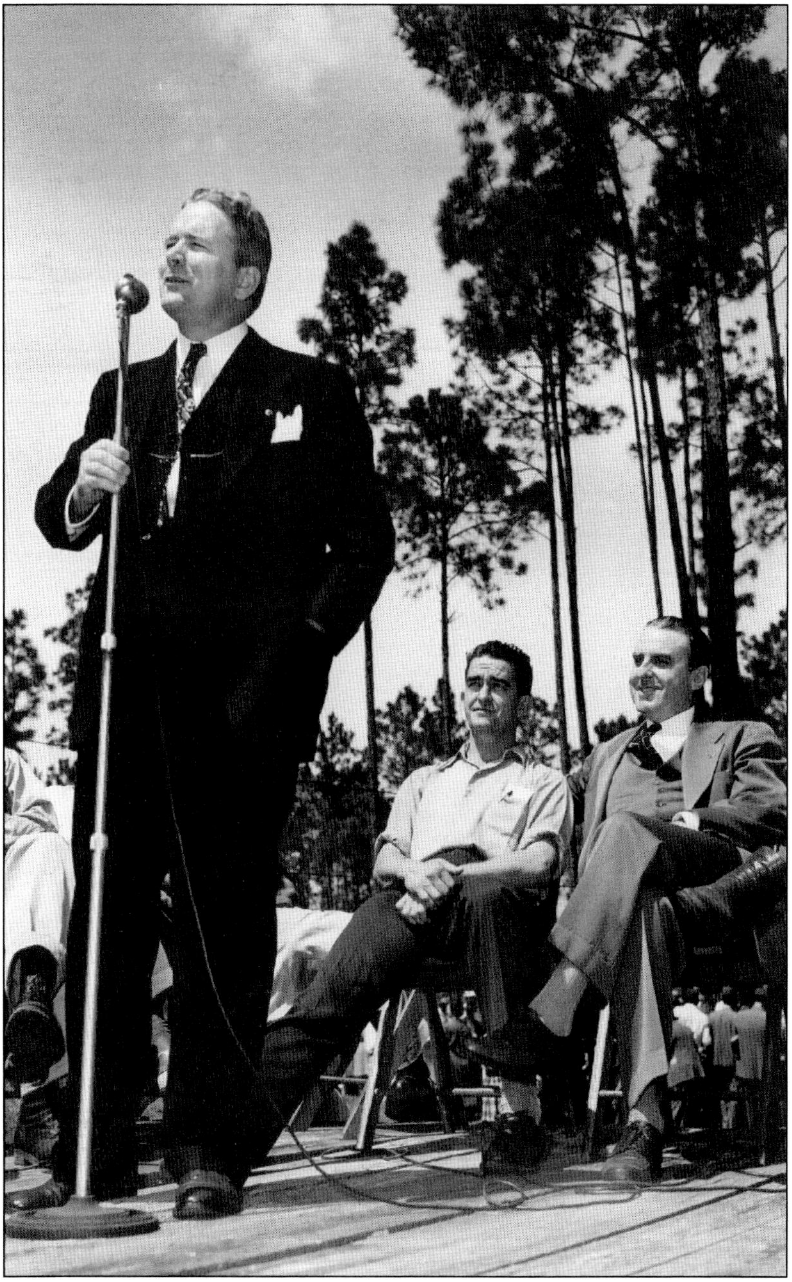

Naturally attractive, the young Fuller Warren was a born campaigner, winning a seat in the Florida House while still a student at the University of Florida. Warren served three terms in the Jacksonville City Commission and made a name for himself as a weekly columnist and author of three books, including *How to Win in Politics*, in 1949. He had a rich, masculine voice that never failed to wow an audience. These assets and accomplishments made him both a formidable opponent and a wildly popular politician. They did not, however, make him a successful administrator or governor. Warren traveled to California just prior to the 1948 campaign, where he met 23-year-old Barbara Jean Manning. The two were married six months into Warren's term as governor, while the previous first lady, Warren's sister Alma, continued to live in the mansion. (SAF.)

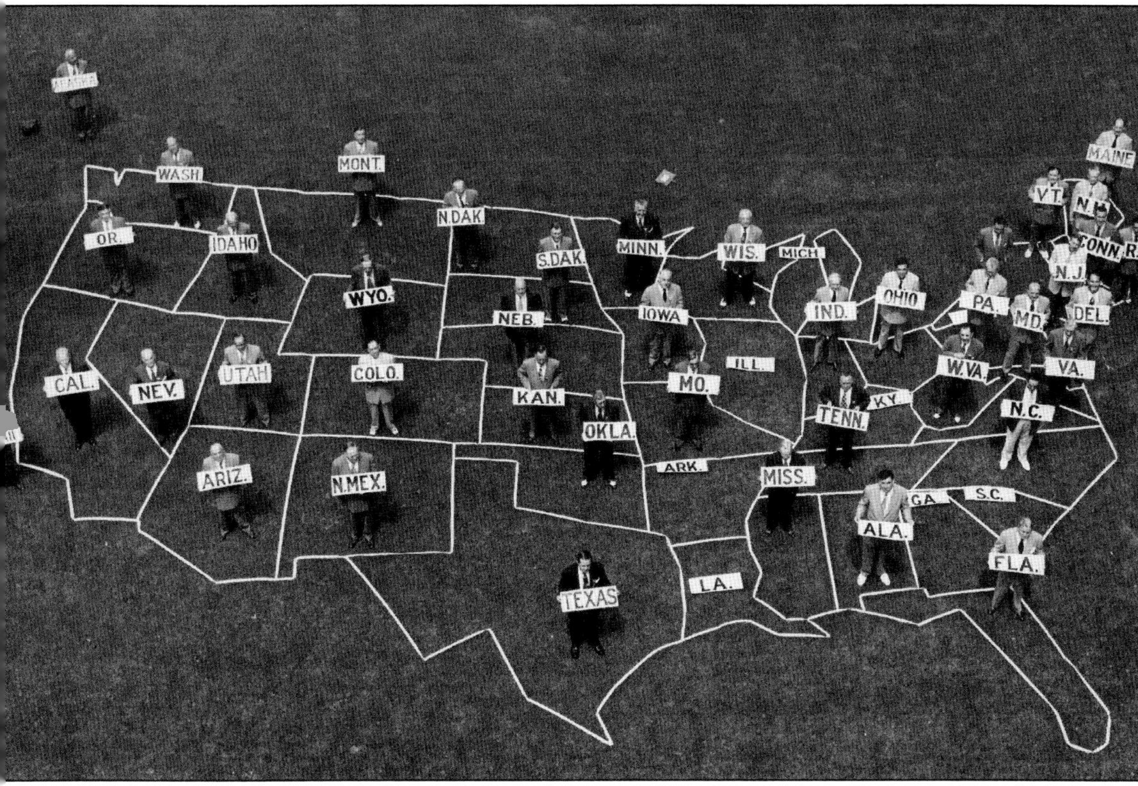

Fuller Warren's legacy is a double-edged sword. He is remembered for starting the state's turnpike and reforestation programs. But his administration was constantly associated with scandal, tainting Warren's achievements. The US Senate committee to investigate crime in interstate commerce discovered links between organized crime and Warren's 1948 campaign. Warren's refusal to testify led one state legislator to introduce a resolution of impeachment. Fuller Warren and his young bride moved to South Florida following the end of his single term. He ran for his old job against Leroy Collins in 1956, losing badly in the primary. A strong supporter of civil rights during the 1948 campaign, he supported segregation in 1956, which further damaged his legacy. Despite having great success early in life, once in office, Warren was not willing to sacrifice his hard-won popularity, and the state soon preferred the talents of more serious-minded public servants. (SAF.)

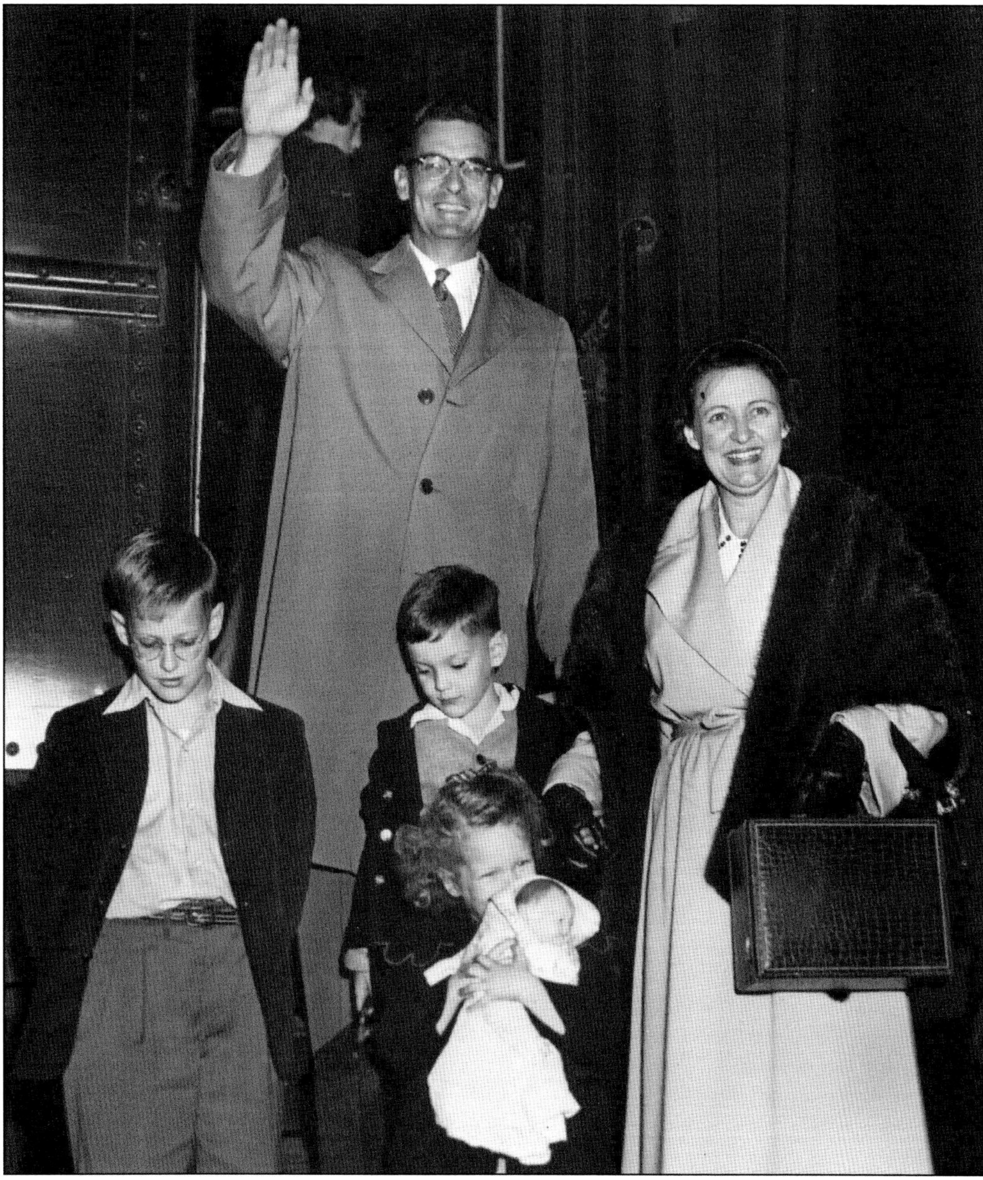

The McCarty family arrives at the Tallahassee train station just prior to Daniel McCarty's inauguration. Described as the first South Florida governor, he was the favorite son of St. Lucie County. Representing the district in the Florida House by the time he was 26, he was named Speaker of the House by the time he was 29. The modest McCarty packed his own bags on his way to Tallahassee, with the entire family, complete with Boston terrier, packed in the station wagon as they left Fort Pierce for their new life as Florida's first family. The three young children took with them all their toys, fishing poles, clothes, and beds. First Lady Olie McCarty had run the family citrus business while McCarty was fighting overseas. Once he was in office, she frequently packed his daily lunches. They were known as a golden couple with a true partnership. (SLC.)

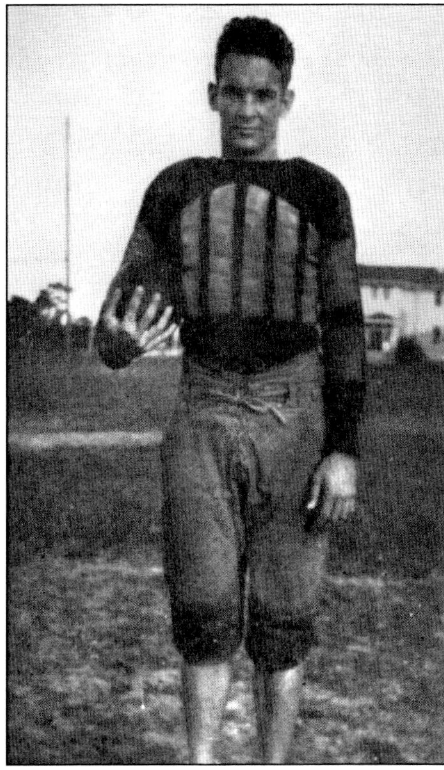

Daniel McCarty, pictured during his high school years, was a popular football player and a student leader. His single mother raised her children to work hard and focus on shaping themselves into model individuals. "Dan" became a father figure to those around him and, by his teens, grew to become the perfect embodiment of what many seek in a leader. (SLC.)

Dan McCarty (standing, left), seen here with his two brothers, started campaigning for governor in 1947 and never stopped. Following his loss to Warren in 1948, he simply refused to stop making speeches. Having been a runner-up to the current governor and actually enhancing his support, unlike the declining political fortunes of Fuller Warren, McCarty was in a great position to be considered something of a shadow governor. (SLC.)

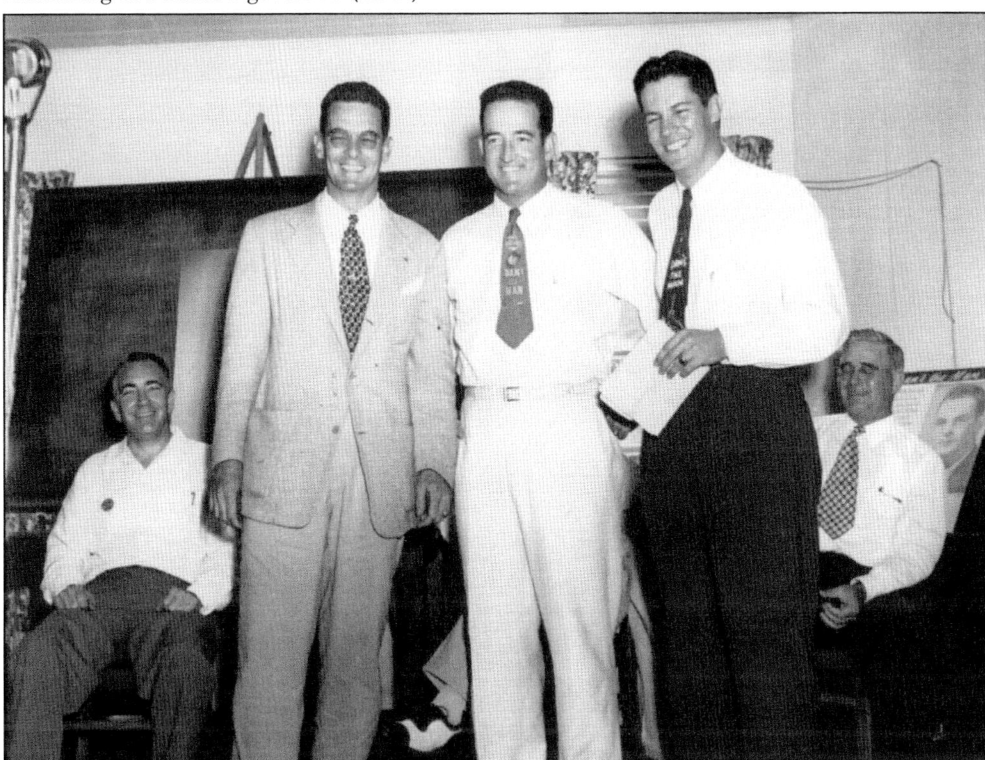

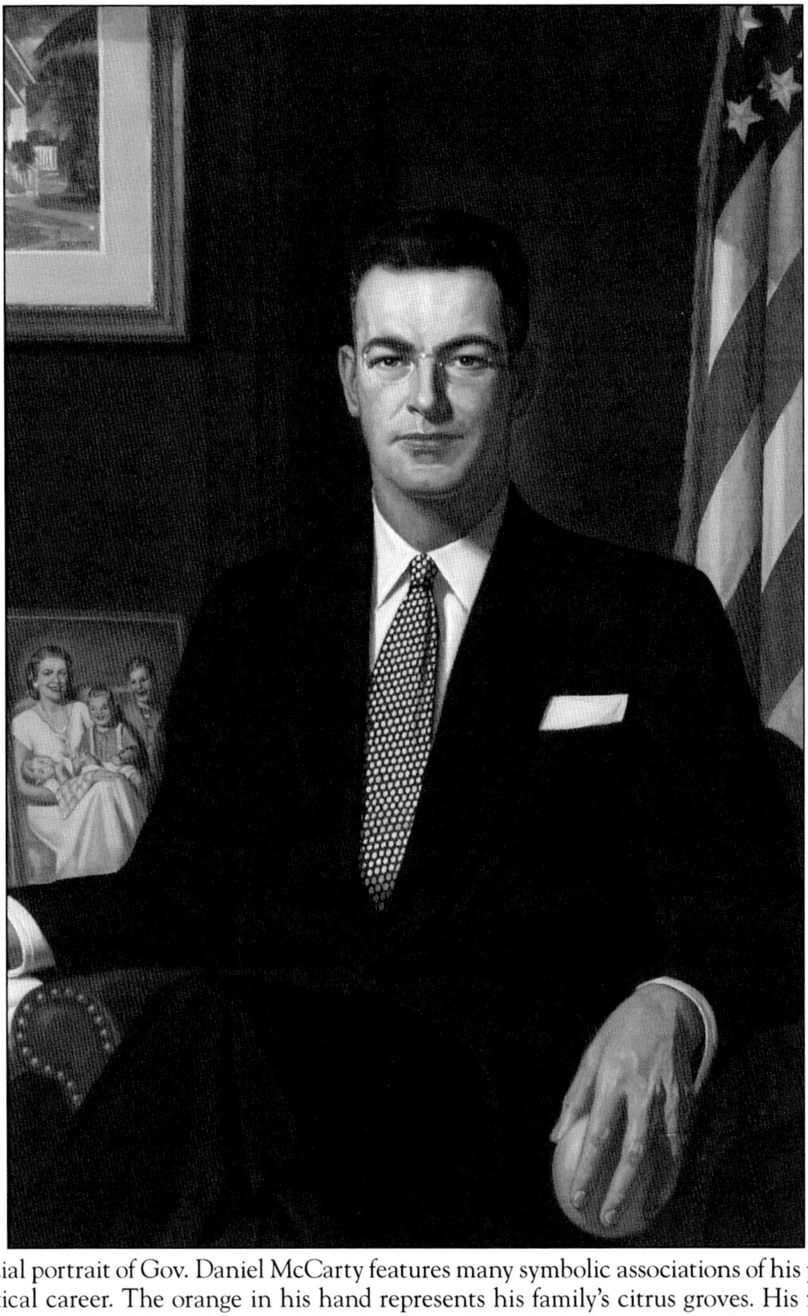

The official portrait of Gov. Daniel McCarty features many symbolic associations of his personal and political career. The orange in his hand represents his family's citrus groves. His family is seen in the painting behind him, and the church in the painting at top was where his funeral would be held. A chain smoker and hard worker, McCarty, 41, suffered a heart attack in 1953. For months, he remained in the mansion to recuperate, only taking up weekly office hours again when Charley Johns made a move to make himself acting governor. By September, McCarty was well enough to take part in a Shriner's parade. It was there that he caught a cold that would turn into pneumonia. His final official workday at the capitol, before he finally gave in to calls for rest, was spent welcoming former campaign volunteers who were shocked at the frail and pale man he had become. He died during the ensuing hospital stay. (MFH.)

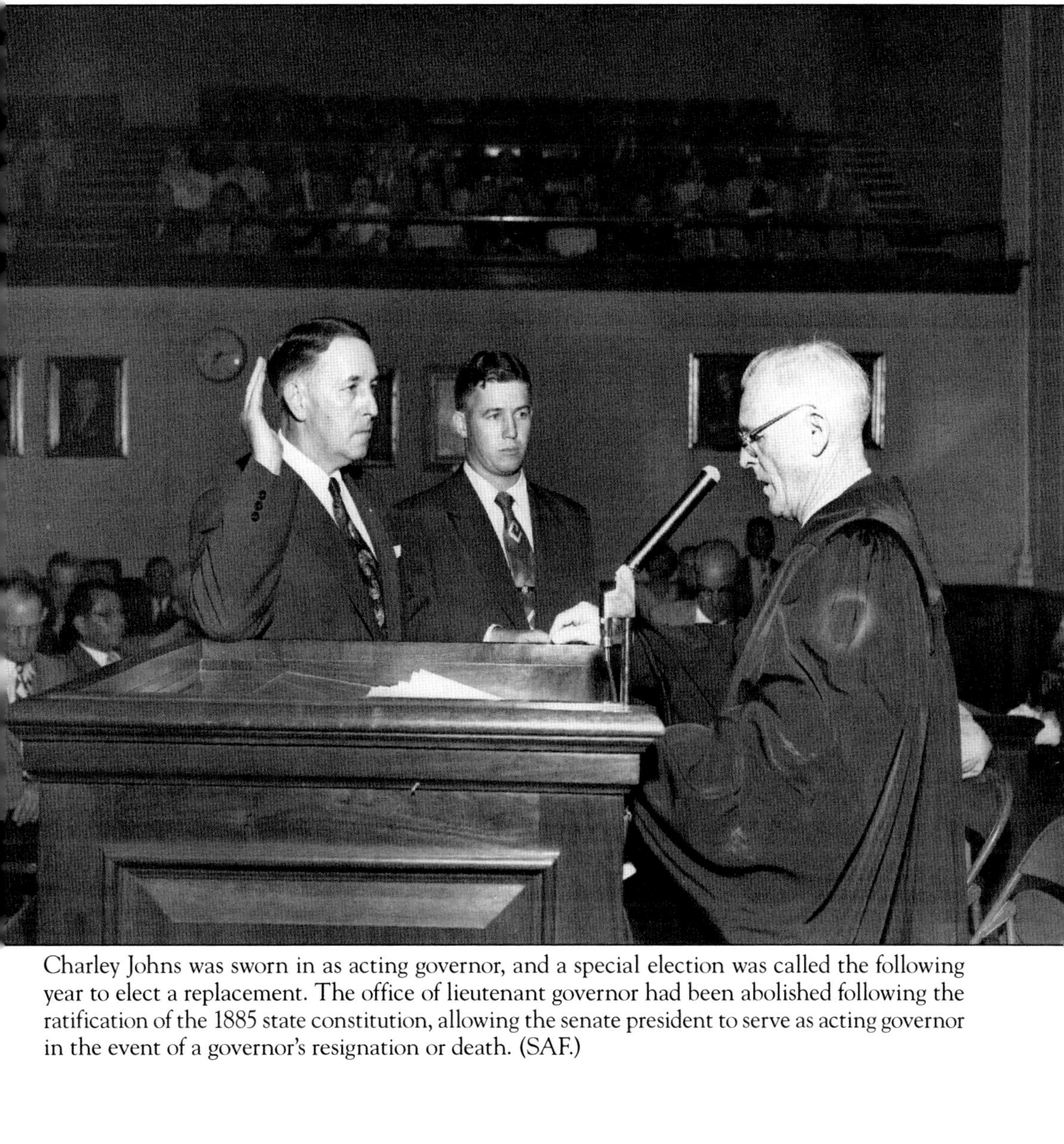

Charley Johns was sworn in as acting governor, and a special election was called the following year to elect a replacement. The office of lieutenant governor had been abolished following the ratification of the 1885 state constitution, allowing the senate president to serve as acting governor in the event of a governor's resignation or death. (SAF.)

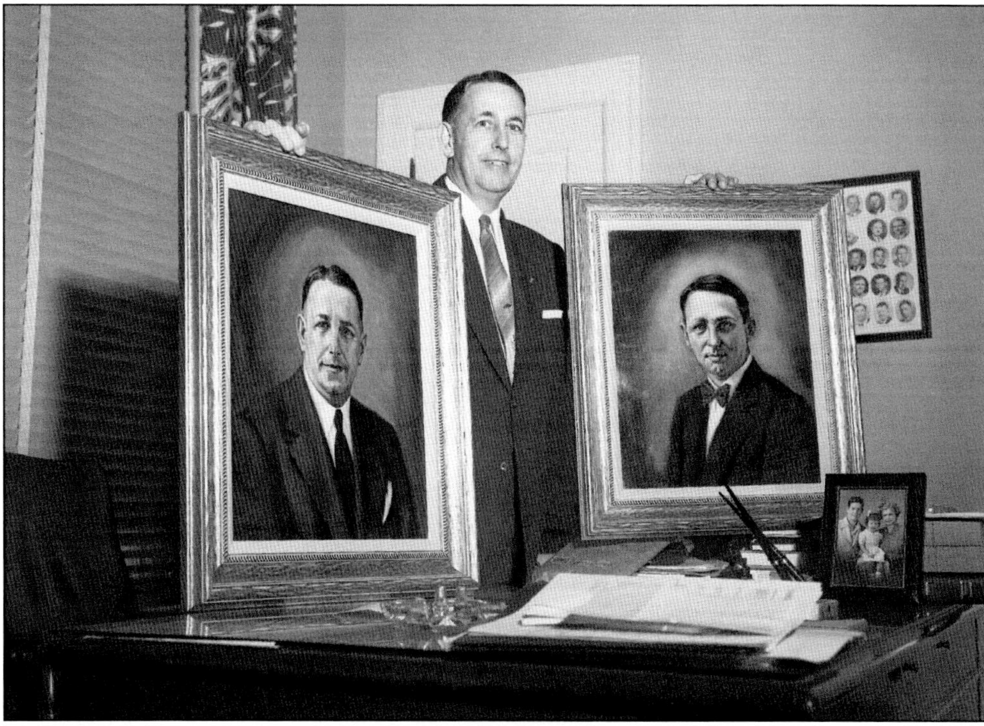

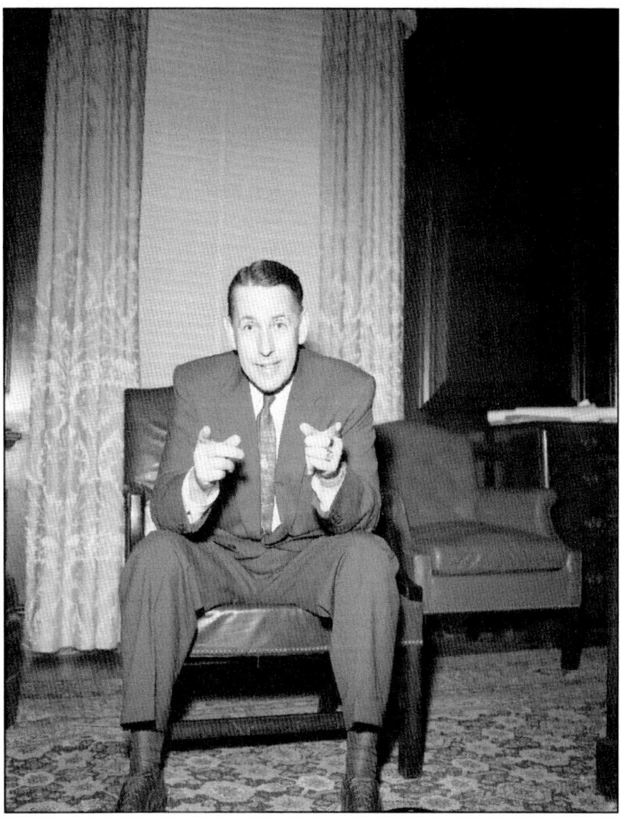

Charley Johns's lifelong dream was to become president of the state senate. Johns is seen above, following his election to that position, holding up his official portrait (left) and that of his brother Markley, who also served as president of the state senate before he died in office. Charley won his late brother's senate seat in 1947. Johns's time in the governor's office was brief and stormy. He seemed to go out of his way to attack all McCarty appointees, and his controversial firing of several for purely political reasons led to his being defeated by Leroy Collins in the special election of 1954. Once out of office, Johns returned to the state senate. (Both, SAF.)

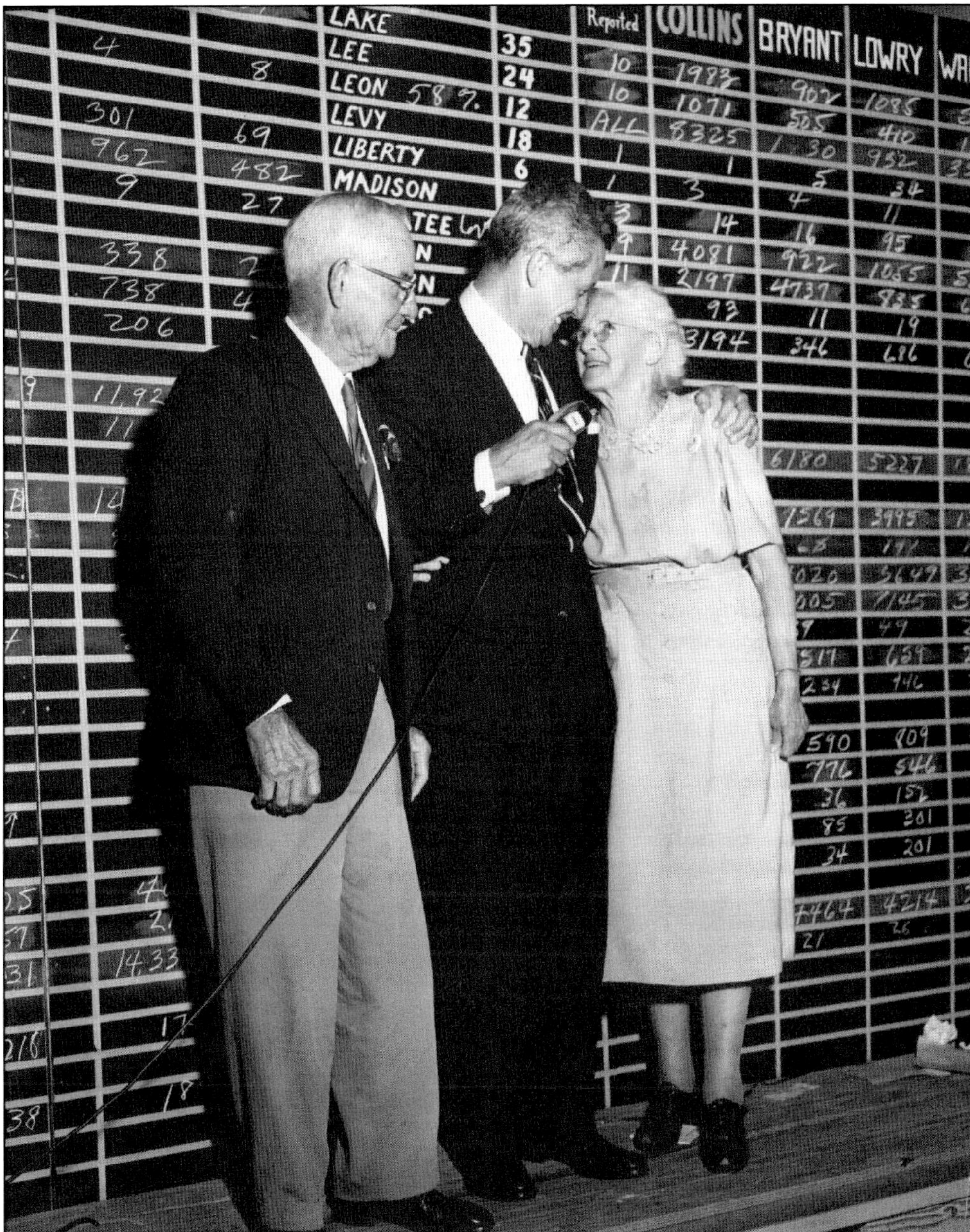

Leroy Collins stands with his parents on primary night as he was announced both the Democratic nominee and the next governor of Florida. Not long after Johns became acting governor, it was obvious that the 1954 race was going to be between Johns, the constitutionally elevated governor, and Leroy Collins, carrying the standard of Daniel McCarty. The primary election results saw Charley Johns win 48 of the state's 67 districts, an impressive total, but a far cry from the landslide McCarty garnered two years earlier. He received just 38 percent of the total vote, while Collins received 33 percent and carried the larger urban strongholds, like Dade County. Following the primary runoff two weeks later, it was Collins who was elected to serve his former friend's final two years in office. (SAF.)

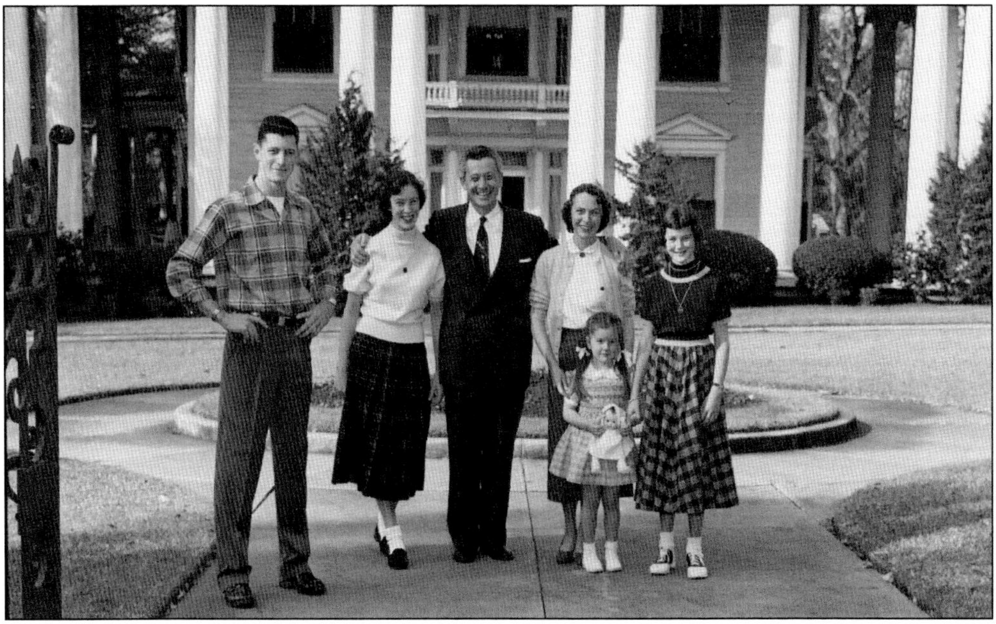

The Collins family (above) poses in front of the mansion's massive veranda and driveway. The mansion was located on busy Adams Street in midtown Tallahassee. Its gate was usually open, and the unpaved north end of the street was a popular area for local children. In 1955, shortly after Leroy Collins was sworn into office, the new chief executive made the decision to demolish the aged first mansion and replace it with a new structure. The Collins' personal home, the Grove, was located next door to the mansion and served as the official executive residence for two years. The new two-story, Colonial-style governor's mansion (below) was completed in time for Collins's second inauguration in 1957. (Above, SAF; below, AC.)

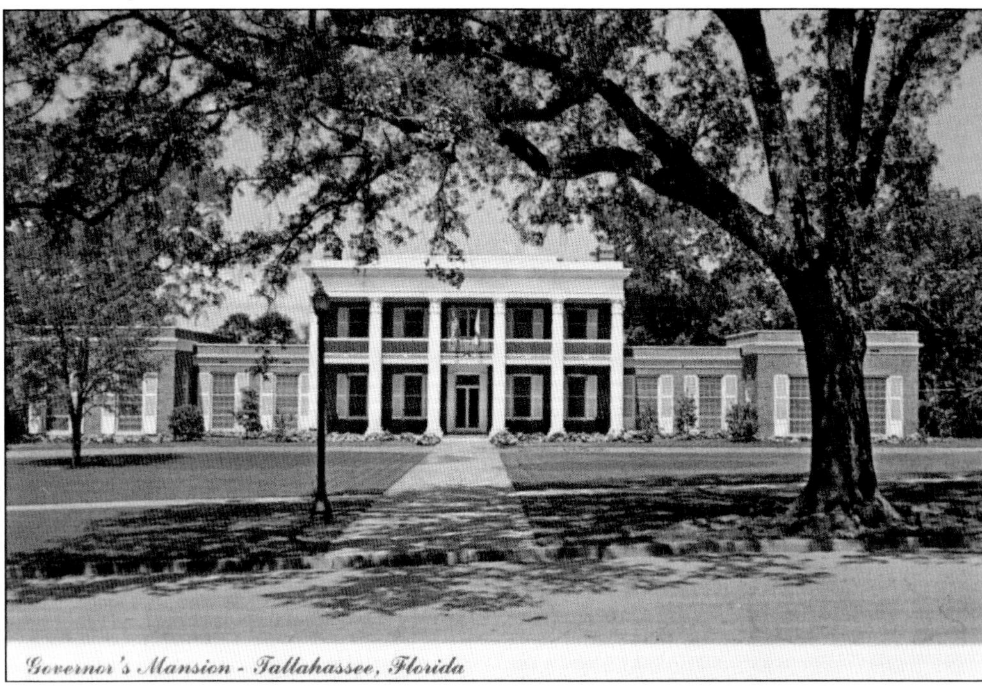

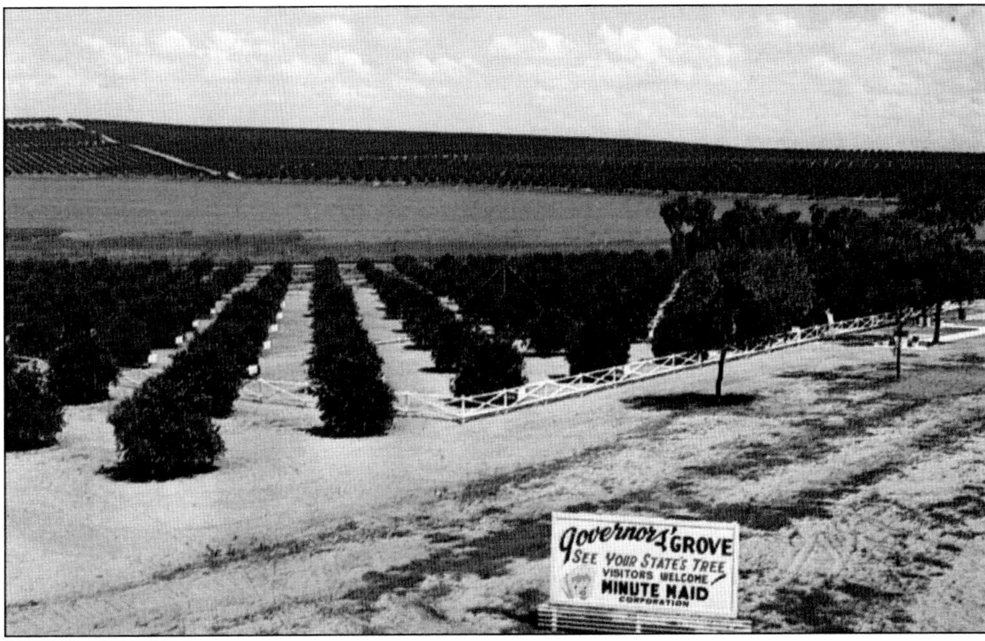

Governors' Grove was located just three miles from Florida's citrus tower in Clermont. During the 1958 governors' conference in Miami Beach, each governor was presented a tree by the Minute Maid Corporation. The company for many years picked and presented the fruit to each governor. In retirement, Leroy Collins served on the Minute Maid board. (AC.)

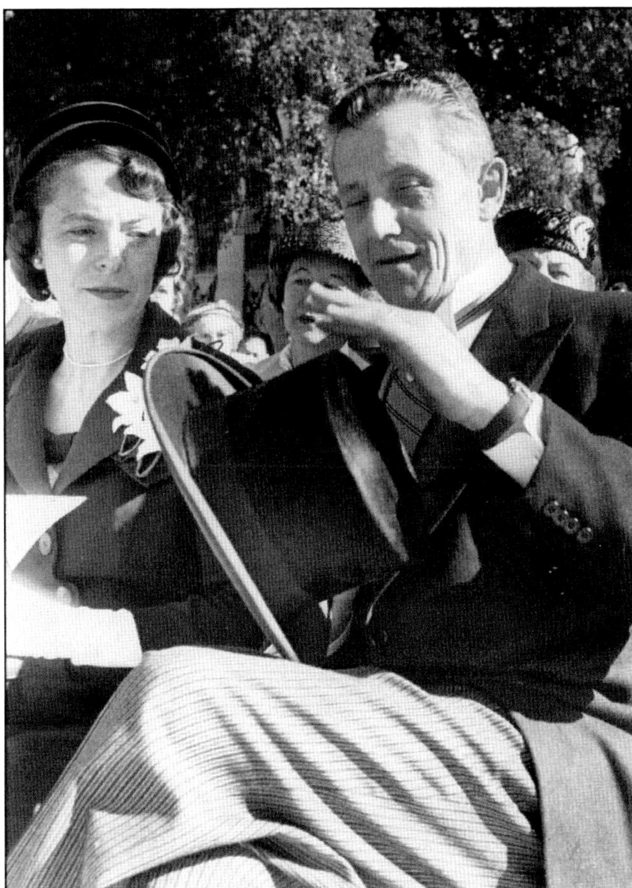

Leroy Collins is seen here with his wife, Mary Call Collins, moments after being sworn in to an unprecedented second term as governor. Months earlier, he had shocked the state by being not only the first governor to succeed himself, but also winning a majority of the Democratic vote in the first primary. Collins faced five opponents for the nomination, including a former and a future governor. (AC.)

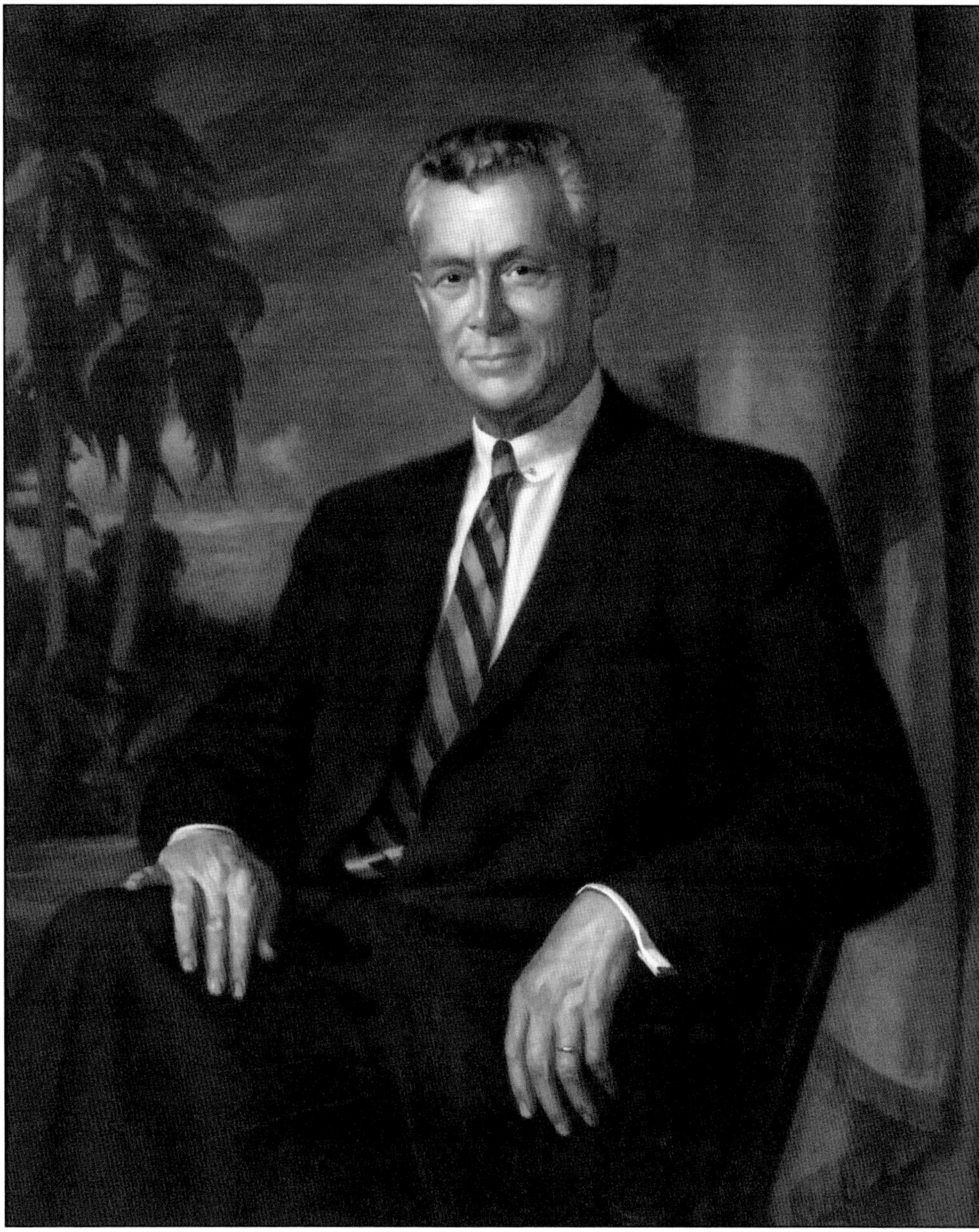

Leroy Collins's official portrait remains in a place of honor outside of the governor's office. He left office after six tumultuous years, an unpopular figure due to his progressive views during the civil rights movement. He is now much revered as both the Floridian of the 20th century and as the greatest governor in the state's history. (MFH.)

Seven

NASA AND DISNEY

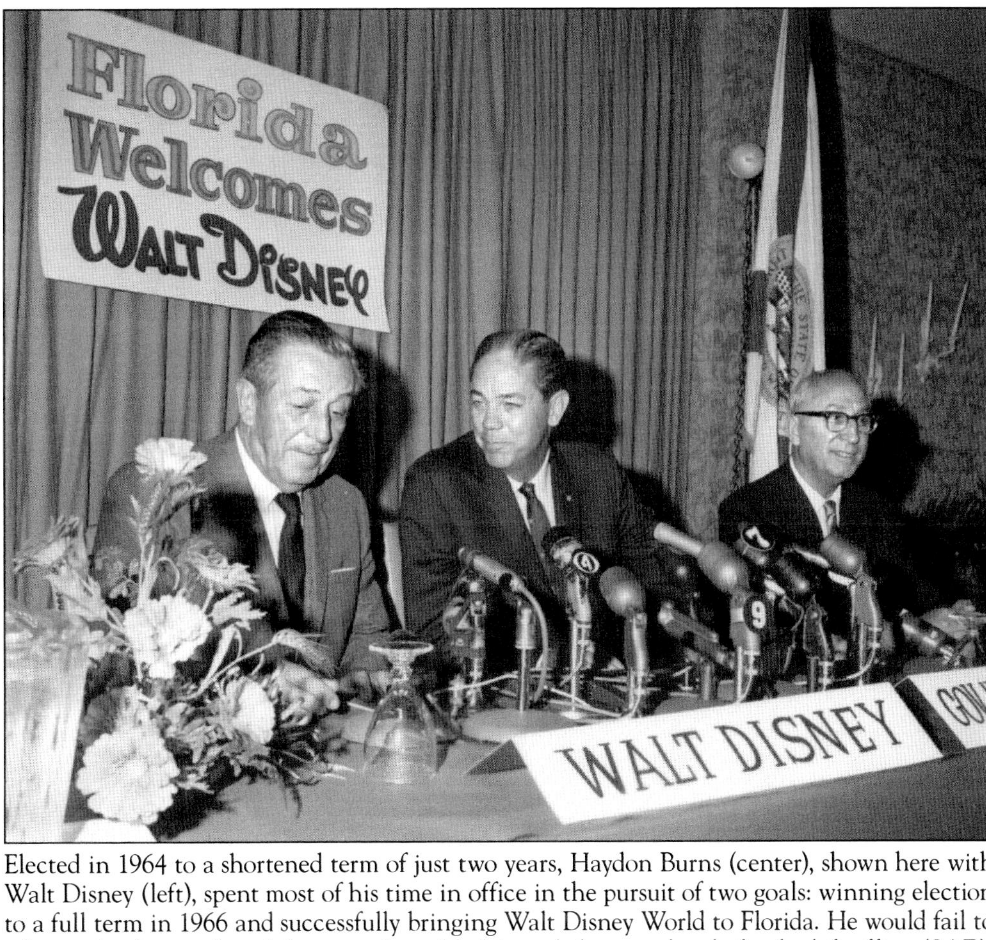

Elected in 1964 to a shortened term of just two years, Haydon Burns (center), shown here with Walt Disney (left), spent most of his time in office in the pursuit of two goals: winning election to a full term in 1966 and successfully bringing Walt Disney World to Florida. He would fail to achieve the first goal, and the second would ultimately be completed after he left office. (SAF.)

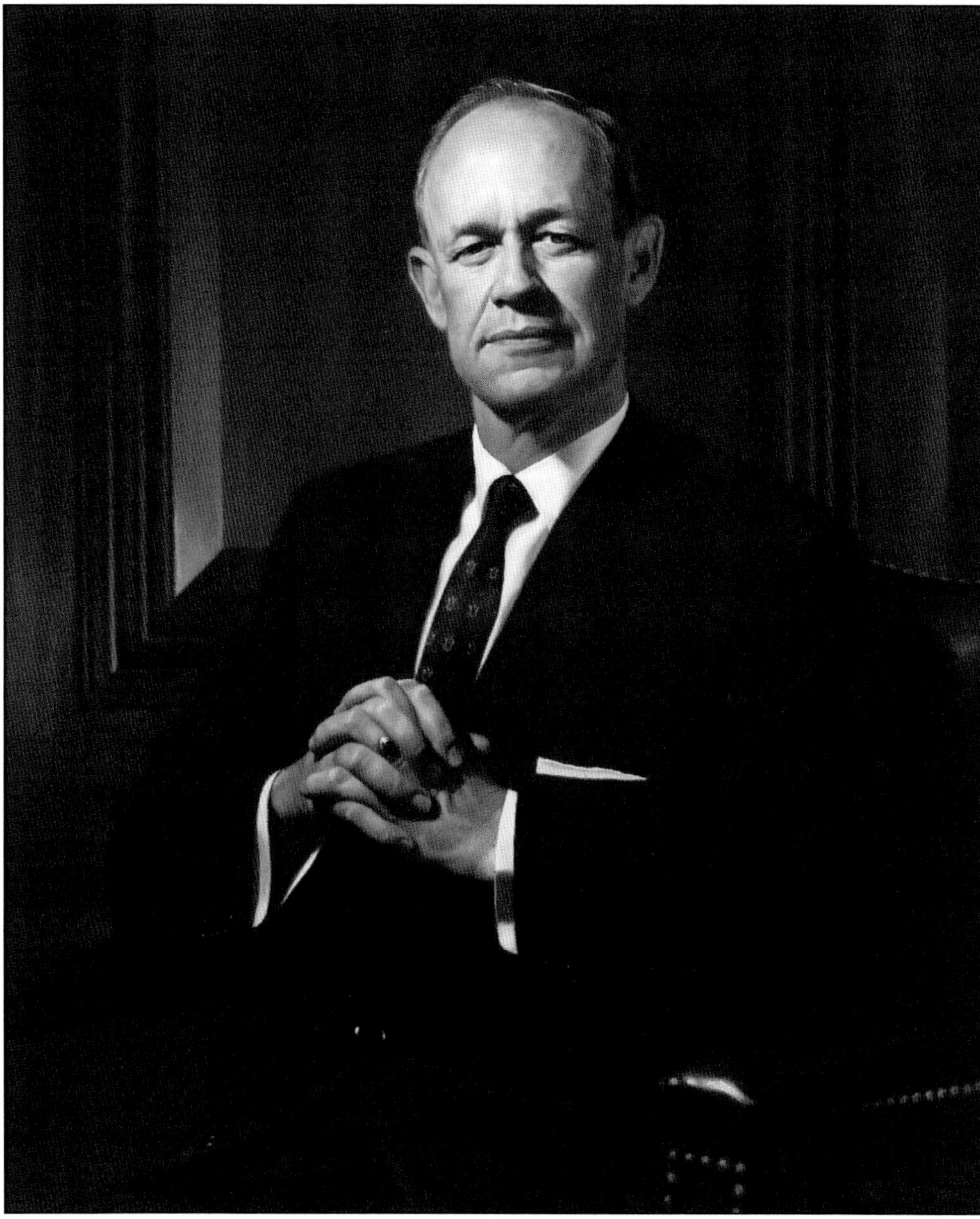

Cecil Farris Bryant, who commonly went by Farris, was born on July 26, 1914. His uncle, Ion Farris, served as Speaker of the House in 1909 and 1913. Uncle Ion was the future governor's hero, and his influence would mold young Farris into an ambitious man in a hurry. The son of a farmer and a bookkeeper, Bryant received a law degree from Harvard Law School in 1938 and made a name for himself as a successful lawyer. Bryant began his political career in 1942, when he was elected a state representative, eventually serving as Speaker in 1953. (MFH.)

Bryant first ran for the governorship against Leroy Collins in 1956. Plagued by a lack of fundraising and poor organization, the campaign was a disaster for Bryant. In 1960, he made another run for the nomination, this time with top-level party financing and a well-structured statewide organization. Traveling around the state in his own plane, which the candidate himself piloted, Bryant won an overwhelming victory in November. (SAF.)

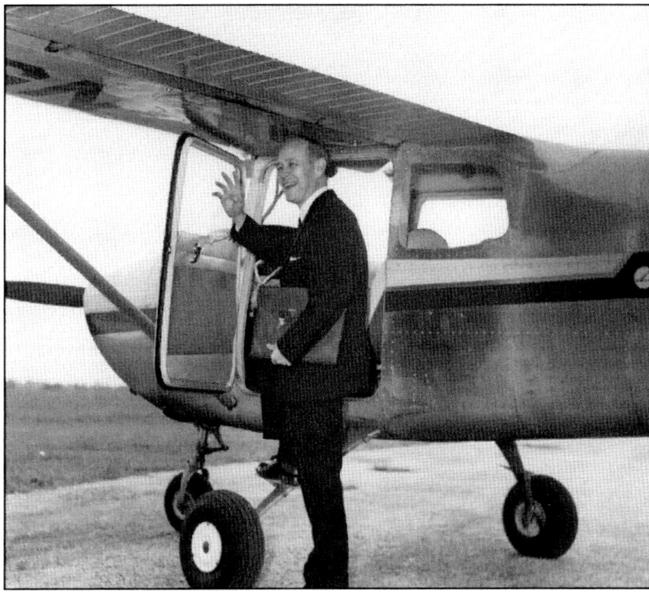

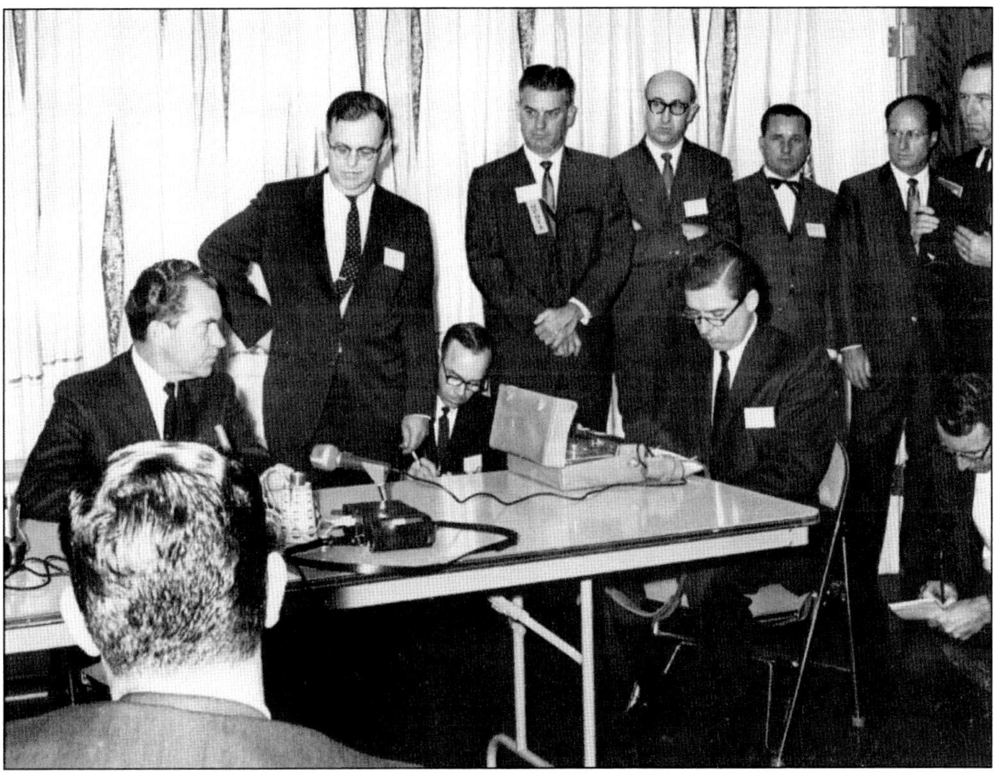

Richard Nixon, seen at left during a crowded press conference, was the Republican presidential candidate in 1960. Due to John Kennedy's pro–civil rights stance, the South, normally a Democratic stronghold, looked promising to Republicans. Nixon's surprise victory in Florida caused the Republican gubernatorial candidate that year to receive nearly 40 percent. The growing strength of Florida Republicans led to the switch of gubernatorial elections from presidential to midterm elections.

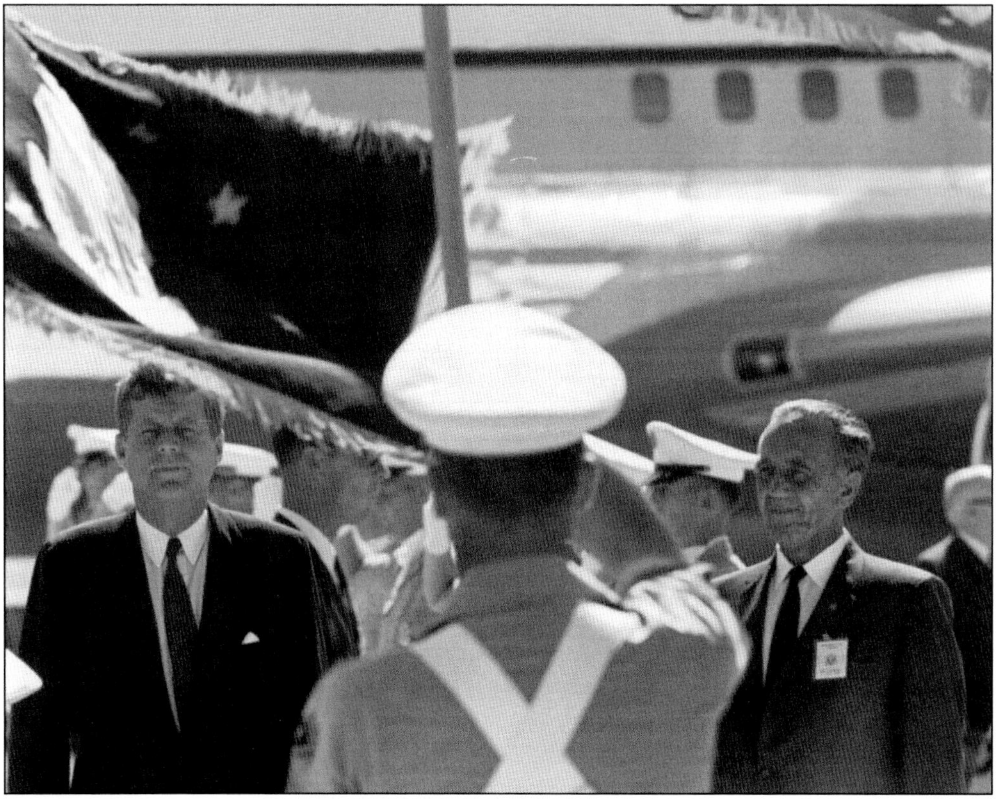

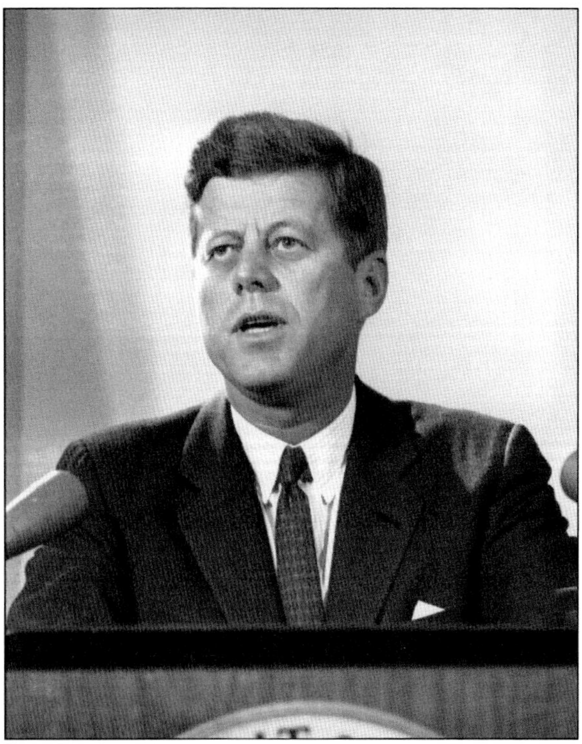

John F. Kennedy, during his brief tenure as the 35th president of the United States, left an impressive mark on the state of Florida. In particular, two events were important for the state: the Cuban Missile Crisis, and Kennedy's speech declaring the goal of a man on the moon before 1970. On October 22 at 7:00 p.m., Kennedy delivered a nationwide address on all major television networks announcing the discovery of the missiles. "It shall be the policy of this nation to regard any nuclear missile launched from Cuba against any nation in the Western Hemisphere as an attack by the Soviet Union on the United States, requiring a full retaliatory response upon the Soviet Union." The state of Florida was the center of national attention during the 13-day confrontation that pushed the world toward nuclear war. (Both, AC.)

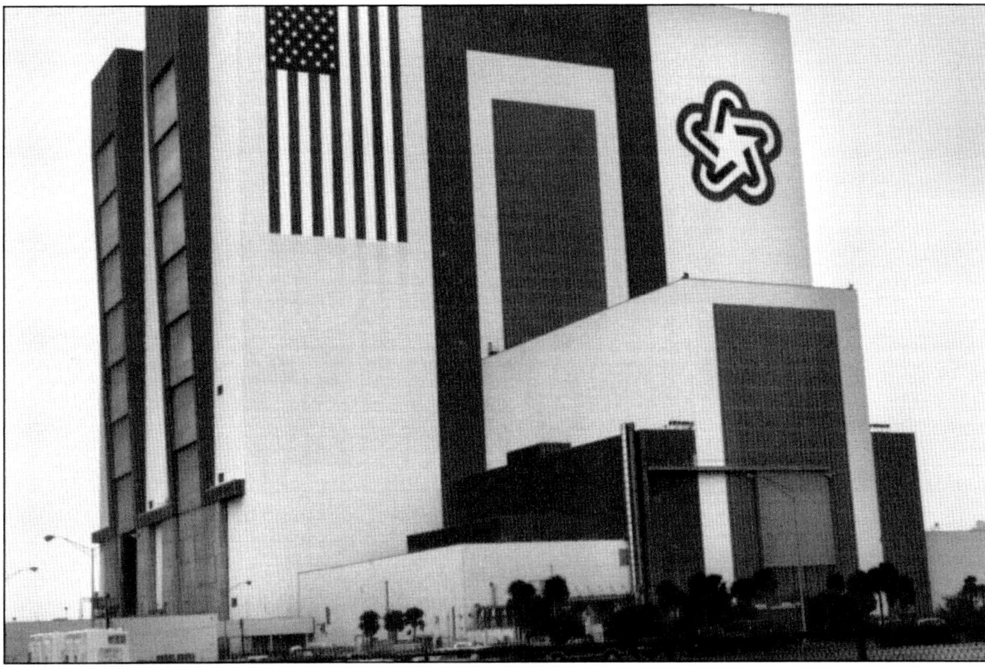

The Vehicle Assembly Building (above) and a Mercury Redstone rocket on display (below) are located at the John F. Kennedy Space Center. The center has been, since 1968, the site for every NASA human space flight. It is located on Merritt Island, midway between Miami and Jacksonville. Like Disney World, it is an important part of Florida's economy, providing employment to nearly 15,000 people. The original name, simply the Launch Operations Center, was changed by executive order to honor the fallen president. Following the conclusion of the Apollo program, the site became home to the space shuttle program. It was also the site at which the tragic events of the *Challenger* explosion occurred. (Both, AC.)

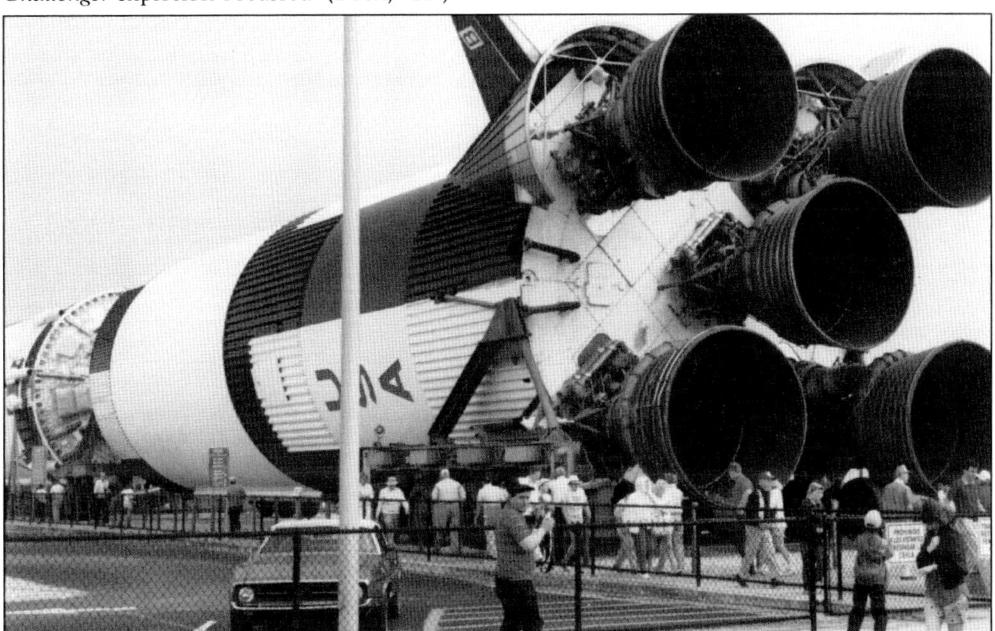

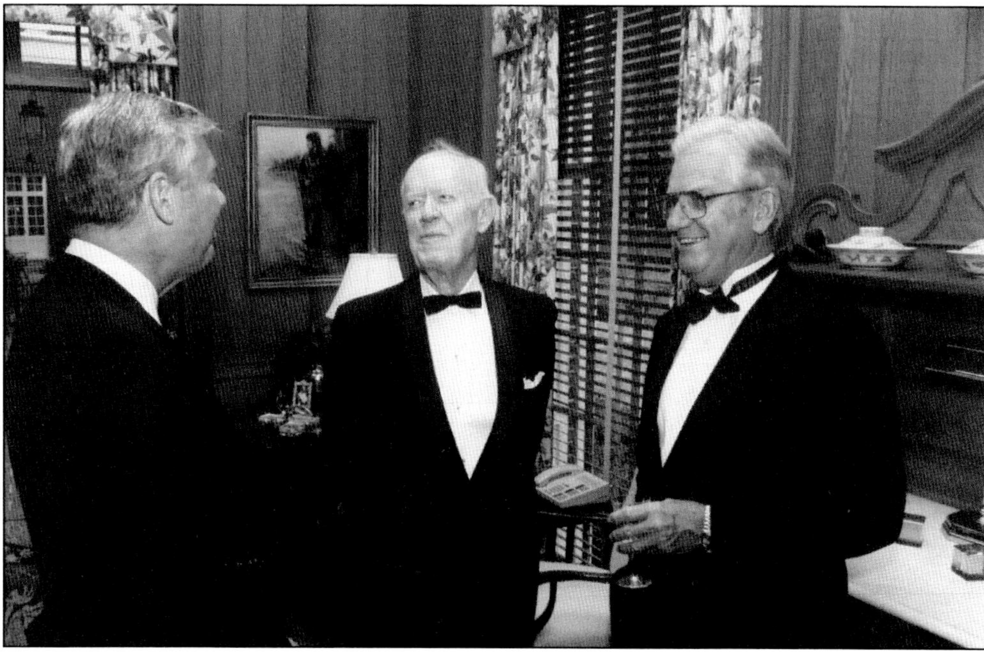

Former governor Farris Bryant (center), seen here with former governors Bob Graham (left) and Wayne Mixson, served on Pres. Lyndon Johnson's National Security Council and in the White House Office of Emergency Planning. In 1970, he ran against Lawton Chiles for the Democratic nomination for the US Senate. Bryant won the first primary but lost the runoff to Chiles. (AC.)

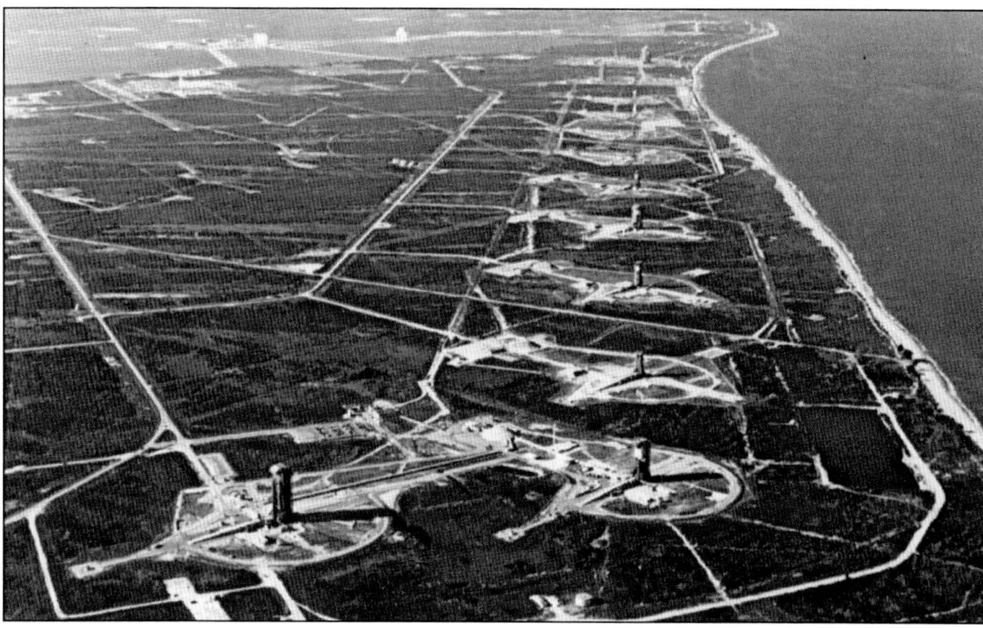

Shown here at John F. Kennedy Space Center is missile row, part of the Cape Canaveral Air Force Station. Many important events in the space race took place on this strip of land, including the launch of the first US astronaut into orbit, the first US lunar landing, and countless space probes. (AC.)

NASA's Gemini-Titan 4, launched from Cape Kennedy, was the second crewed mission of the Gemini series, carrying James McDivitt and Edward White on a four-day, 98-hour flight. It was during this mission that the first spacewalk by an American took place. This flight, like all of the Gemini series, was designed to experiment with space travel prior to the Apollo program. (AC.)

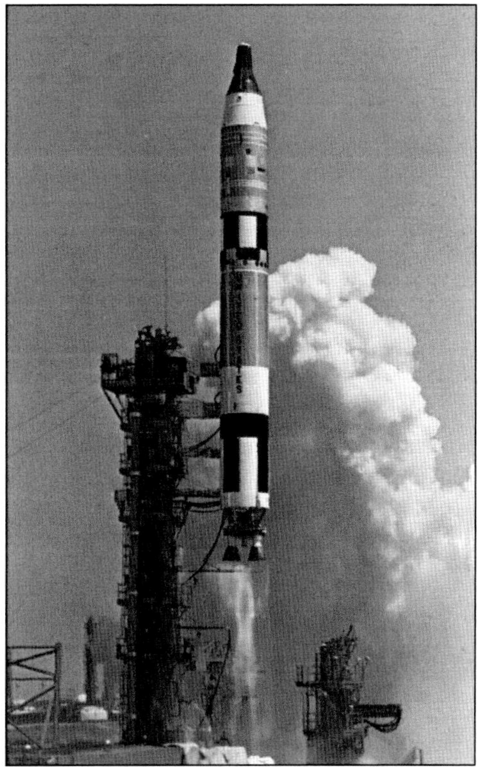

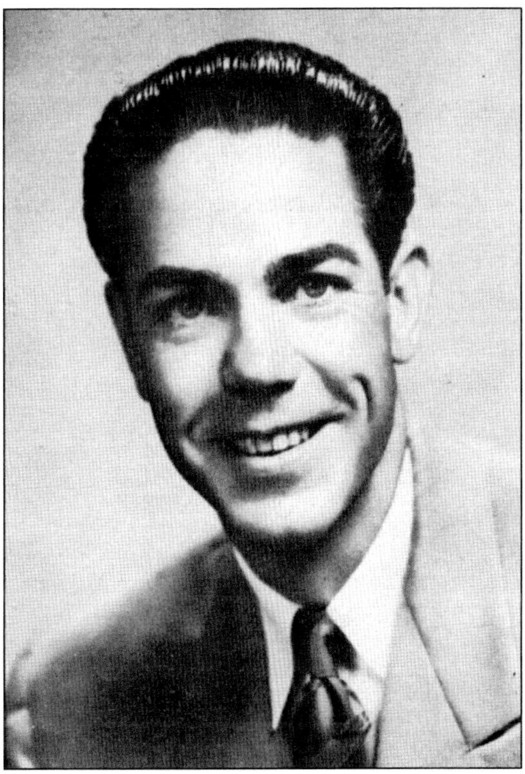

Haydon Burns, seen here shortly after being elected mayor of Jacksonville in 1949, won four consecutive terms as mayor and proved to be a brilliant promoter for the city's interests. Under his leadership, Jacksonville became the insurance capital of the South and home to both a baseball and a hockey team. (JHS.)

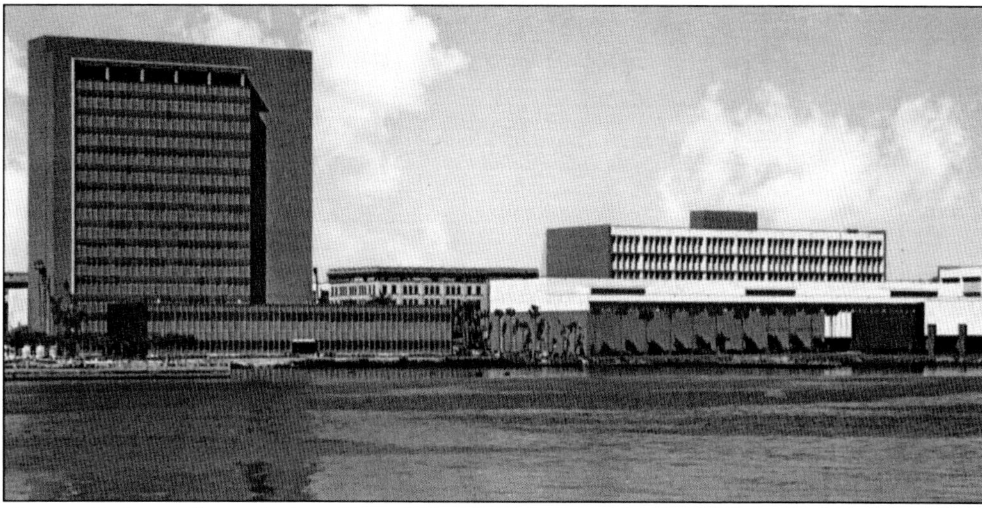

The new Jacksonville city hall and Duval County courthouse (above) were located on the St. Johns River. It was during Haydon Burns's long tenure as mayor that this new facility was put into use as the center of all governmental operations in the county. The 13-story building became Jacksonville's Annex when the city's government moved to another structure in the 1990s. (AC.)

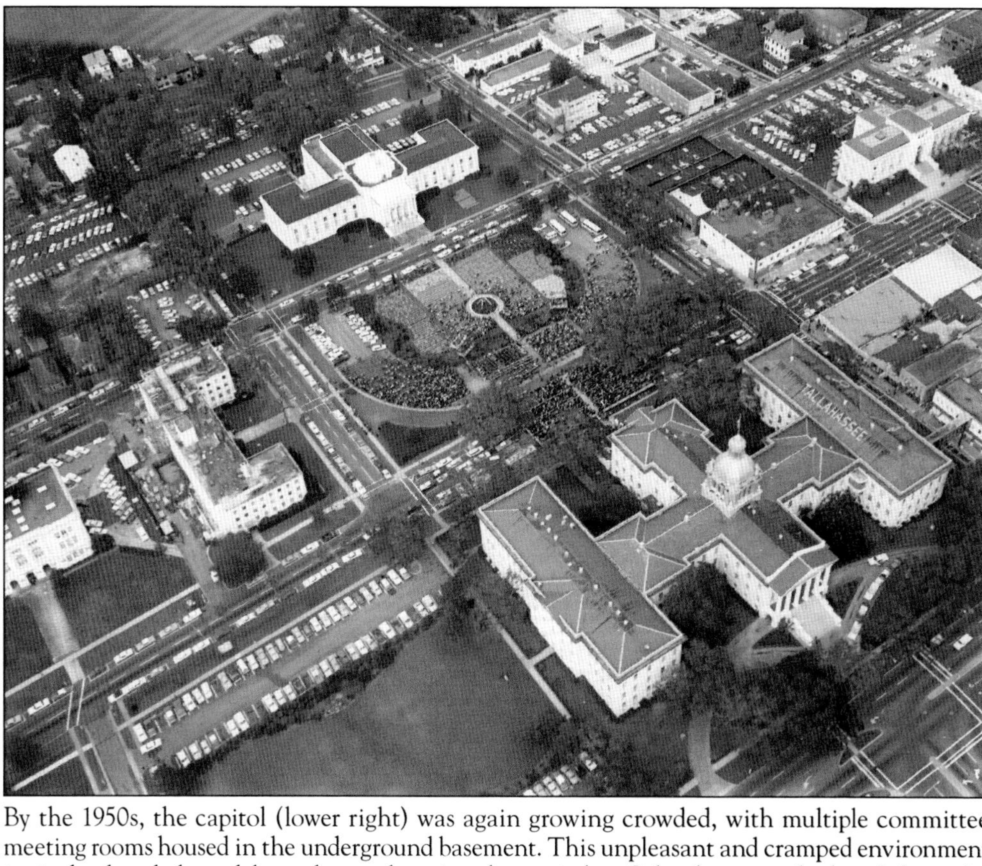

By the 1950s, the capitol (lower right) was again growing crowded, with multiple committee meeting rooms housed in the underground basement. This unpleasant and cramped environment ignited a decade-long debate about relocating the capital to Orlando or simply demolishing the existing structure prior to the creation of a new, larger capitol. (SAF.)

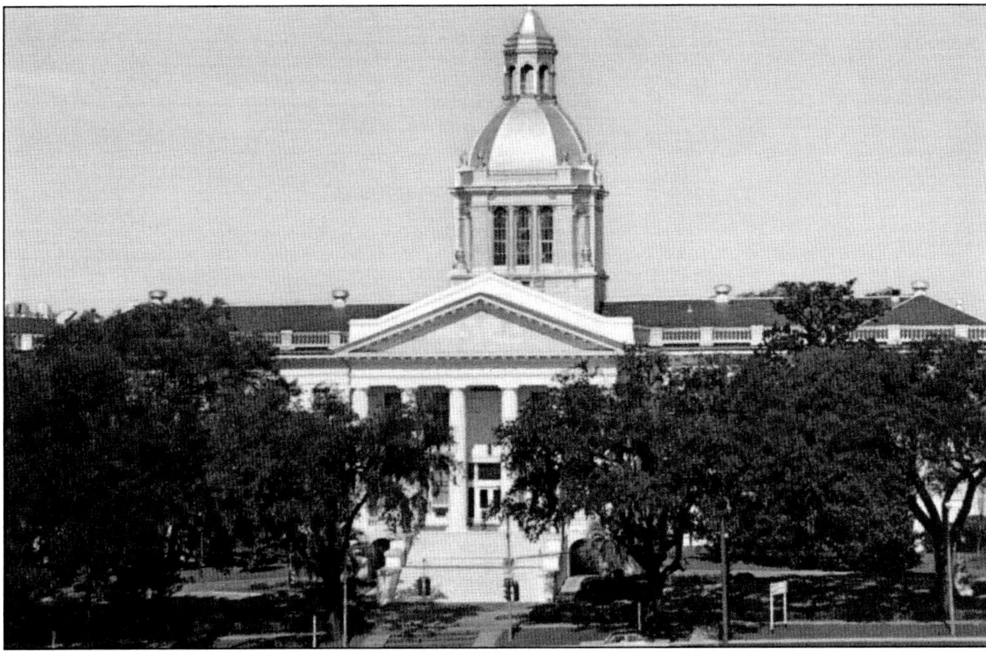

After much protest from citizens, the plans to either abandon Tallahassee or demolish the capitol were discarded in favor of a new building alongside the historic capitol. Governors Burns and Kirk redesigned the governor's suite in the historic capitol, turning their offices into showcases for the entire state. The outdated capitol itself was cause for much embarrassment to lawmakers. (WM.)

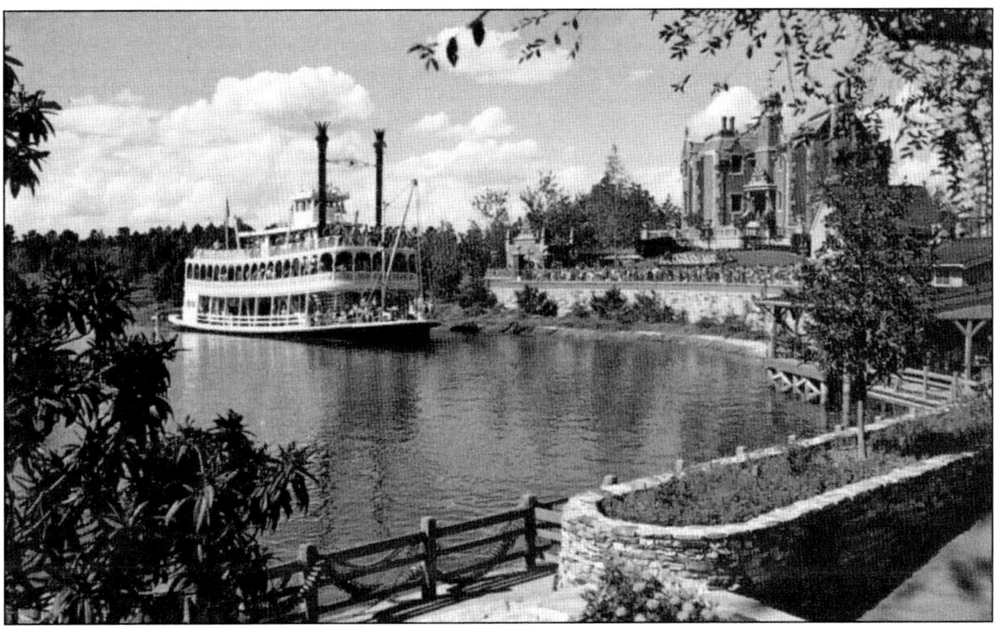

Cruising the Rivers of America, an authentic steam-powered stern-wheeler moves across Liberty Square in the Magic Kingdom. The search for a second Disney amusement park began around 1959. Walt Disney had grown tired of the separate small businesses that had opened near Disneyland in an effort to cash in on its success. (AC.)

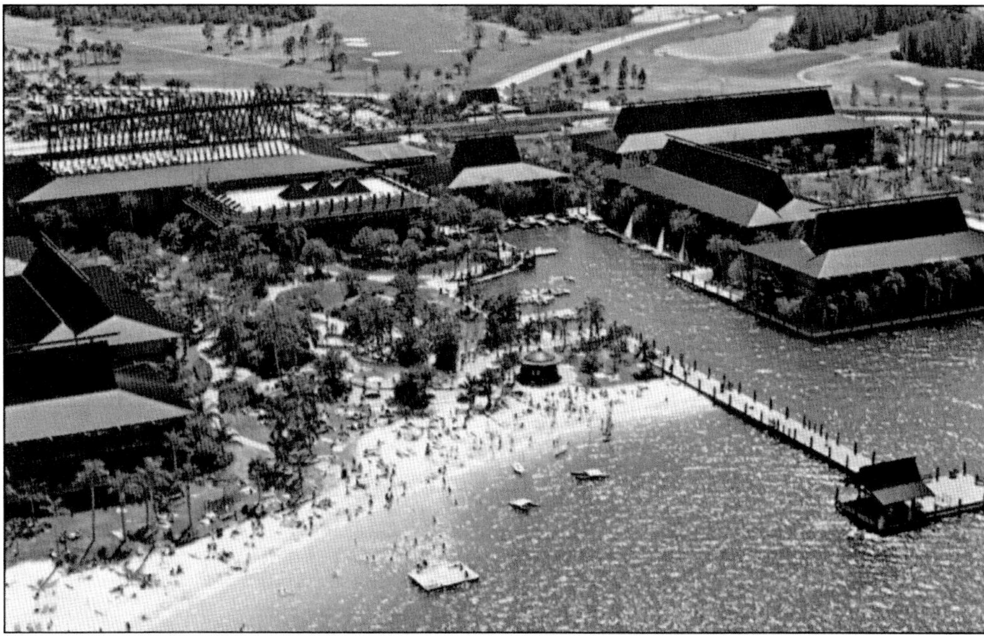

Shown on this page are the famous contemporary and Polynesian Island Village Resorts. Walt Disney said the major difference between Disneyland and Disney World was a blessing of size. These resorts and others like them were part of Disney's plan to include hotel accommodations in the outlying areas of the park. The 43 square miles of Disney World is twice the size of Manhattan and is completely enclosed by swampland. The Disney empire was simply stretched too thin in the 1950s to allow the purchase of more land for development. Disneyland has long suffered from the boundaries of its original 160 acres. The Orlando area allowed Walt Disney greater control and room for future expansion. Throughout the 1960s, Disney quietly used multiple dummy corporations to buy up land in a successful effort to keep prices down. (Both, AC.)

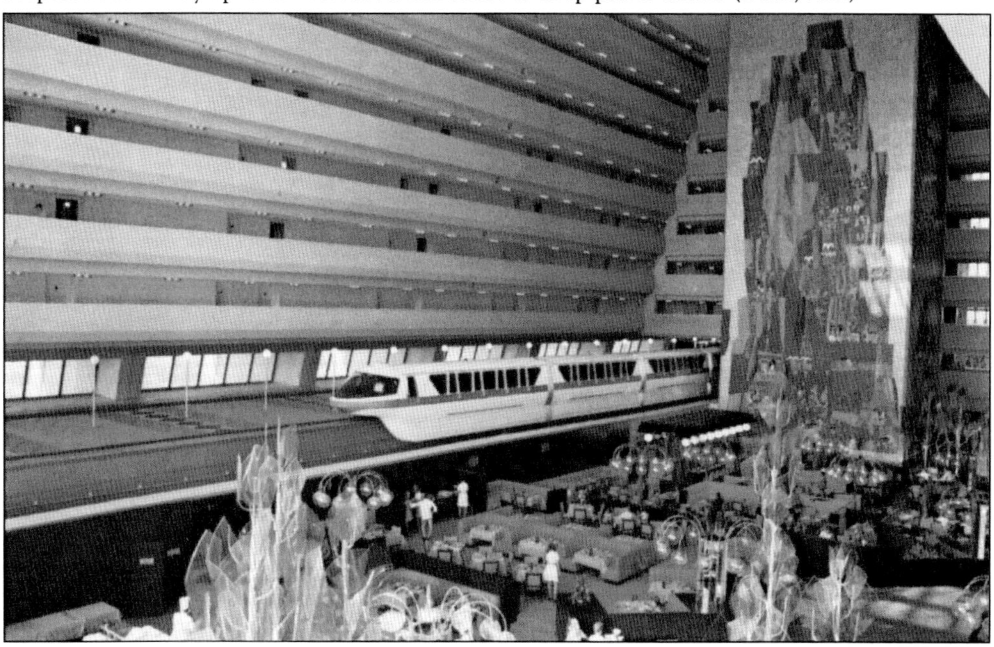

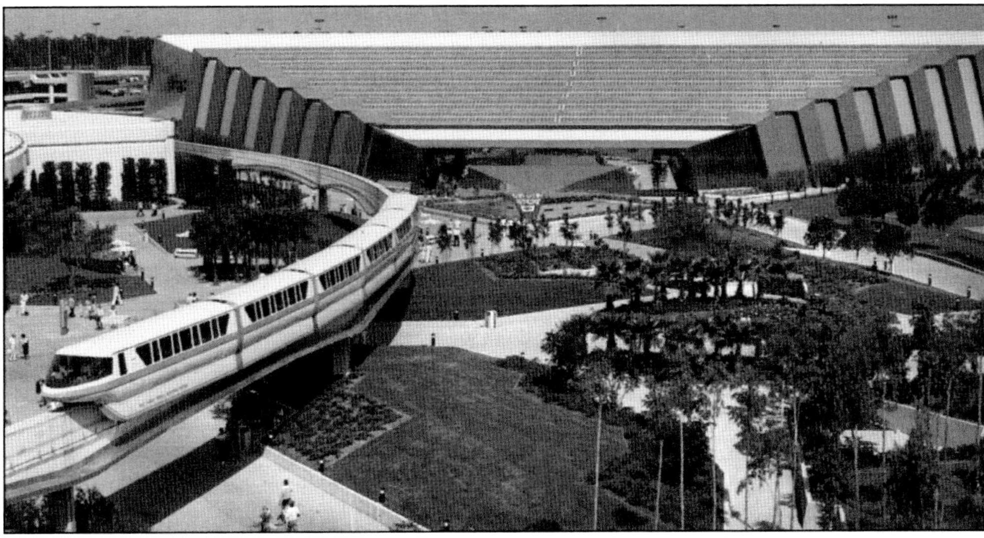

Epcot was Walt Disney's prototype for a futuristic community known as Progress City. He envisioned it to be a real community, with both urban and suburban sensitivities. The functional Disney resort would serve as a communal link to its population. The park does have elements of this original concept and has often been a public showcase for exciting new technology. The scope of Disney's vision has since been hemmed in by the realities of a modern world. (AC.)

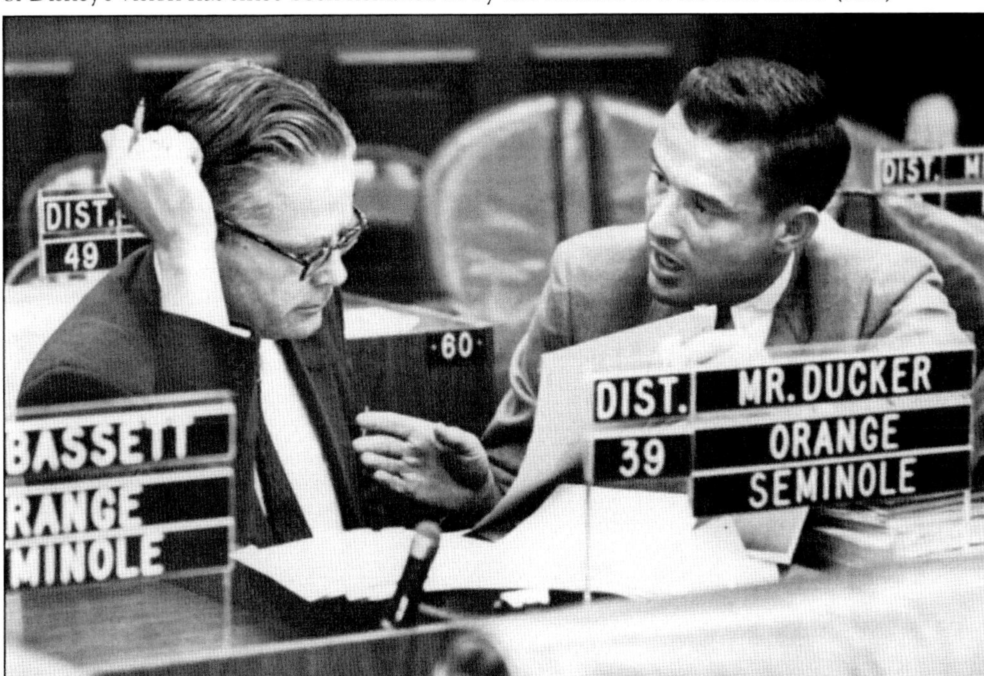

State representatives Robert Rust (right) and John Ducker discuss legislation creating a special district for Disney World. Roy Disney, following his brother's death, lobbied hard for the creation of the Reedy Creek Improvement District. It contained the towns of Bay Lake and Reedy Creek, designed as an incorporated city that would receive tax-free bonds and exemption from future state land laws. Gov. Claude Kirk signed the district into law in May 1967. (AC.)

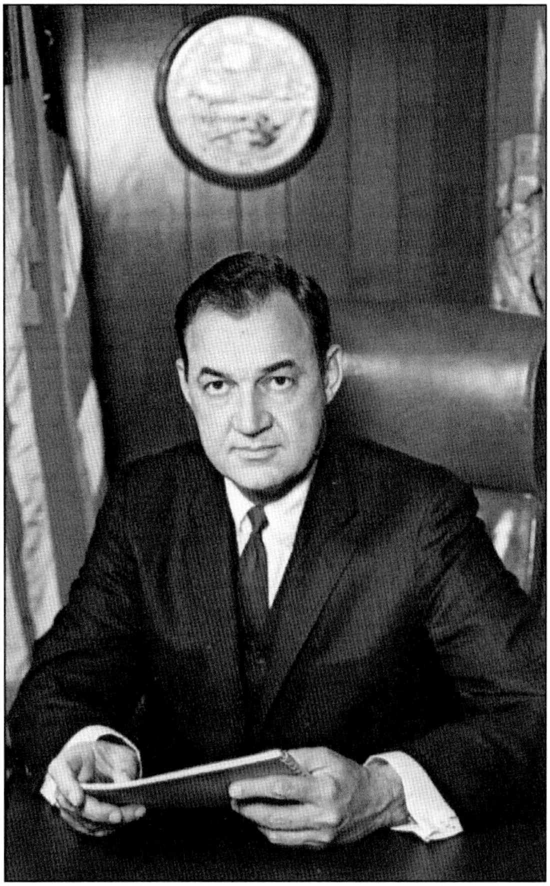

Claude Kirk, elected in 1966, was the first Republican governor in the state since Reconstruction. After a bitter Democratic primary election, defeated incumbent Haydon Burns refused to endorse nominee Robert High, leading to a mass conservative exodus from the Democratic Party. Kirk scored a huge upset to become governor, defeating Robert King High, the mayor of Miami, 55 percent to 45 percent.

Shown here is Saw Grass Recreation Park, two miles north of Fort Lauderdale. After several decades of being overdeveloped and drained, the Everglades underwent a program of conservation, largely credited to Governor Kirk. While his views on school busing and the controversial statewide teachers' strike of 1968 undercut his administration, Kirk's views on the environment became his lasting legacy. (AC.)

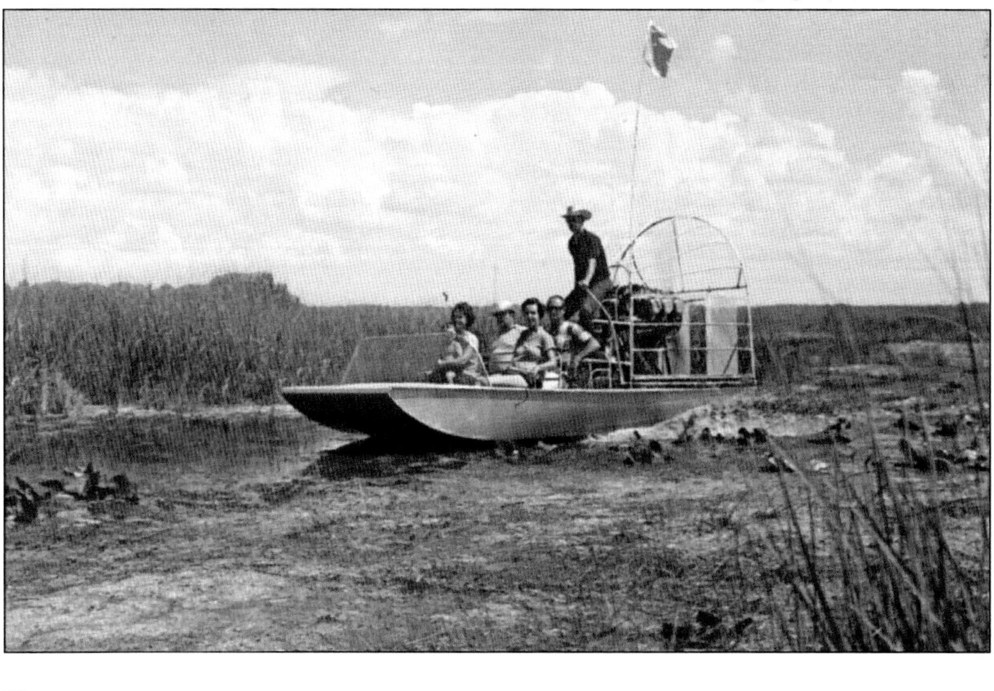

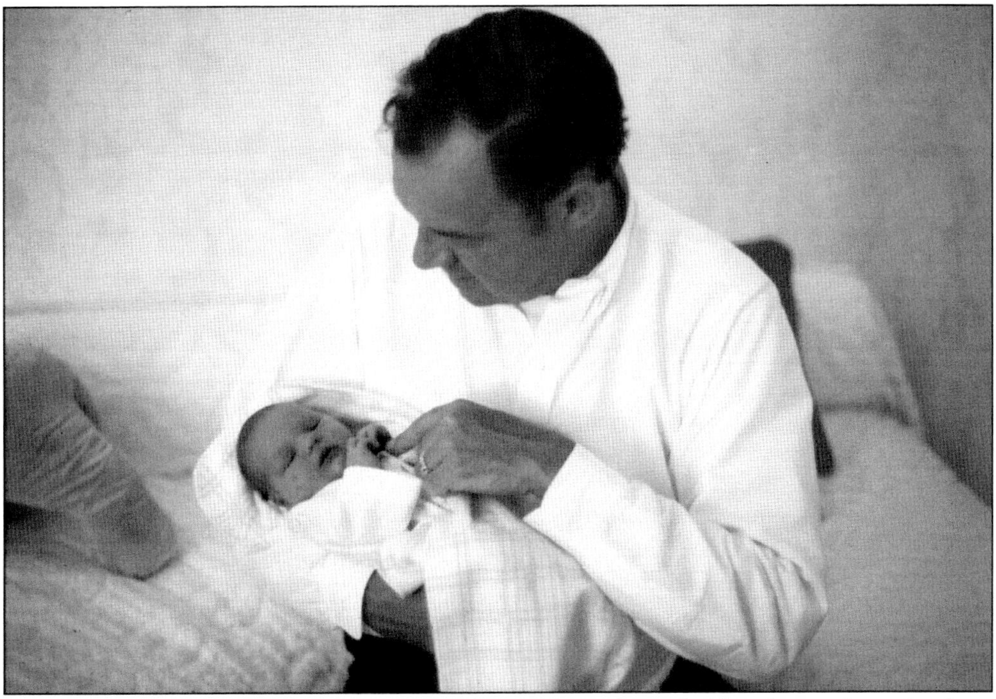

Gov. Claude Kirk is seen here at his private Palm Beach residence, holding his newborn daughter. A young divorcée when he came into office, Kirk married German-born Erika Mattfeld. At the inaugural ball, he introduced her to the press as "Madame X." They had two children while he was in office: Claudia in 1968, and Erik in 1970. (SAF.)

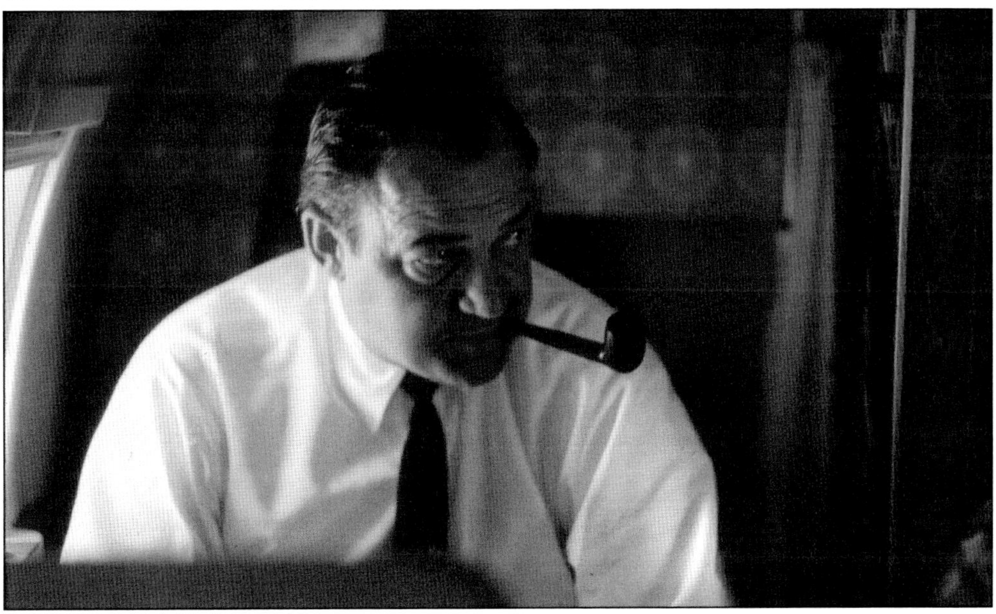

Claude Kirk, shown here on the official state jet, frequently used public funds to promote himself as a potential vice presidential candidate in 1968. His efforts proved fruitless and severely weakened his support among Republicans at home. After being turned down for the No. 2 spot on the Republican ticket, Kirk faced a strong challenge from Jack Eckerd for the Republican nomination. (SAF.)

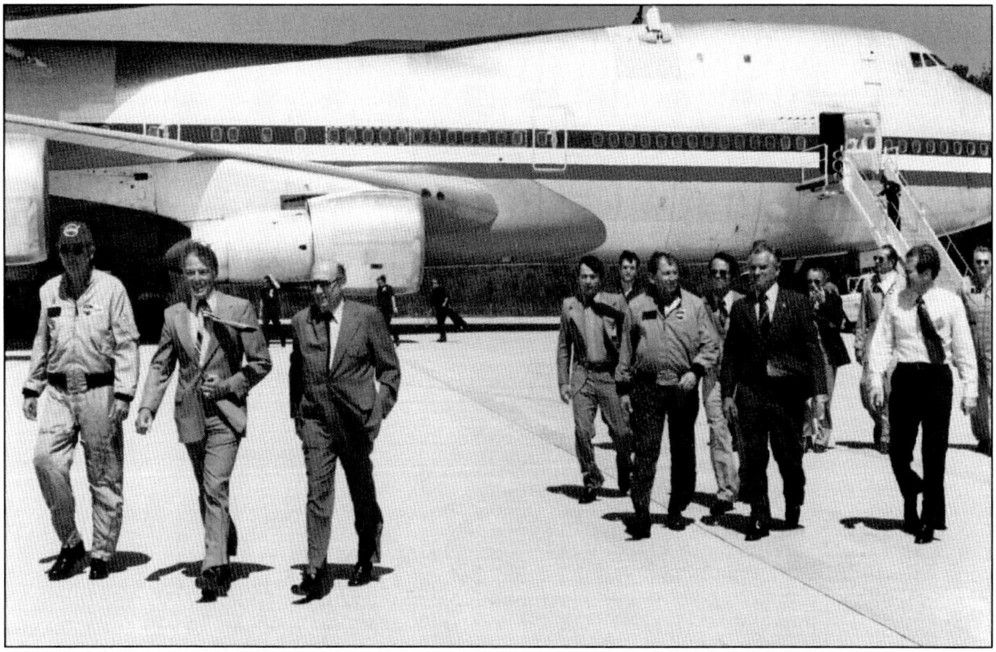

Future US senator Bill Nelson (far right) and Gov. Wayne Mixson (second from far right) served as guests of honor for the arrival of the first space shuttle at Cape Canaveral. The shuttle, a partially reusable human spaceflight vehicle, was strapped on top of a Shuttle Carrier Aircraft 747-100. This particular carrier aircraft, N905NA, was part of the American Airlines fleet. It transported the *Enterprise* in 1978. (WM.)

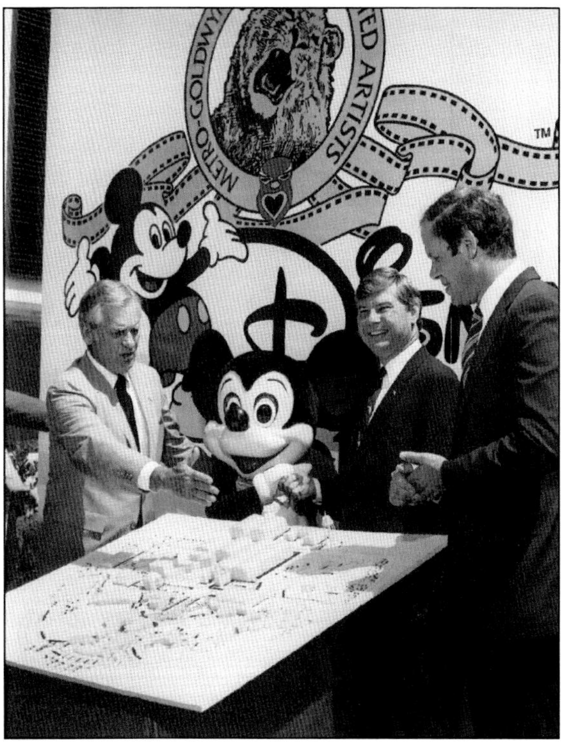

Disney CEO Michael Eisner (far right) presents a model of the future Disney MGM studios to Governors Graham (second from right) and Mixson. At this time, the governor's office was involved, largely due to Disney's original desire to turn the location into a television and motion-picture production facility. The state had greatly expanded its push to attract production companies to Florida. (WM.)

Eight

Golden Age

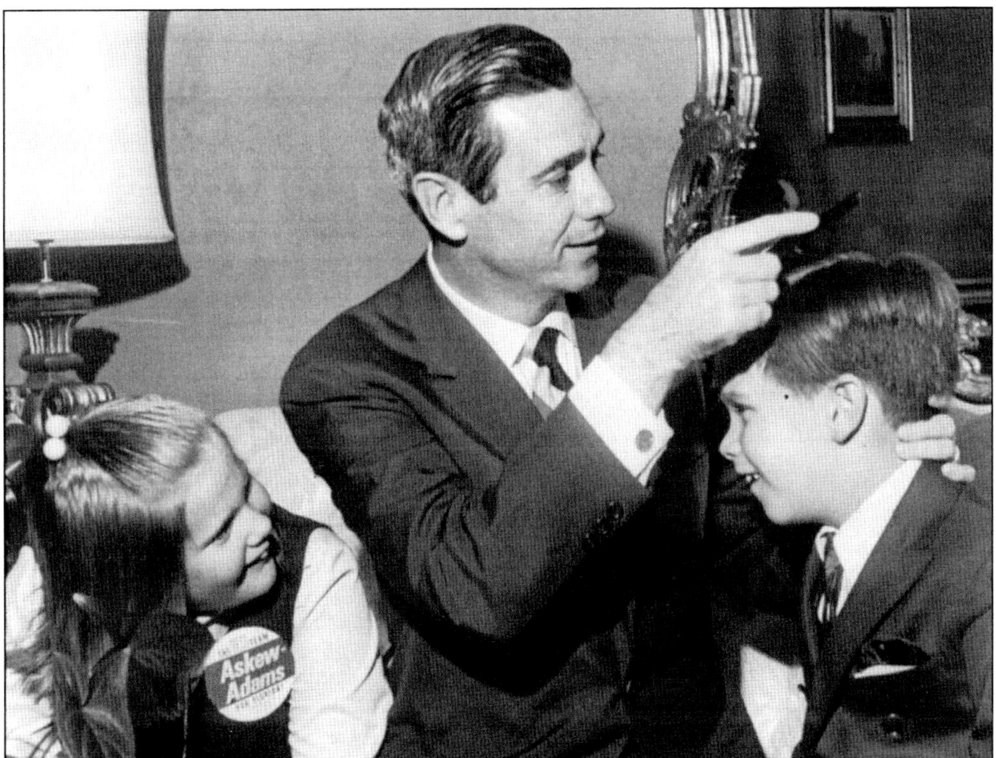

Reubin Askew, then the Democratic gubernatorial candidate, combs his son Kevin's hair while his daughter Angela looks on with amusement. Raised in a modest three-bedroom home, the Askew children described the executive mansion as a wonderland with boundaries. The governor, for his part, forbade the serving of alcohol during state receptions. (AC.)

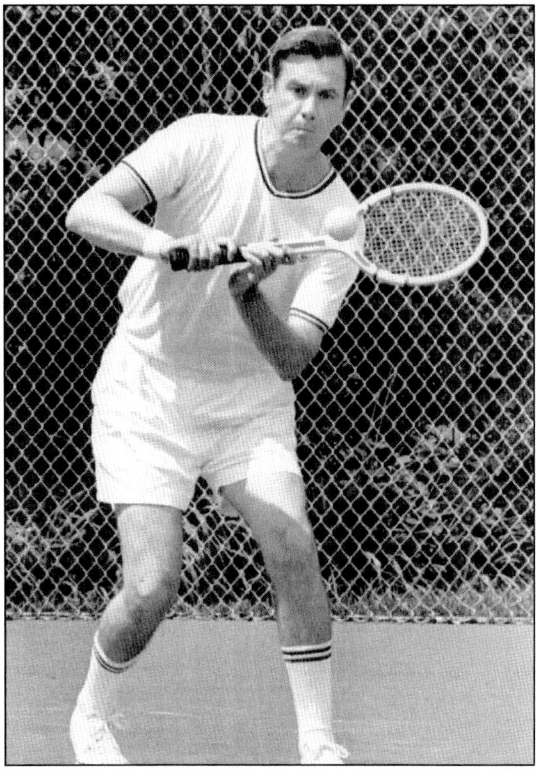

Always active and ambitious, Reubin Askew spent many hours playing heated tennis matches with members of his staff and legislative opponents. Despite his natural good nature, Askew hated to lose. Any staffer who proved more accomplished on the court than Askew would stop receiving invitations. The governor possessed a very developed sense of morality and was usually very combative during legislative sessions. (AC.)

Future governor Lawton Chiles walks the length of the state in his wildly successful bid for the US Senate in 1970. Vastly outspent in the Democratic primary by former governor Farris Bryant, Chiles walked 1,000 miles across the state to bring his message to the public, earning him the lifelong nickname "Walkin' Lawton." (SAF.)

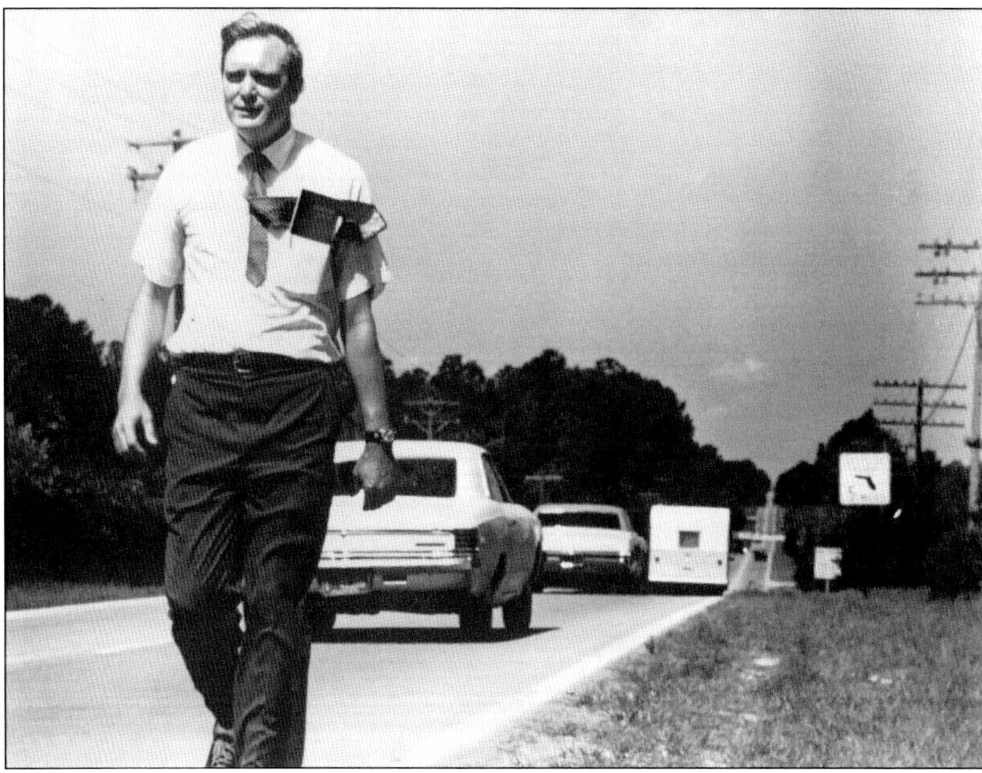

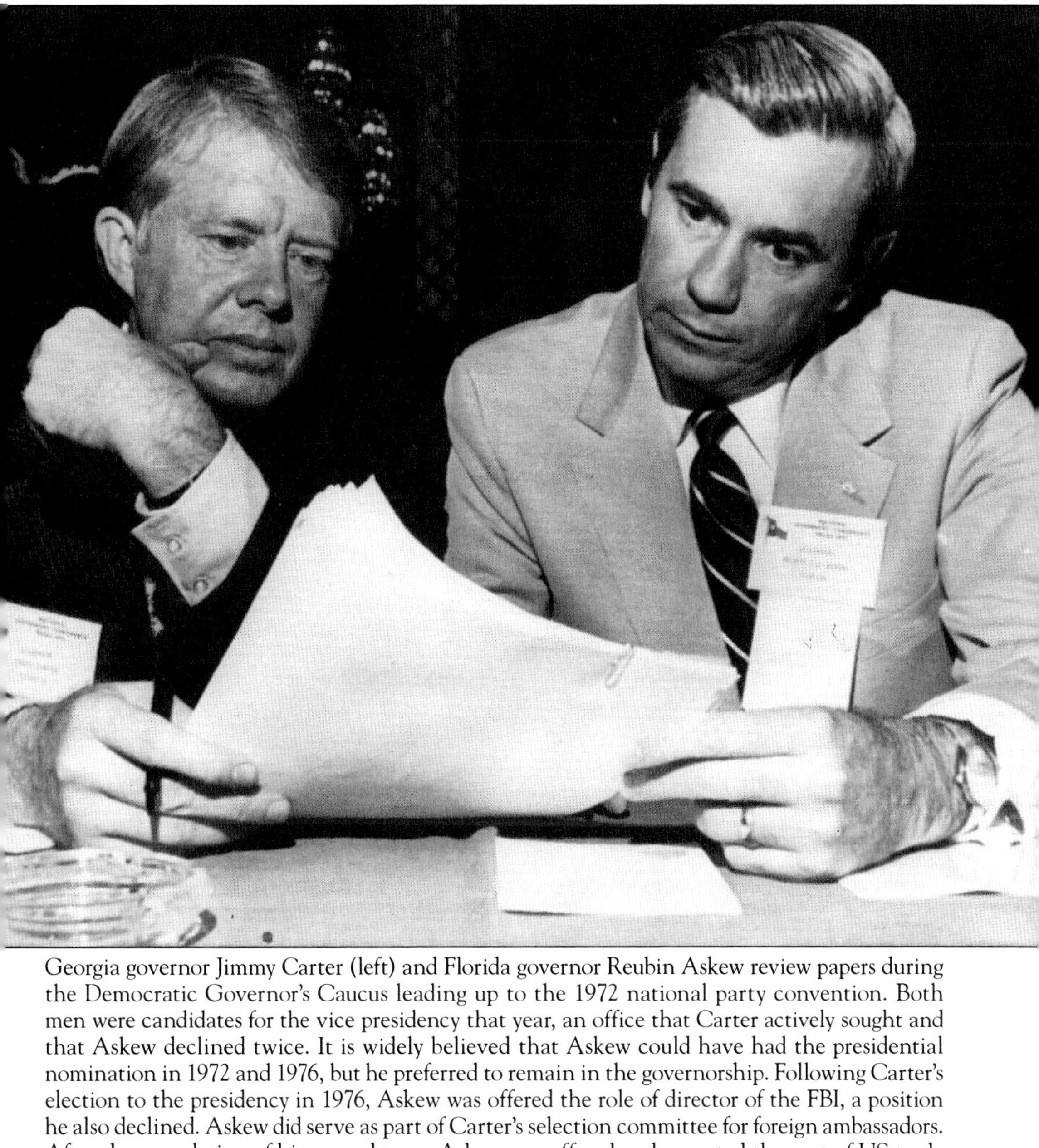

Georgia governor Jimmy Carter (left) and Florida governor Reubin Askew review papers during the Democratic Governor's Caucus leading up to the 1972 national party convention. Both men were candidates for the vice presidency that year, an office that Carter actively sought and that Askew declined twice. It is widely believed that Askew could have had the presidential nomination in 1972 and 1976, but he preferred to remain in the governorship. Following Carter's election to the presidency in 1976, Askew was offered the role of director of the FBI, a position he also declined. Askew did serve as part of Carter's selection committee for foreign ambassadors. After the completion of his second term, Askew was offered and accepted the post of US trade representative, serving until Carter's term ended in 1981. Askew was the first trade representative who held the title US Trade Representative, not Special Trade Representative. The post was both a cabinet-level position and an ambassadorship. (AC.)

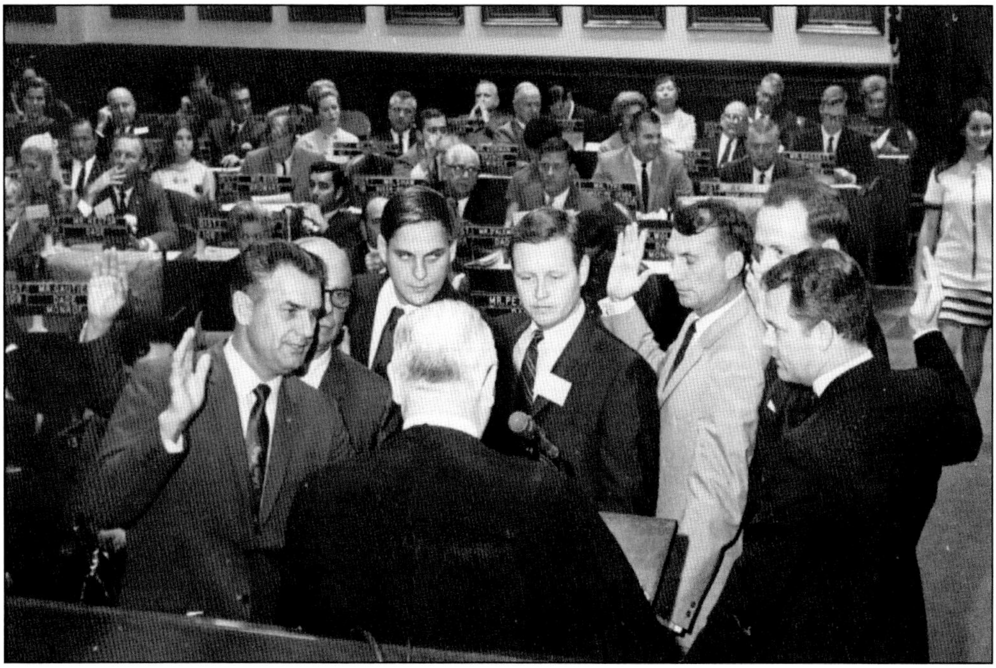

Shown on this page are swearing-in ceremonies for members of the legislative classes of 1967 (above) and 1972 (below). These two memberships have often been called the cream of the golden age crop. Under their leadership, the state government went from being ranked 49th nationwide in the early 1960s to being dubbed one of the finest lawmaking bodies of the 20th century. These lawmakers would help end school segregation in Florida, create the state's corporate tax laws, and pass the Sunshine Amendment. Florida's first solar program became a model for the nation. (Above, WM; below, AC.)

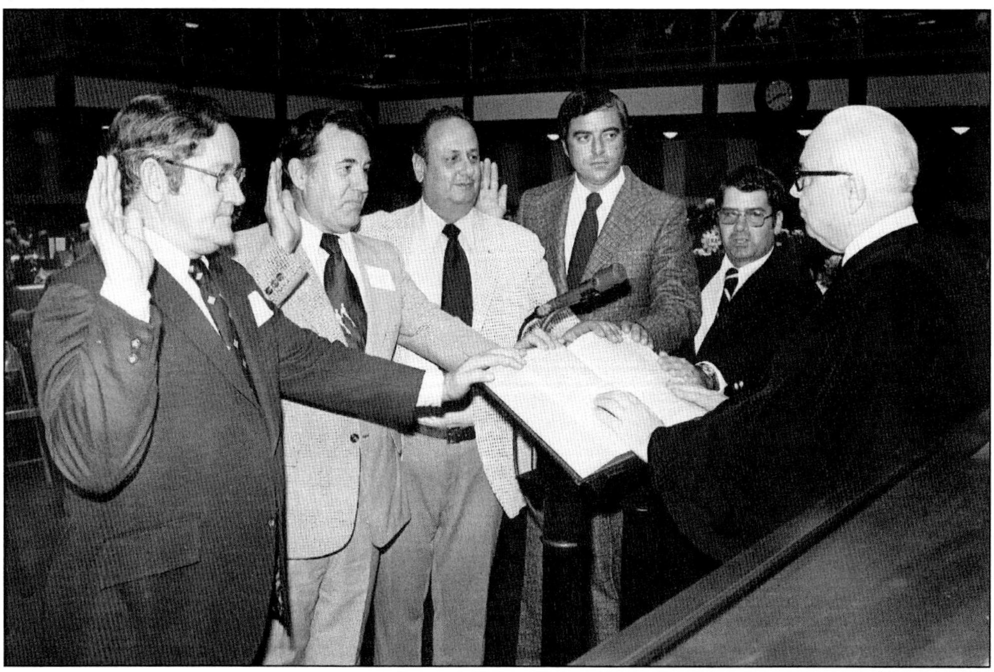

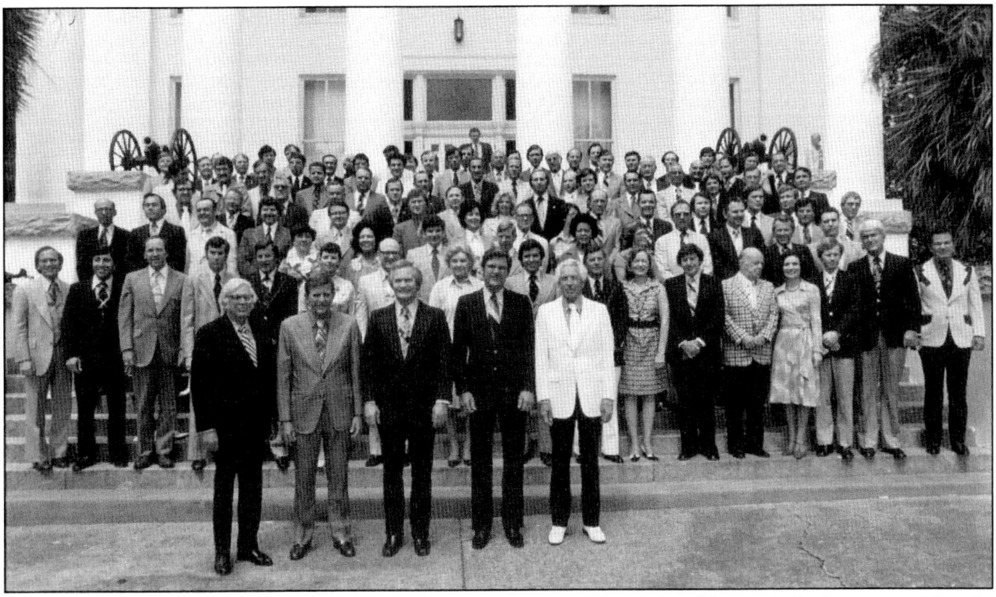

Under the speakership of Donald Tucker (first row, center), pictured here with the entire Florida House of Representatives, the house chamber would be rebuilt alongside the new capitol building. While many members during this period began to move into spacious private offices in the new capitol office complex, other members had to share offices with each other. This helped create close working friendships among many members. (Mark Foley.)

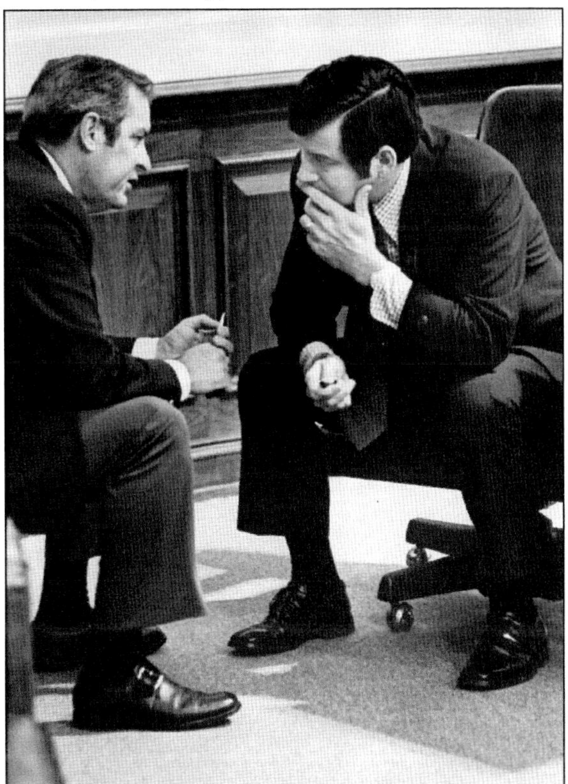

State senators Jim Williams (left) and Dick Pettigrew discuss an upcoming bill to change the voting age to 18 on the senate floor. Interaction between legislators in both chambers has been described as both open and engaging. There were always four or five small groups talking and debating at a time. (Jim Williams.)

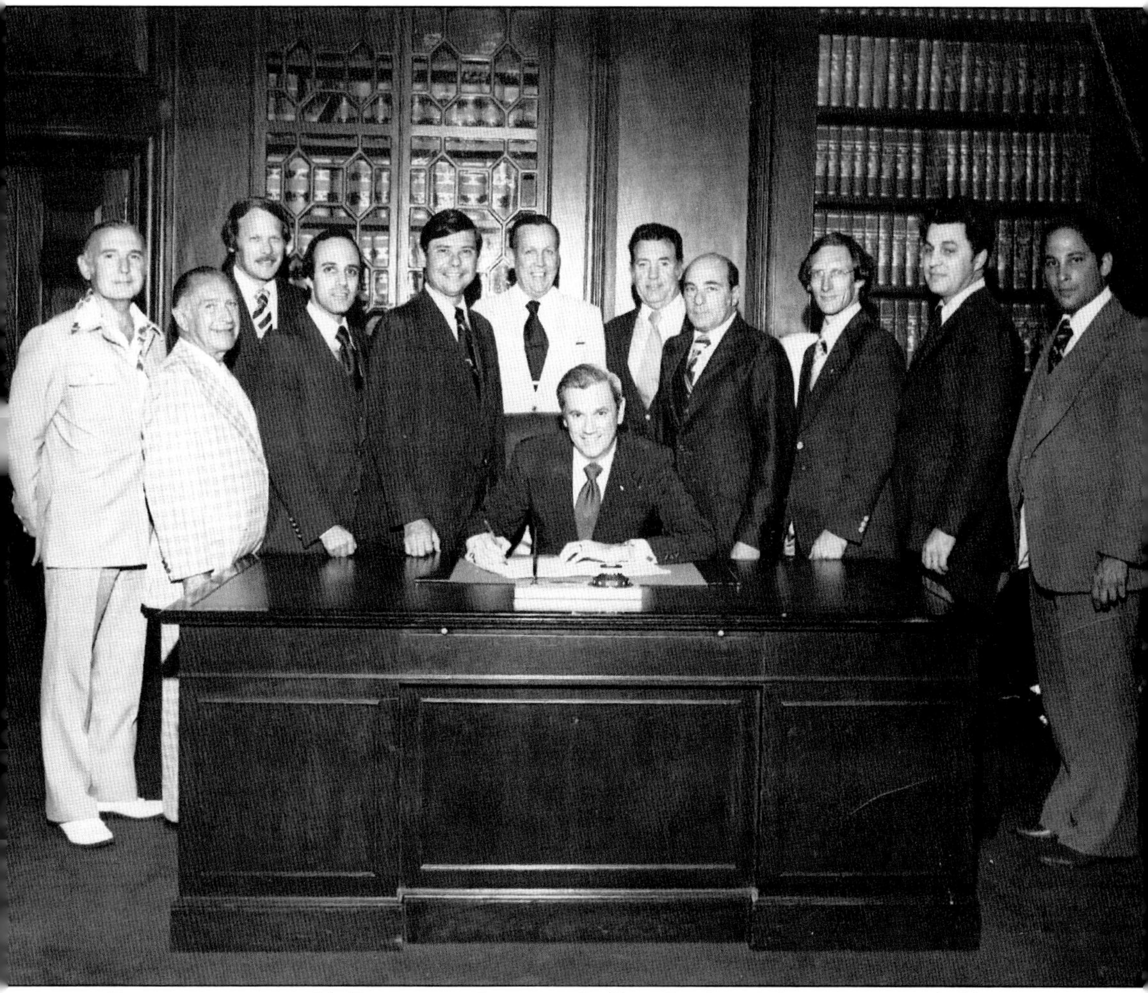

During a ceremonial bill signing in his capitol office, Reubin Askew is surrounded by members of the Florida Senate and House. Future governor Bob Graham (fifth from the left) was at this time the leading candidate to replace Tom Adams as Reubin Askew's running mate in 1974. Askew's relationship with the legislature was rocky at times. A no-nonsense chief executive, he was not afraid to guilt a lawmaker into voting his way on an issue. His sometimes-heated conversations with Speaker Tucker have become legendary, as both men fought for dominance over state affairs. (AC.)

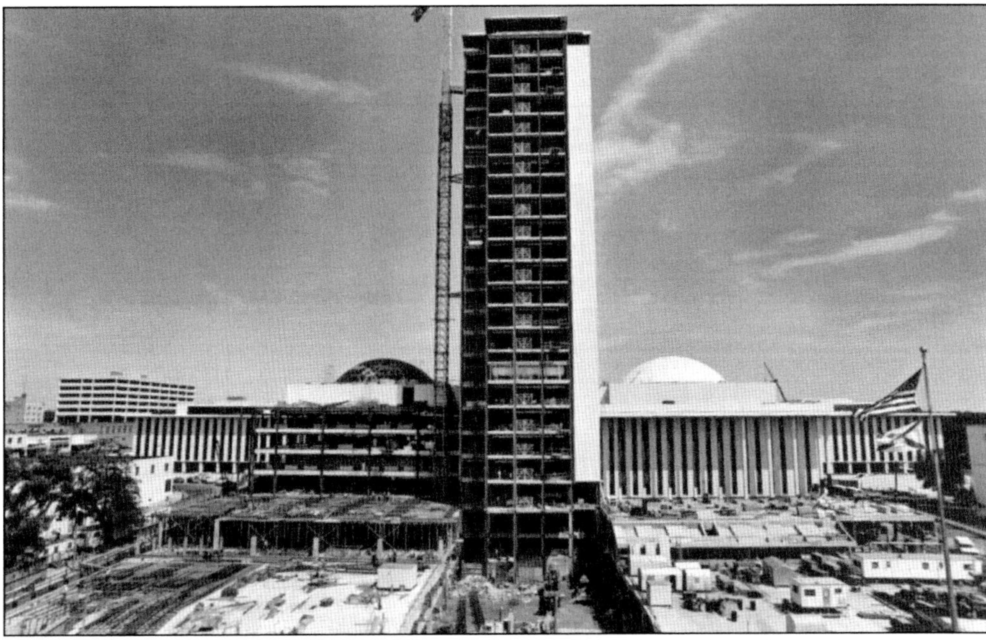

In 1973, land was cleared for the foundation of the new capitol complex. The modern House and Senate office buildings would be built that year, and members of both chambers enjoyed, for the first time, the comforts of a sizable workspace. The 22-story capitol tower took nearly four years and $43 million to construct. In 1978, the legislature approved a budget of $7 million to restore the old capitol to its 1902 appearance. This was done mainly to provide much-needed space between the two capitol buildings. The most recent additions to the historic capitol, including its enlarged dome and cupola, were dramatically demolished in 1980 by a wrecking ball. The historic capitol museum opened with much fanfare in 1982. (SAF.)

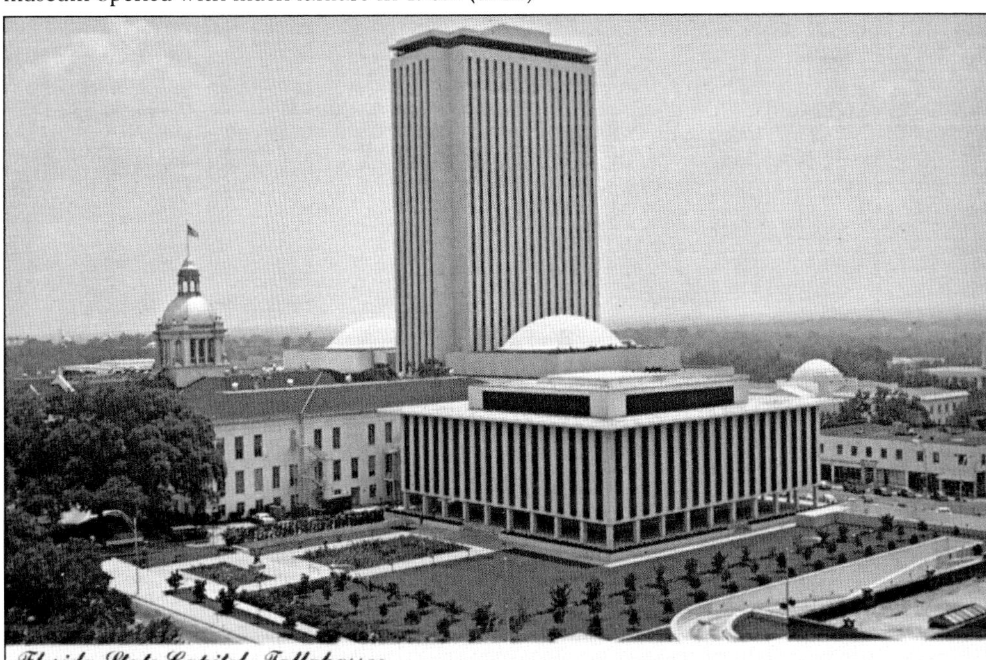

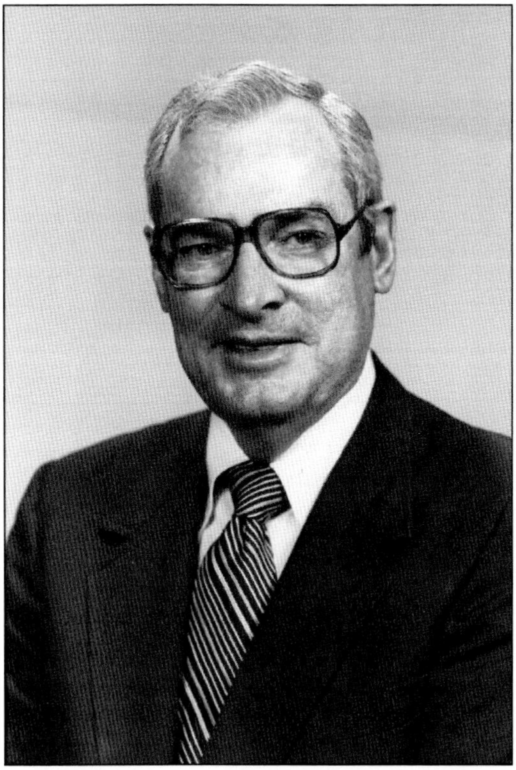

In 1974, Reubin Askew and his lieutenant governor, Tom Adams, were barely speaking. Adams had been accused of using state employees to operate his farm. Shortly before Askew's reelection announcement, he decided to throw Adams off the ticket. The governor selected state senator Jim Williams, pictured here in 1974, as his running mate. The two men won by nearly 65 percent that November and formed a fruitful partnership over the next four years. (Jim Williams.)

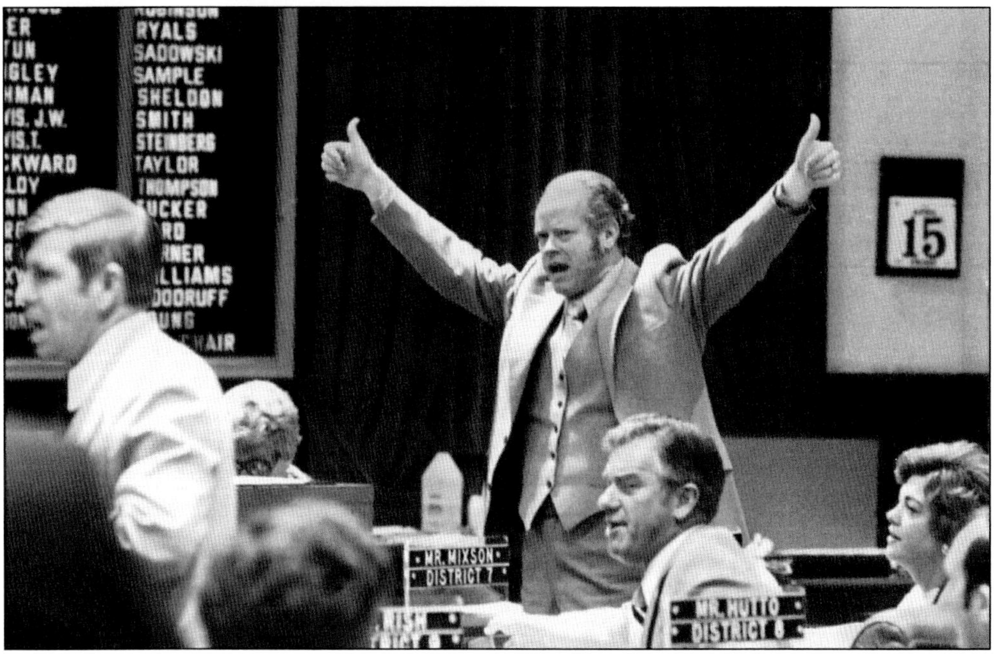

Legislators vote in the old house chamber just before the close of another session. With their own private offices, lawmakers could still be found eating, drinking coffee, chain-smoking, or simply socializing in the House chamber. The lawmakers of the golden age were known for their close friendships and nonpartisan approach to governing. (Mark Foley.)

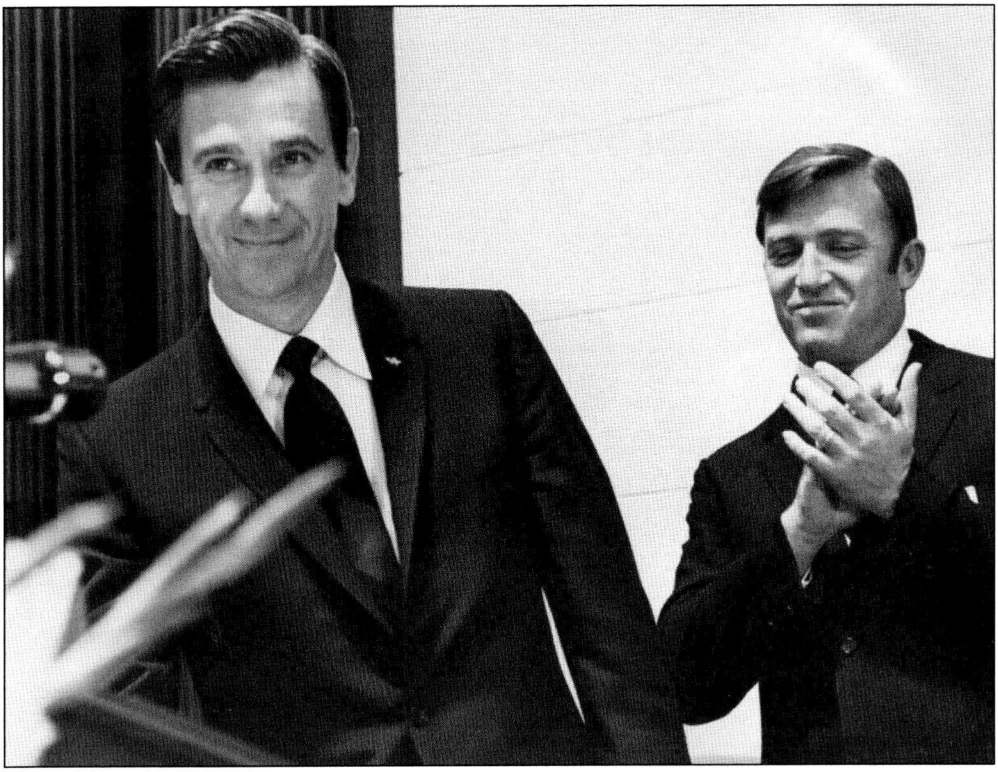

Reubin Askew (left) was a transformational figure often regarded as Florida's bridge between its past and future. He pushed for open government and tax reform. Askew was the best man to govern the state during this period of transition. Even his former opponent Claude Kirk agreed that his landslide defeat against Askew in 1970 was best for the state. Askew was, in many ways, an antipolitician who was led by a moral rather than a political ideology. Some of his critics called him stubborn or pious. Supporters admired his fearless nature and toughness when dealing with legislatures. Askew is regarded as the finest Florida governor since Leroy Collins and a leading voice in the New South movement of the 1970s. (SAF.)

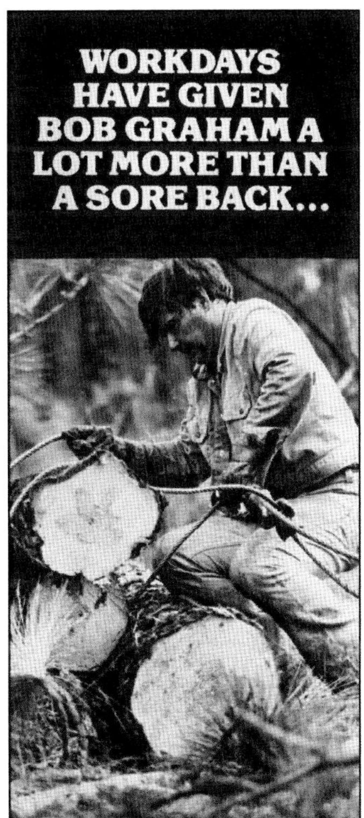

Running for the governorship with hardly any name recognition, Bob Graham took part in a series of workdays to help better understand the common hardships of the average Floridian. Graham worked a variety of jobs, from short-order cook and bellhop, to social worker, plumber, and housewife. Here, he ties steel cables around timber. This approach would prove incredibly successful in the 1978 election. (AC.)

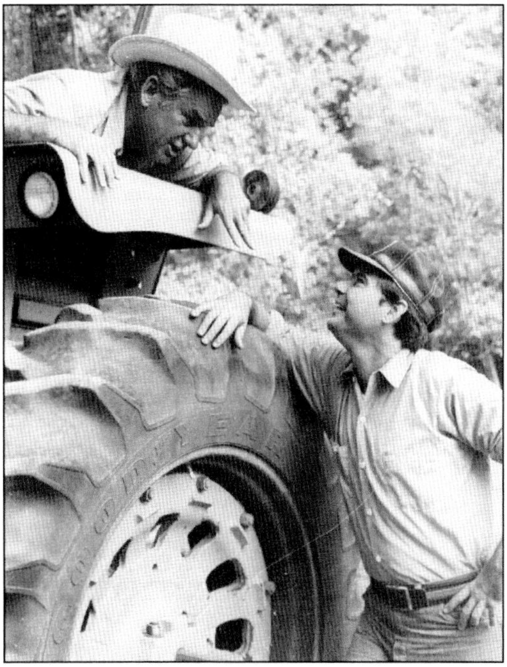

Over time, the selection of lieutenant governor has become an important factor in the overall success of a gubernatorial candidacy. This was certainly true when unknown state senator Bob Graham (right) from South Florida picked conservative representative Wayne Mixson (left) from North Florida as his running mate. This selection has often been regarded as the perfect example of a balanced statewide ticket. (WM.)

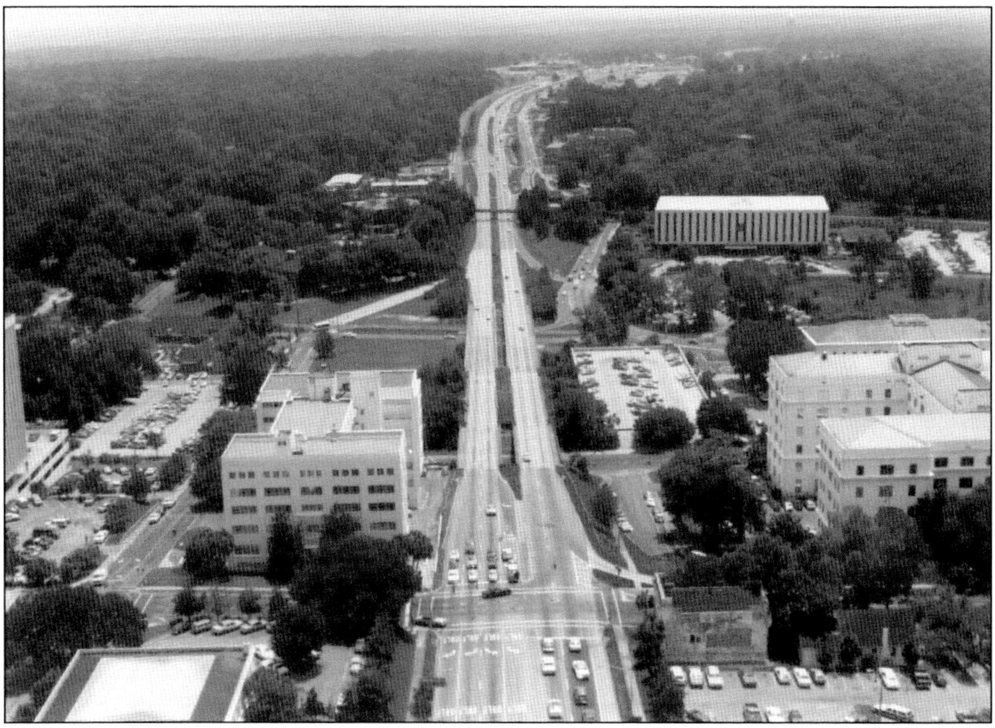

Appalachee Parkway is seen in a photograph taken from the top floor of the new capitol building at the time of its completion. The office buildings in the background are the Farris Bryant Building (right foreground), home to the Florida Fish and Wildlife Conservation Commission, and the Haydon Burns Building (right background), which houses the Florida Department of Transportation. (WM.)

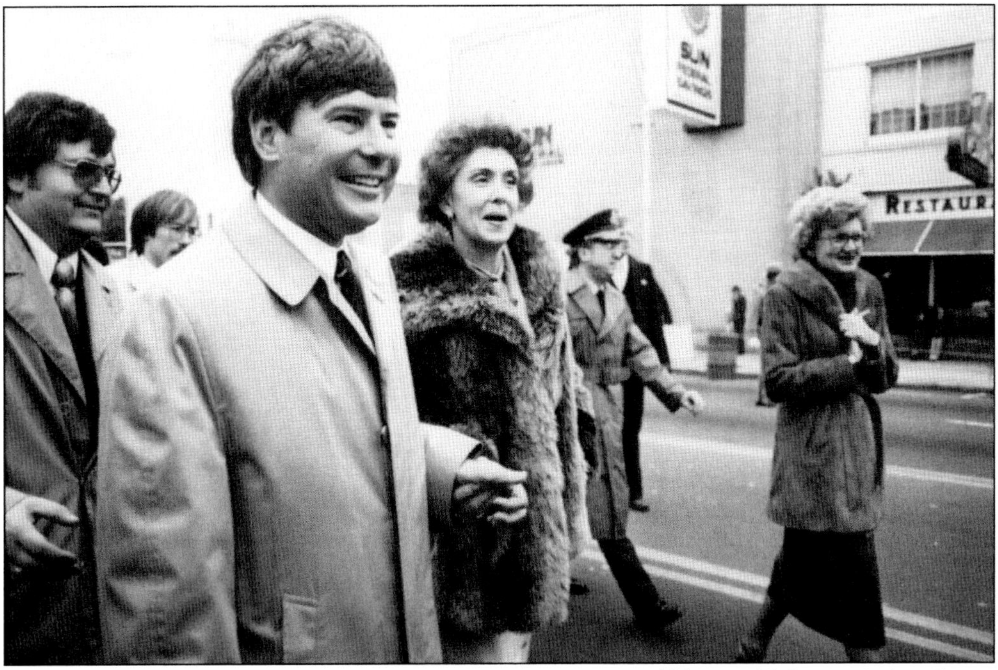

There was an old saying among politicians in the state: "It would be a cold day in Hades when a man from Miami Dade was elected governor." When Bob Graham, the first governor from Miami Dade, was sworn in, Tallahassee experienced a cold snap. Throughout the inauguration, the crowd huddled under blankets as a gentle snow fell from the sky. This was the first inauguration to take place on the steps of the new capital building. (Both, WM.)

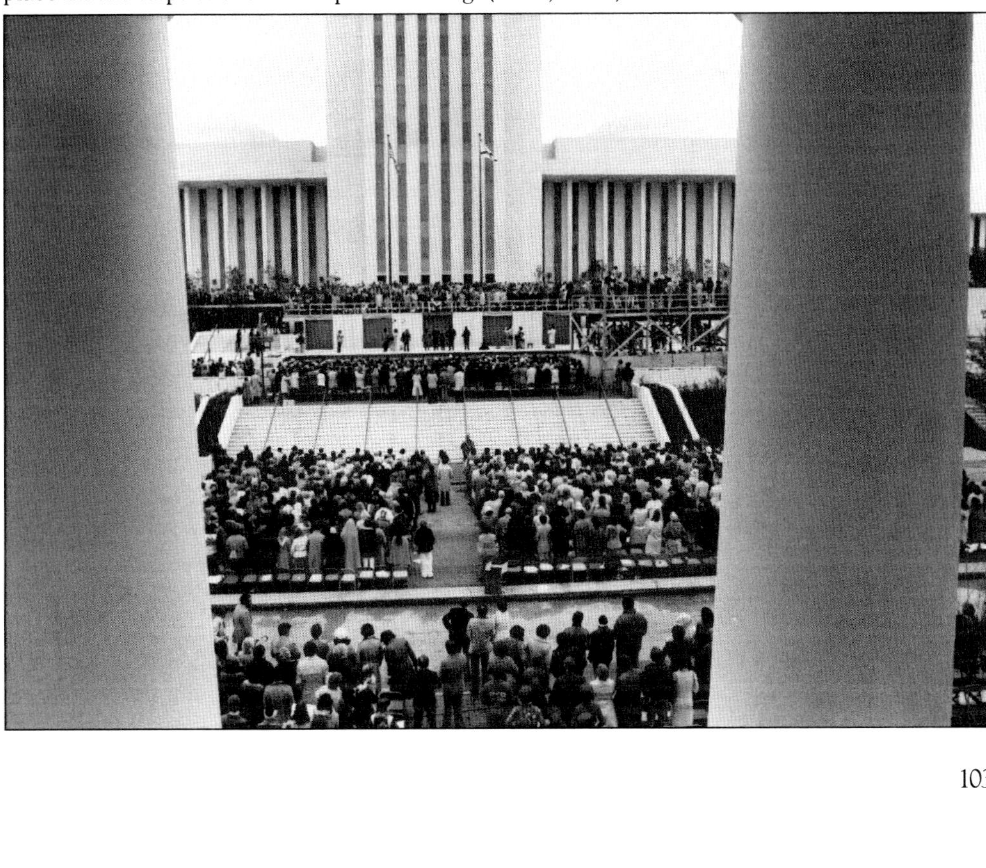

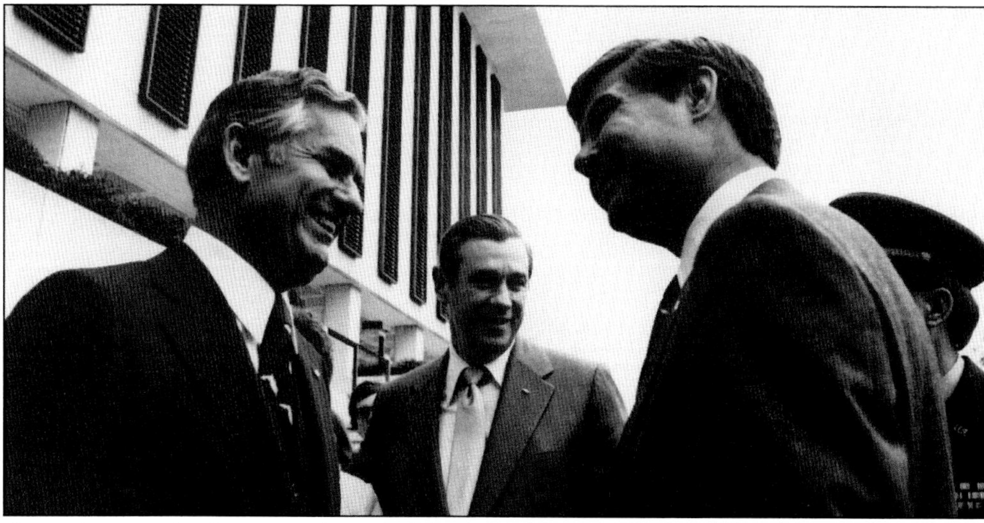

Shown here are the three main figures of Florida's golden age. Reubin Askew (center) stressed open government and tax reform, Bob Graham (right) looked for a balanced approach for economic expansion and environmental protection, and Wayne Mixson (left) worked tirelessly to attract both investors and international trade to Florida. During their governorships, the state's growth was boundless and its leadership truly extraordinary. (WM.)

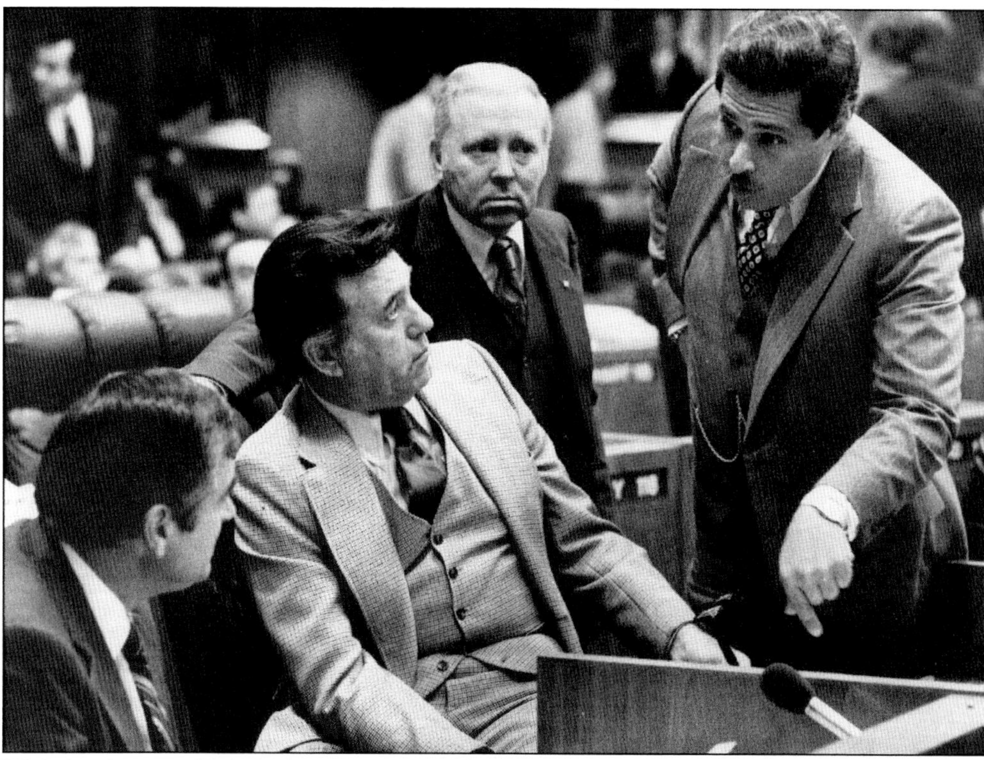

With the election of Bob Graham as governor, the tone of state government changed. The governor's office now worked alongside the legislature to create a moderate balance between conservation and commercial expansion. The legislature's output during this period was staggering, with reforms to education, energy, and the creation of thousands of new jobs. (Walt Young.)

Bob Graham's two terms in office are usually considered the peak years for the Florida golden age. Companies flocked to the state, and Florida had one of the highest GDP rates in the country. Graham's focus on education resulted in the state's university system being considered one of the finest in the country. Graham left the governorship with an 83-percent approval rating. (WM.)

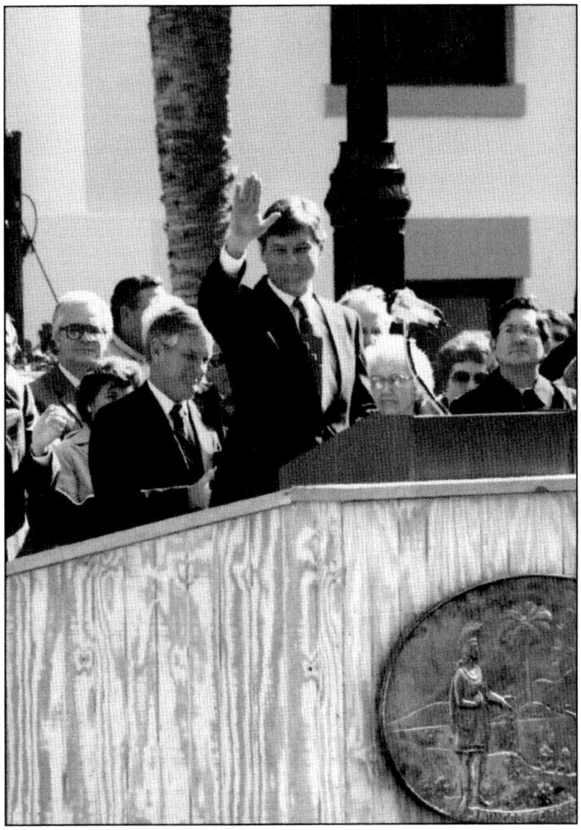

The Grahams left the executive mansion early, choosing to move their belongings in early December 1986. This left the mansion to Governor-elect Bob Martinez and his family. The Martinezes began renovating the upstairs residence nearly three weeks prior to the governor officially taking office. During this period of transition, the state saw the unprecedented three-day term of another governor, who also chose to reside at the mansion. (WM.)

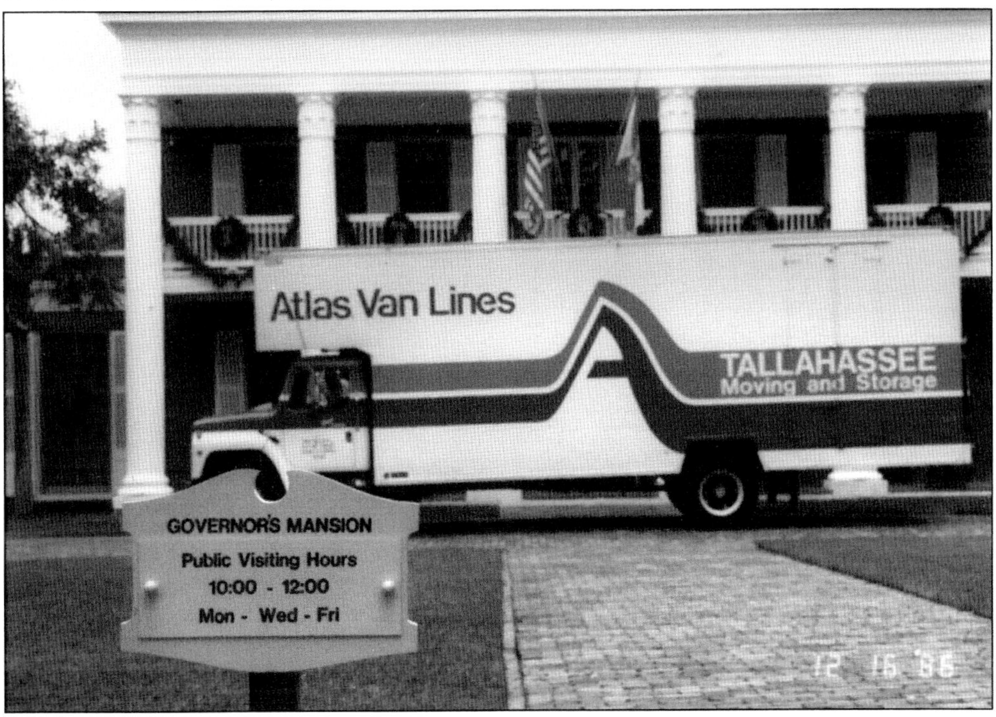

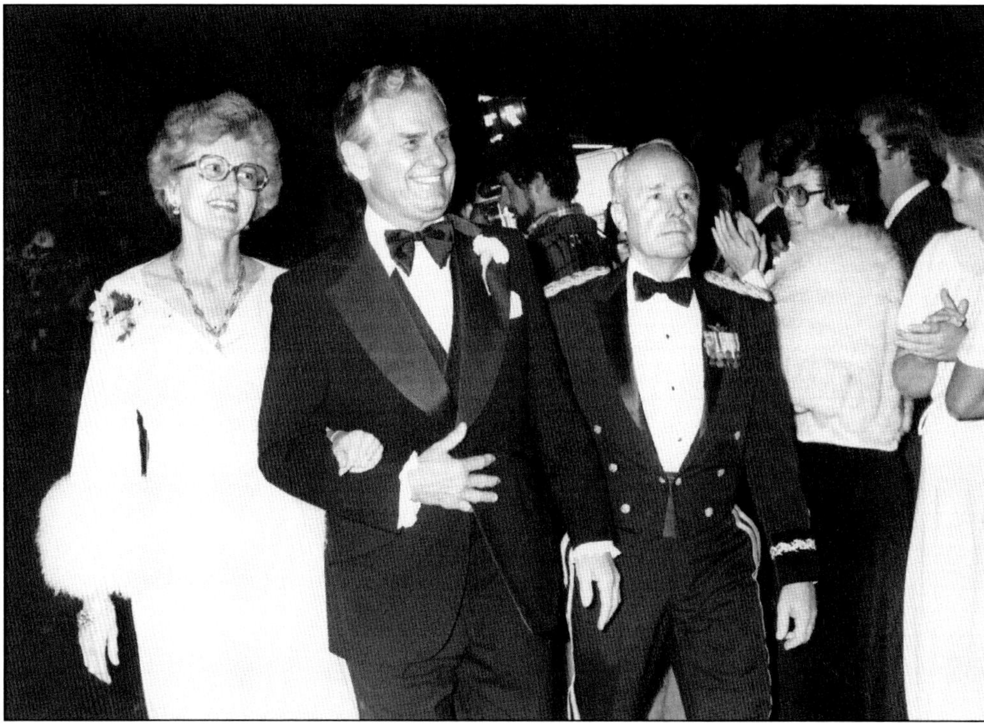

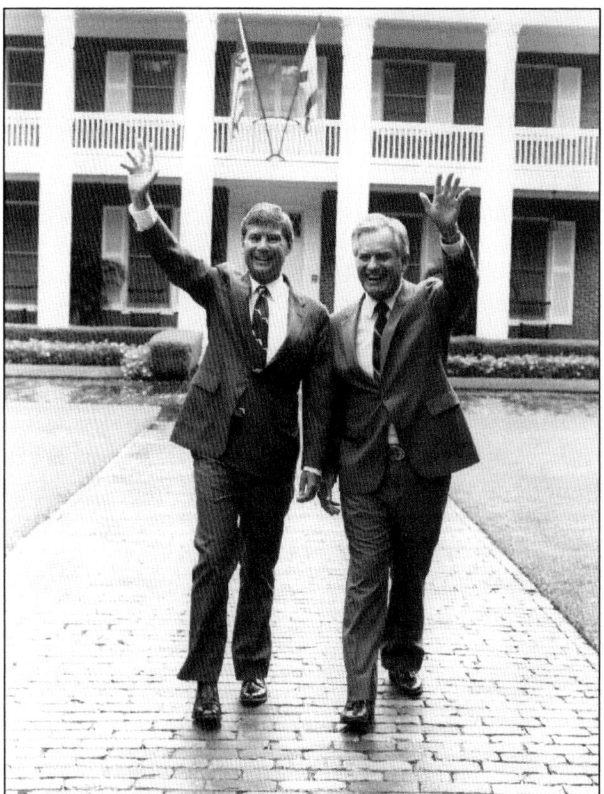

Lt. Gov. Wayne Mixson and his wife arrive at the 1979 inaugural ball. Mixson was the first lieutenant governor in Florida history to serve two consecutive terms in that office. In his other role as secretary of commerce, Mixson was a successful spokesperson for the state. (WM.)

With the election of Bob Graham (left) to the US Senate, the start of his senate term overlapped the remainder of his tenure as governor. According to state law, Graham's lieutenant governor, Wayne Mixson (right), had to serve the remaining days of the administration. Upon taking the oath of office, Mixson served as the state's 39th governor for three days. (WM.)

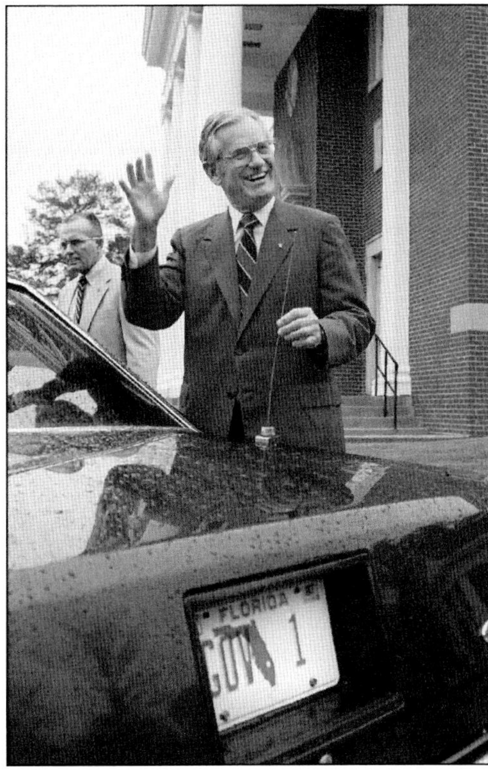

Guarded by Secret Service agents dressed in plain clothes, Wayne Mixson and his wife, carrying two overnight bags, made the brief journey from their family home to the state capitol. It was Mixson's first official act as governor-elect. While the majority of his three-day tenure included celebrating the past eight years of the Graham-Mixson administration and receptions for Governor-elect Martinez, Mixson still had a full workload as governor. Before resigning office, Governor Graham created a backlog of appointments for Mixson to fill. Mixson also conducted one final cabinet meeting and spent three nights as the mansion's official resident. (Both, Mark Foley.)

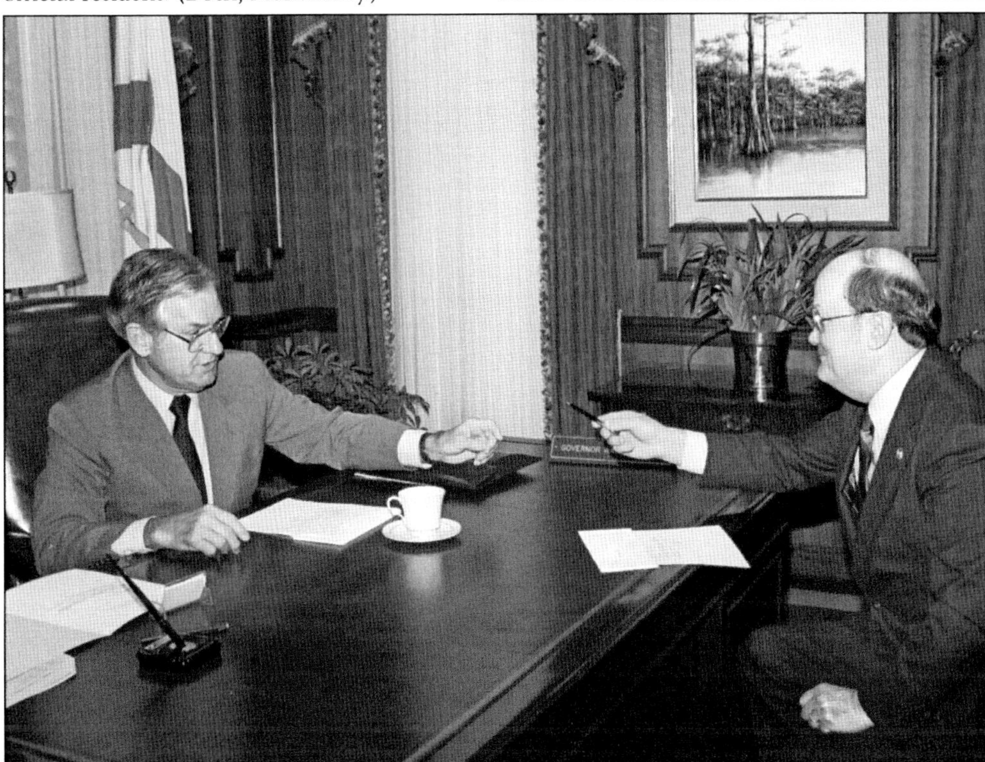

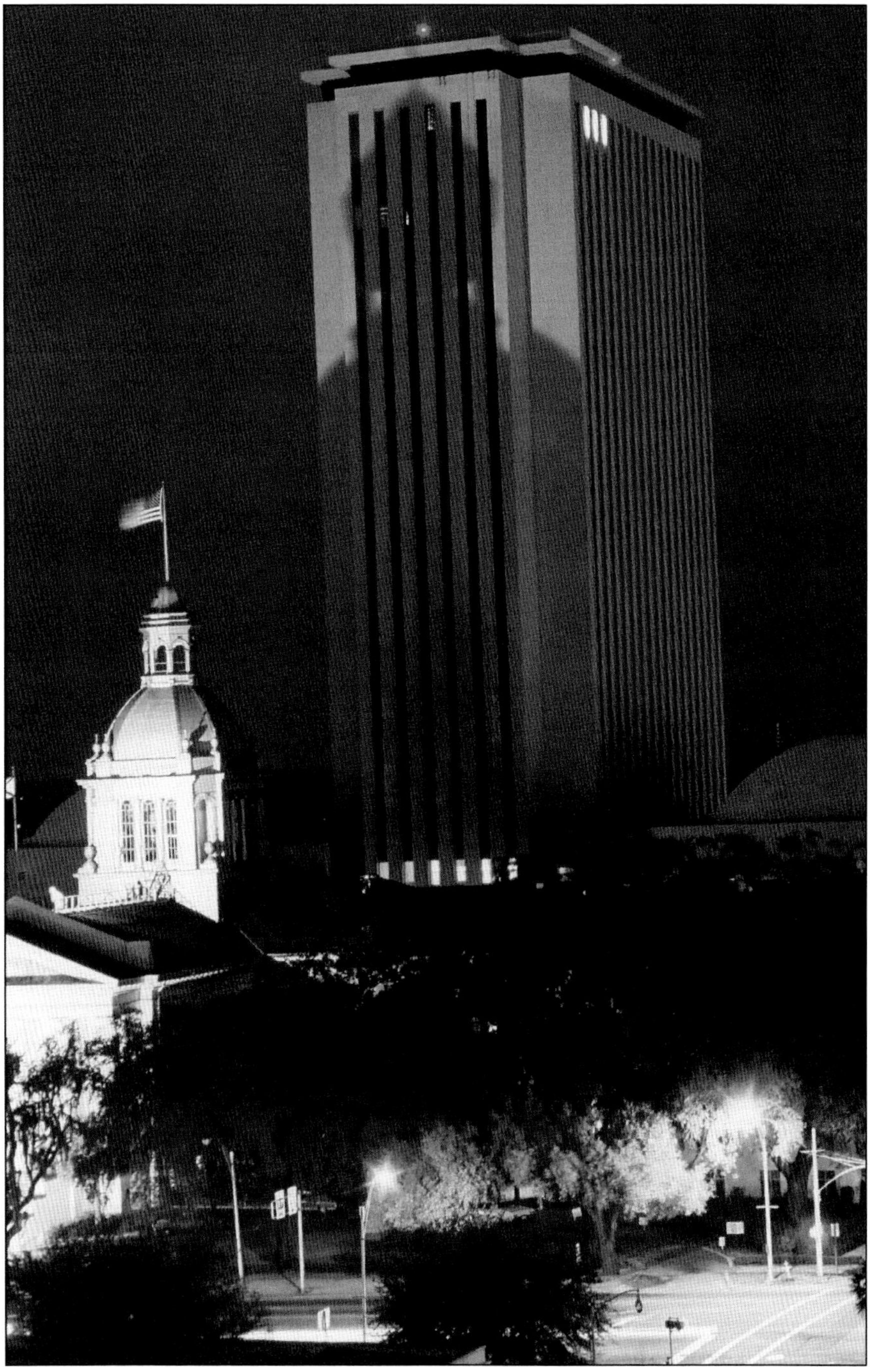

The historic capitol, like the golden age itself, casts a long shadow over Florida's current political landscape. Florida's golden age began with Claude Kirk's call for a special legislative session during his inaugural address, and it ended following Bob Martinez's election 20 years later. During this period, the state's legislature modernized with reapportionment and quickly became the finest legislative body in the nation. Every governor or lawmaker elected since has tried to match its level of unparalleled achievement. (SAF.)

Nine

NATIONAL STAGE

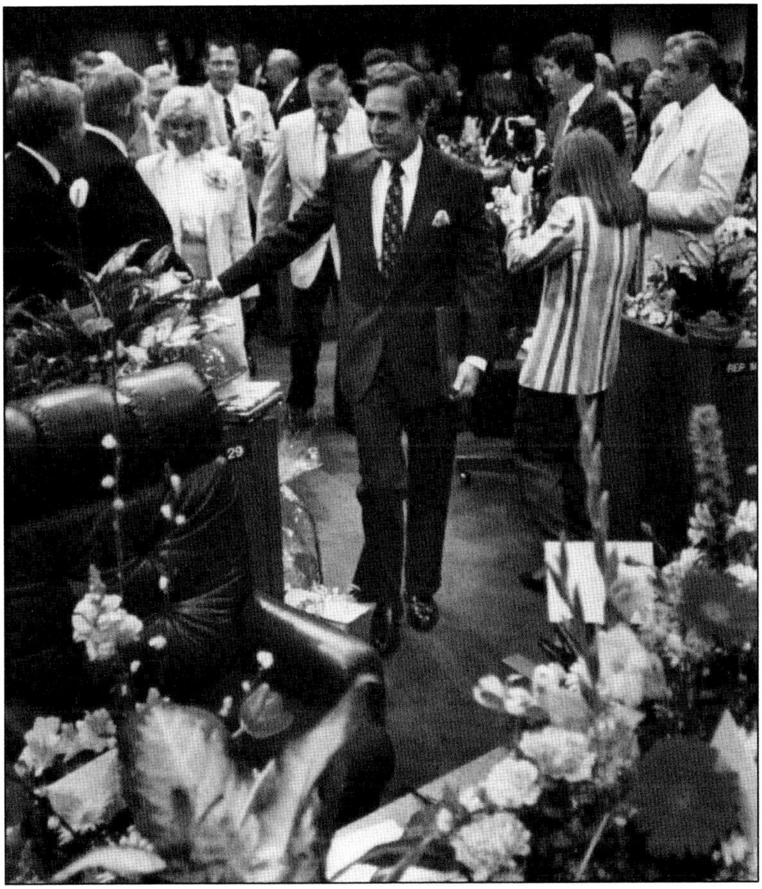

Bob Martinez was born on Christmas Day 1934 in Tampa, the son of Spanish Americans. Prior to entering public office, Martinez worked as an educator, director of the Hillsborough County Teachers Association, labor advocate, and restaurant owner. A Democrat for most of his life, Martinez switched parties in 1983 and came to symbolize the great Republican conversion that took place in Florida during the Reagan years. (SAF.)

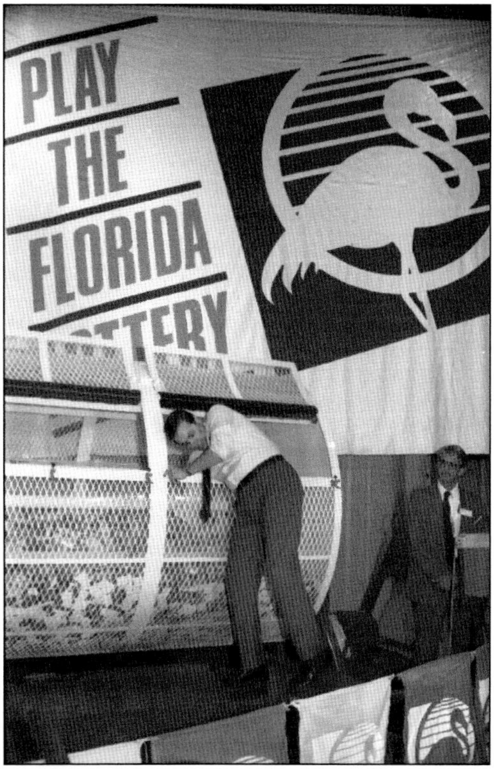

Gov. Bob Martinez digs into a large bin of entry tickets to pick the finalists for Florida's first lottery. He was only the second Republican in the 20th century to win the governorship of Florida. Like Claude Kirk two decades earlier, Martinez benefited greatly from a divisive Democratic primary battle. (SAF.)

Martinez served two terms as mayor of Tampa before entering the race for governor. His time as mayor saw dramatic improvements for the city of Tampa, but his lack of legislative experience weakened his relations with lawmakers. While he was elected to the governorship with a mandate, the legislative branches were still decidedly Democratic, and the bulk of his agenda was defeated by the opposite party. (AC.)

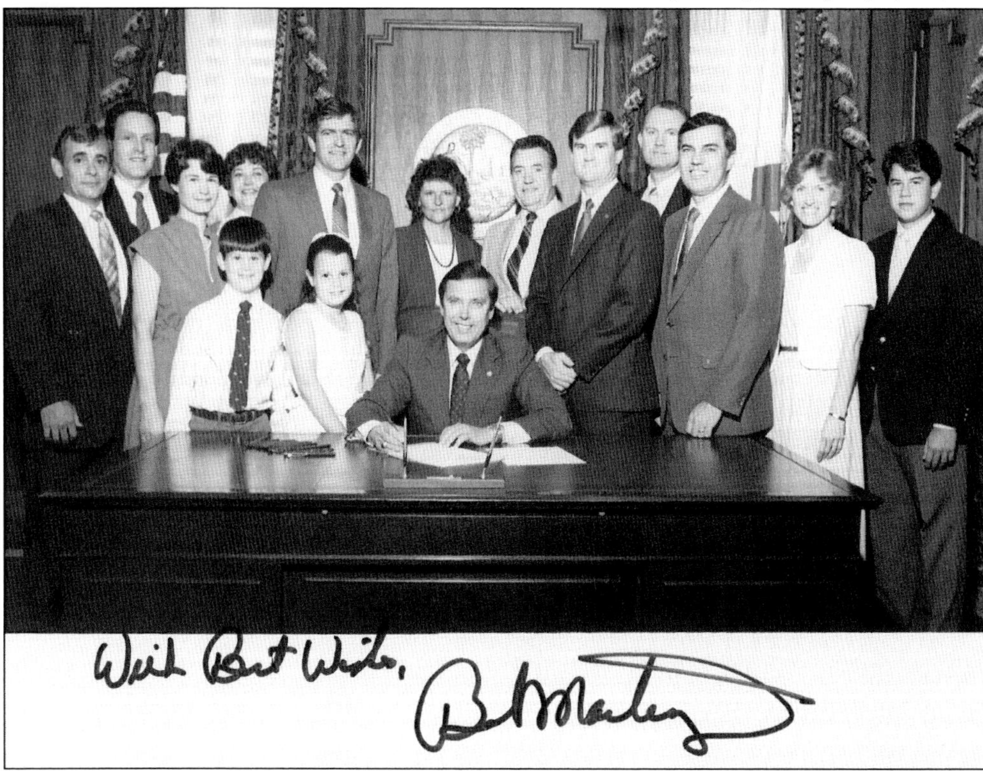

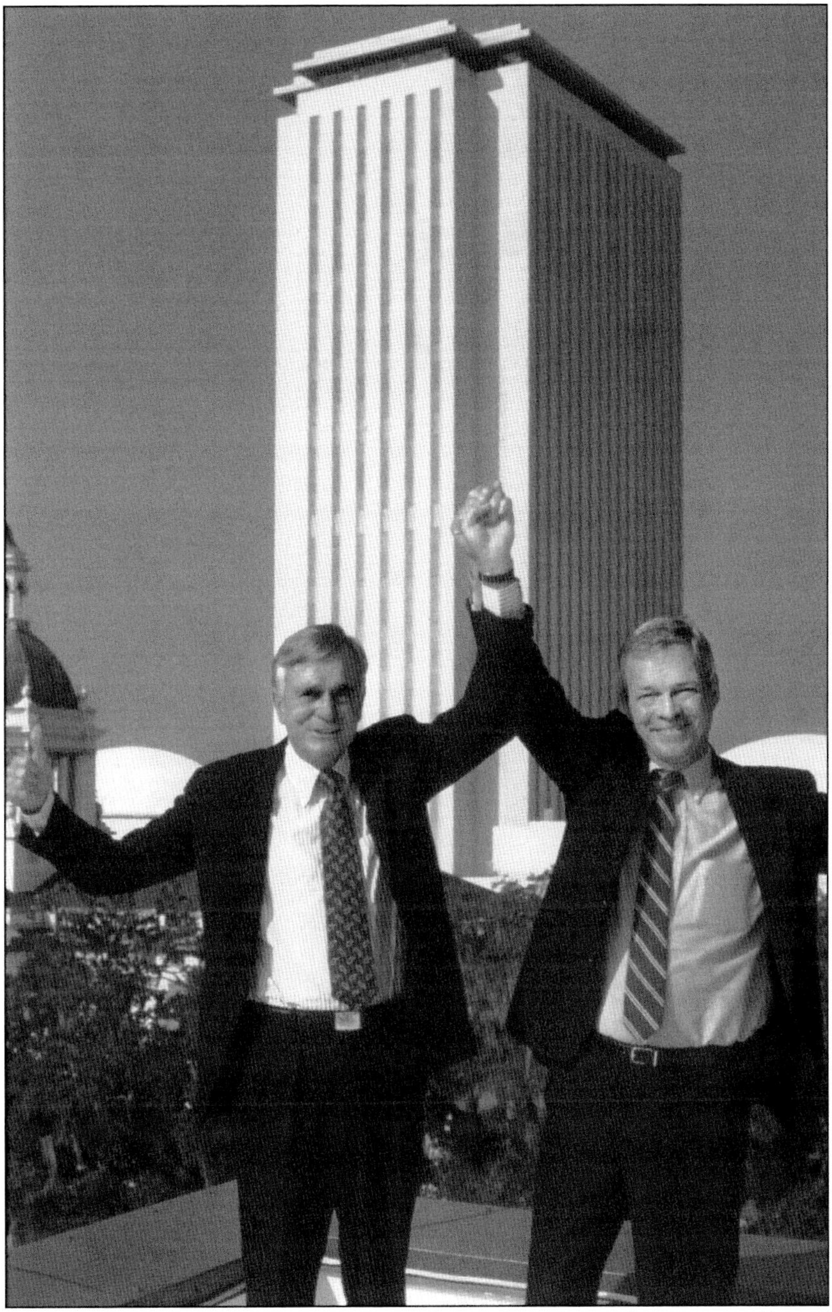

In 1988, Sen. Lawton Chiles (left) decided to retire from politics for good. Lawton and his wife, Rhea, settled down in Tallahassee, and the former senator became a college professor. Yet, following two years and many pleas from party leaders, Chiles made a triumphant return to politics. Alongside running mate and friend Buddy MacKay (right), Chiles won the governorship of Florida in 1990 with a resounding victory. The folksy campaign was seen by many to hearken back to his days as Walkin' Lawton. The two candidates were labeled "Butch Cassidy and the Sundance Kid," their main campaign headquarters were housed in an old used-car dealership, and they refused to accept individual campaign donations over $100. (SAF.)

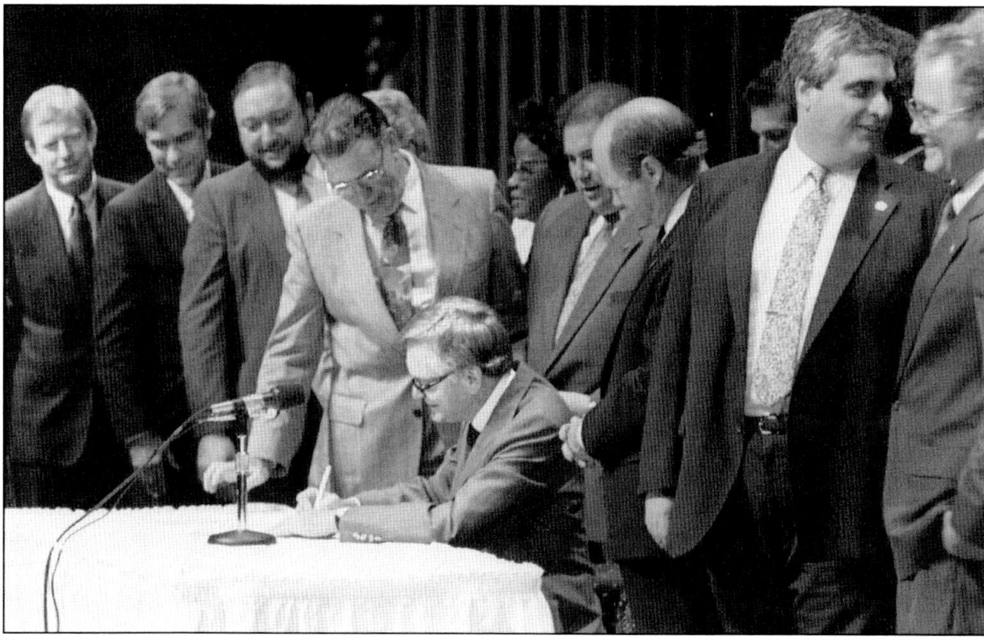

During his first term as governor, Lawton Chiles established the Florida Department of Elder Affairs. In this photograph, Chiles signs the bill into law. The Chiles administration also appointed an unprecedented six out of seven justices of the state supreme court. His work to reinvent state government led to the complete overhaul and reorganization of countless government departments. (Walt Young.)

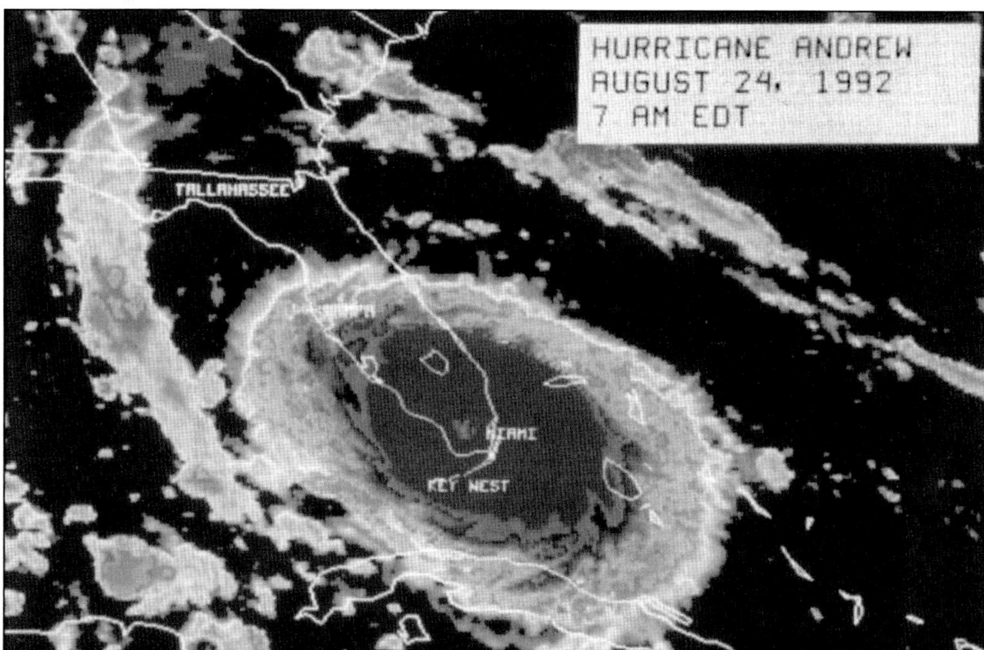

Hurricane Andrew struck the Florida coast on August 24, 1992. It caused nearly $25 billion in damage to the state. It left hundreds of thousands homeless and resulted in a series of new building laws in Florida. The hurricane was also terribly destructive to the state's wildlife. (AC.)

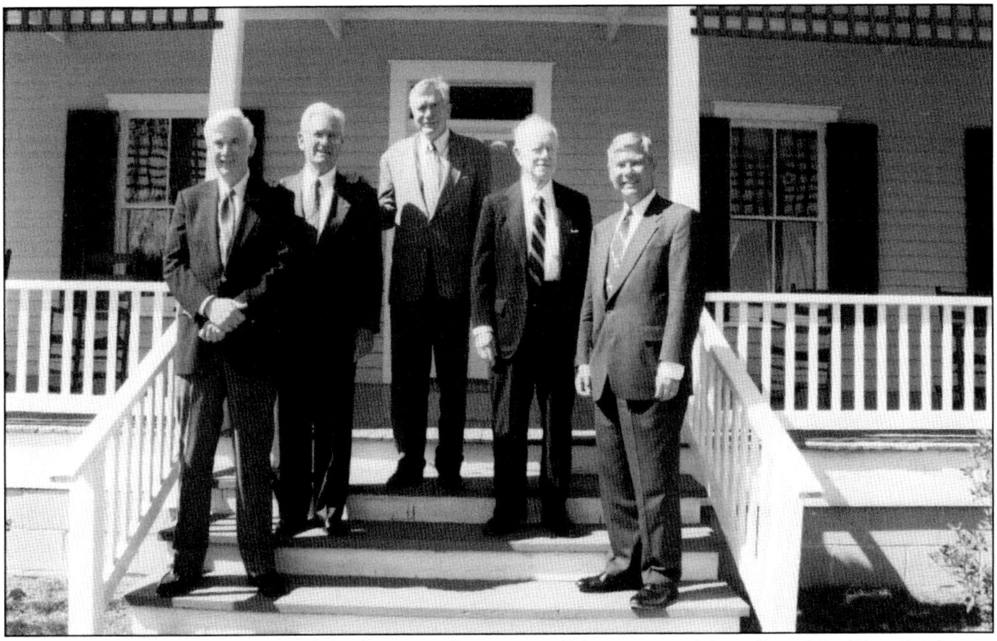

While in Washington, Rhea Chiles became the principal designer and founder of the Florida House, a national showcase for the state. As first lady, she was devoted to transforming the governor's mansion into both a home and a public shrine to the governorship. The Chiles were lovers of the Kennedy mystique of Camelot and worked to bring a populist version of that to Florida. These two photographs were taken during the first couple's promotion efforts for the book *700 North Adams Street*, a privately produced photography book on the history of the governor's mansion. Events like these were commonplace during Chiles's administration and helped establish the close connection that many former governors have with each other. Pictured above are, from left to right, Reubin Askew, Wayne Mixson, Lawton Chiles, Farris Bryant, and Bob Graham. Seen below, from left to right, are (first row) First Ladies Graham, Chiles, Askew, Collins, and Mixson; (second row) Farris Bryant, Bob Graham, Lawton Chiles, Reubin Askew, and Wayne Mixson. (Both, WM.)

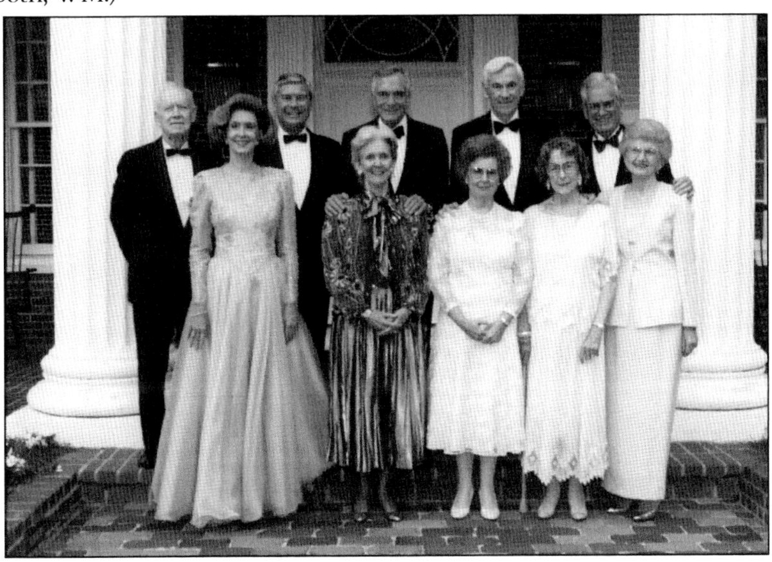

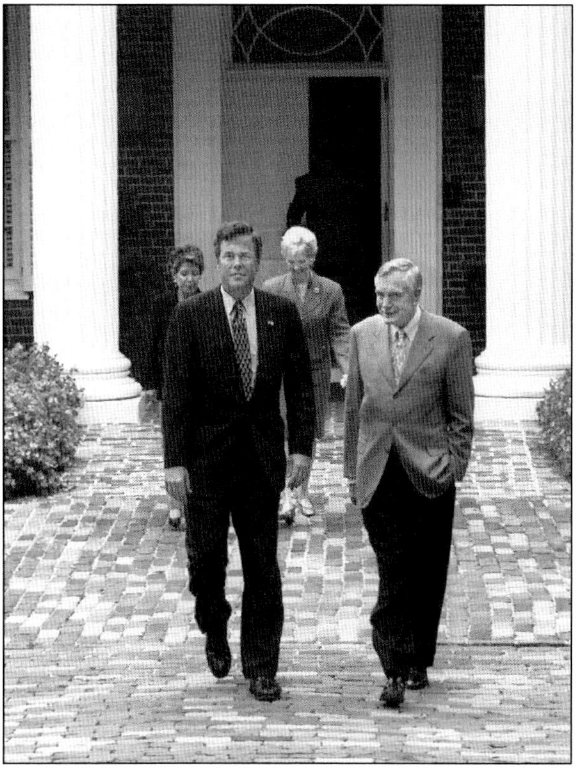

In one of the most competitive and dramatic gubernatorial elections in state history, Lawton Chiles (right) narrowly defeated Jeb Bush (left) for the governorship, 50.7 to 49.2 percent. The election took place during the Republican wave of 1994. Lawton Chiles was one of only two Democratic governors to win reelection that year. (SAF.)

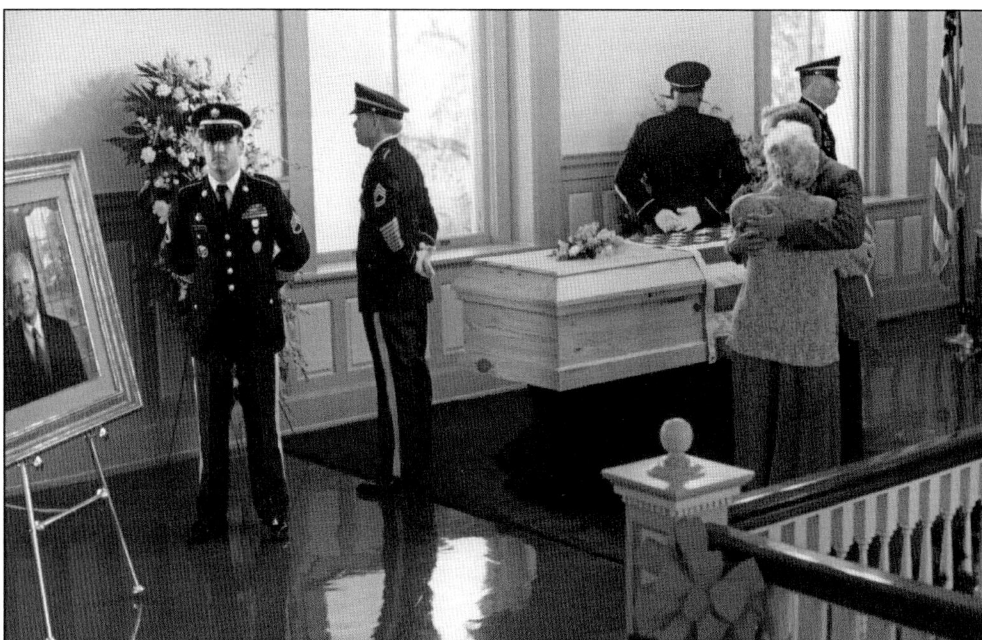

First Lady Rhea Chiles embraces her son Bud Chiles while observing the closed casket of Gov. Lawton Chiles. Governor Chiles, who had a history of heart issues, was found in the governor's mansion next to his exercise bicycle by a law-enforcement agent. The governor was pronounced dead on the scene, and the entire state went into a period of mourning. (SAF.)

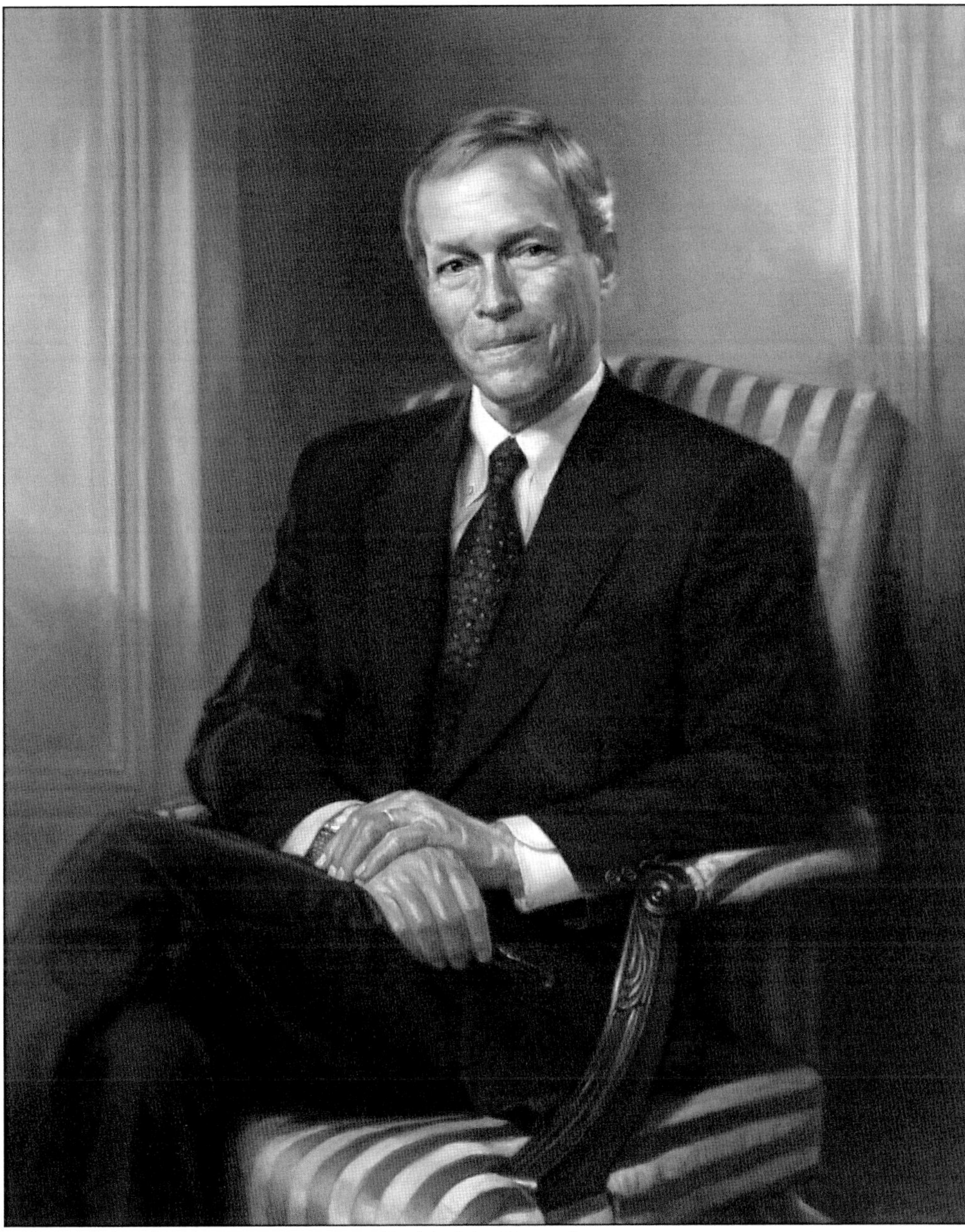

Following his brief stint as governor, Buddy MacKay, a former state representative, senator, and US congressman, was appointed by Pres. Bill Clinton as a special envoy for the Americas. As lieutenant governor, MacKay was given many duties and played an important role in Chiles's cabinet, including being cochair of the Florida Commission on Education, Reform and Accountability. He is widely considered one of the most significant and powerful lieutenant governors in state history. (MFH.)

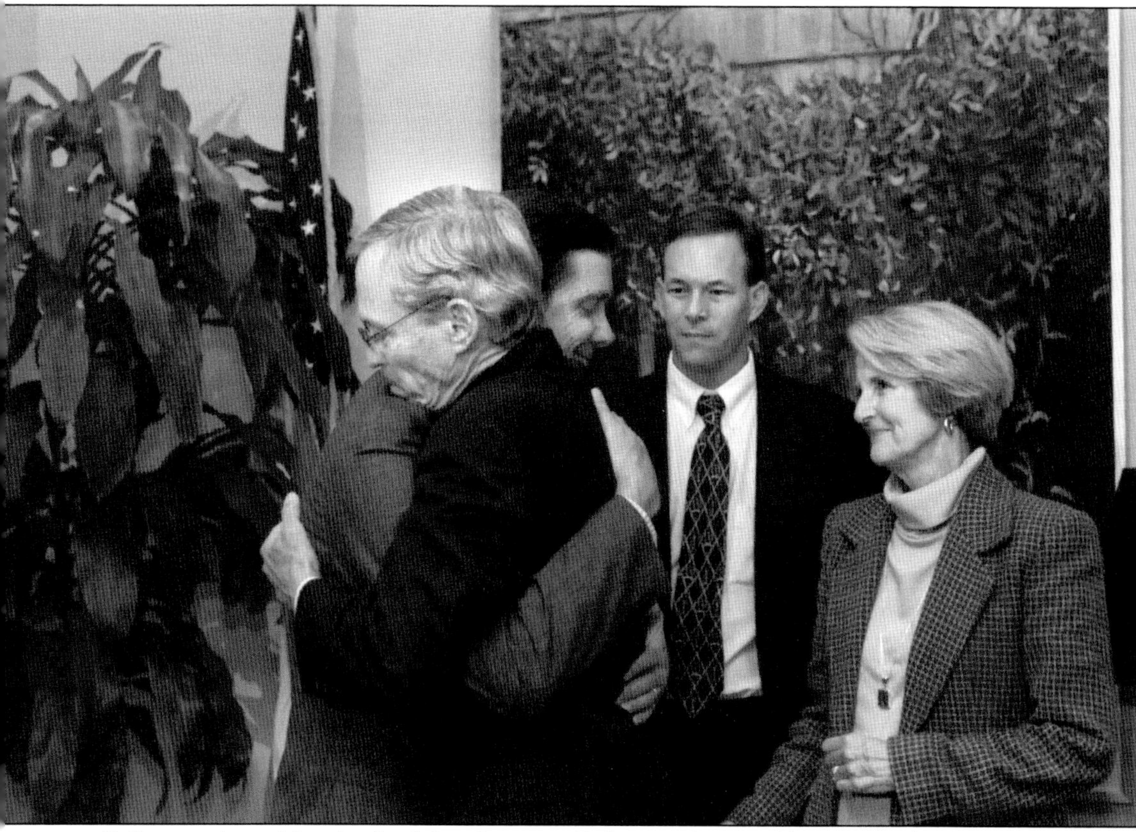

Following the sudden death of Gov. Lawton Chiles, Lt. Gov. Buddy MacKay (embracing, right) was sworn in as the 42nd governor at his capitol office. The two-minute ceremony took place around 12:30 a.m., due to the MacKays being away on business. It had been a little over a month since he lost in a landslide to Governor-elect Jeb Bush, and the next 24 days would see MacKay lead the state through the remainder of the governmental transition. MacKay publicly stated that there was no joy in his unexpected term as governor. He refused to move into either the governor's mansion or the governor's capitol office suite. He was the first lieutenant governor to assume the office of governor due to the death of a predecessor since Marcellus Stearns. Despite keeping a low profile during his tenure, MacKay made 56 appointments to various boards and offices, including two judgeships. He also helped negotiate a conservation plan for the Everglades. (SAF.)

A young Jeb Bush (left) is shown in his capitol office during his time as secretary of commerce. In 1987, Governor Martinez appointed Bush to the position after his tireless efforts to bring Dade County into the Republican fold. He served in this role until 1988, when he resigned to work for his father's presidential campaign. (SAF.)

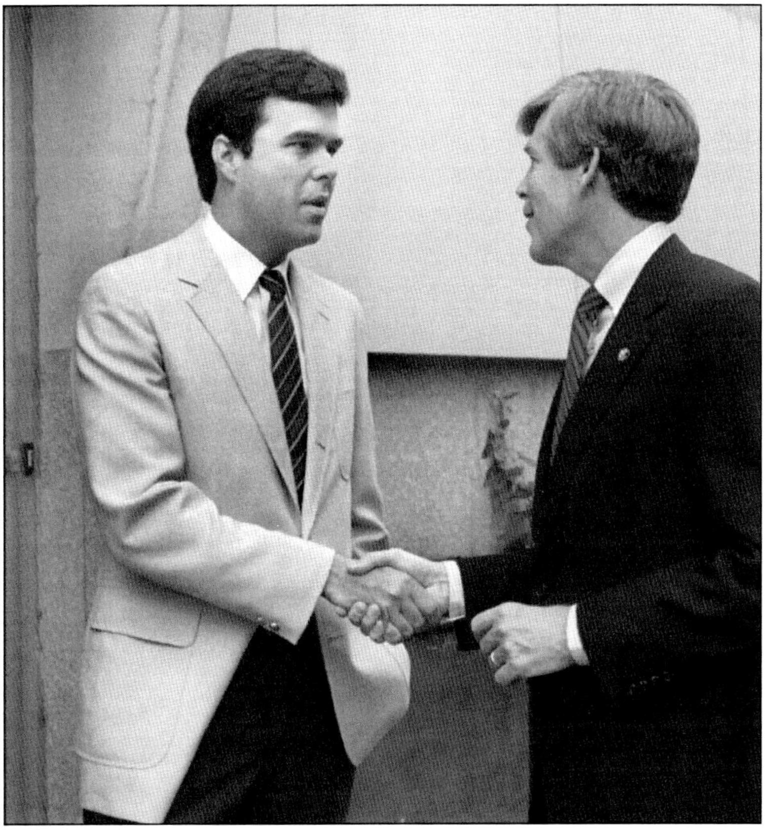

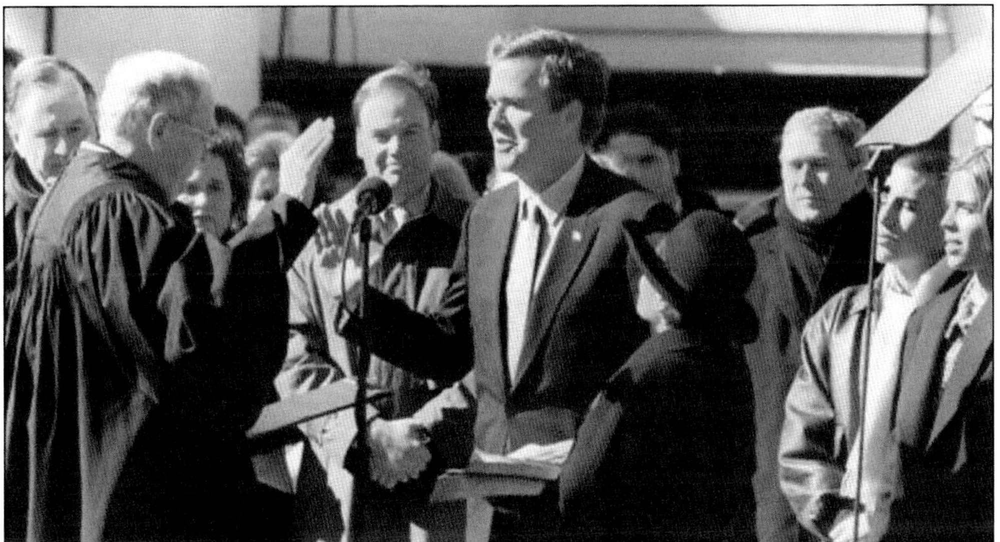

Jeb Bush, who had run for governor in 1994 as the Republican nominee, faced no primary challenge in 1998. He was well ahead of Democratic nominee Buddy MacKay in every poll and had raised nearly $30 million. In the general election, he beat MacKay 55.2 to 44.7 percent and carried all but nine of the state's sixty-seven counties. (SAF.)

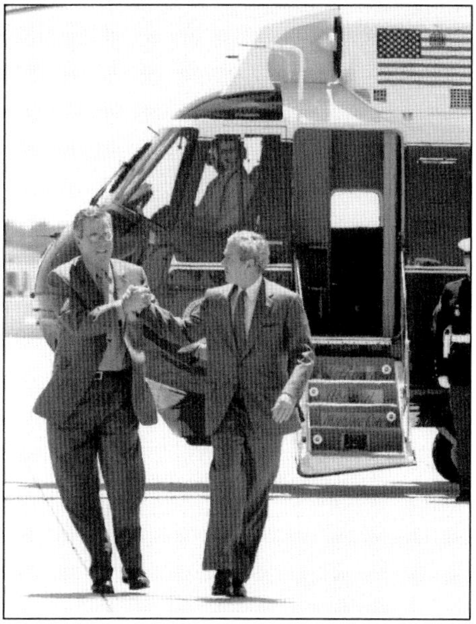

Pres. George W. Bush (right) made numerous visits to Florida to support his brother for reelection in 2002. Democrats had made Jeb Bush (left) their biggest target that year. The election was notable as the first time a Republican was reelected to the governorship. It was the most costly campaign in the state's history, and the Department of Justice sent observers to certain polls. (AC.)

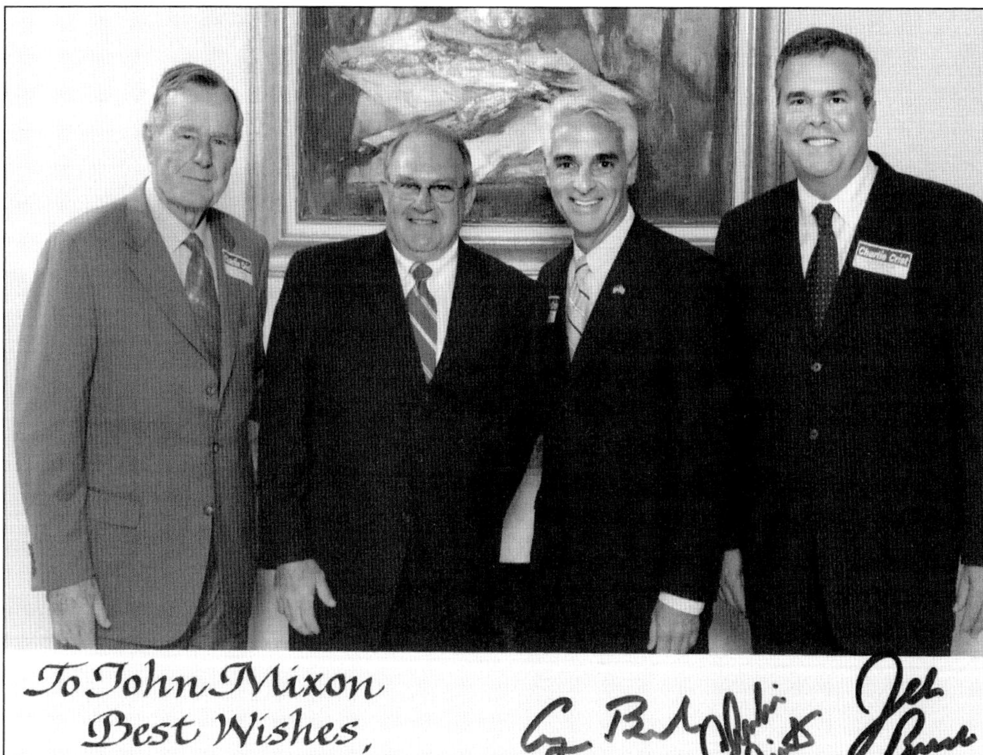

In 2006, the Republican nominee for governor was Charlie Crist (second from right), then Florida's attorney general. Previously, he was elected the state education commissioner and served in the Florida Senate. Both George H.W. Bush (left) and George W. Bush campaigned for Crist. Yet, toward the end of the general election, Crist began to distance himself from the Bush family as 2006 turned into a Democratic wave year. John Mixon is second from the left, and Jeb Bush stands far right. (Dr. and Mrs. Mixon.)

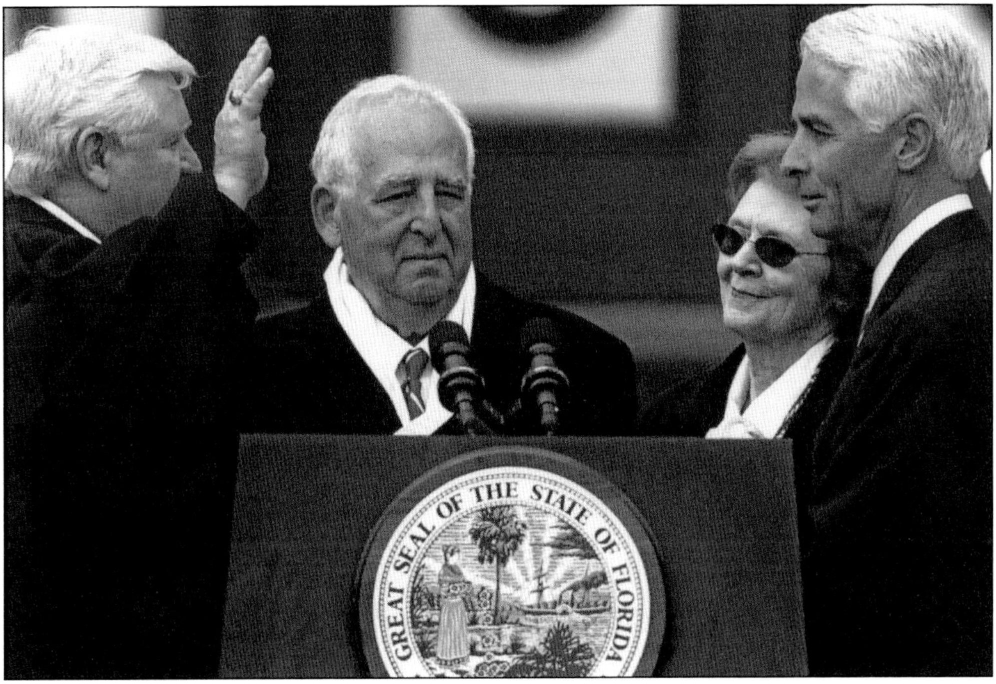

These photographs were taken during Charlie Crist's inauguration in January 2007. Above, Governor-elect Crist takes the oath of office. Below, five living governors share the stage. They are, from left to right, Reubin Askew, Claude Kirk, Charlie Crist, Bob Martinez, and Jeb Bush. Crist was wildly popular for the first three years of his term, with approval ratings hovering around 65 percent. This was due in large part to his laid-back nature and moderate approach to governing. He was short-listed as a vice-presidential candidate in 2008 and surprised everyone when he declined to run for a second term in 2010. He chose to run for the US Senate instead, losing the Republican primary to Marco Rubio. Crist then changed his party affiliation to Independent and served the remainder of his term in office as Florida's only governor without a party. (Both, SAF.)

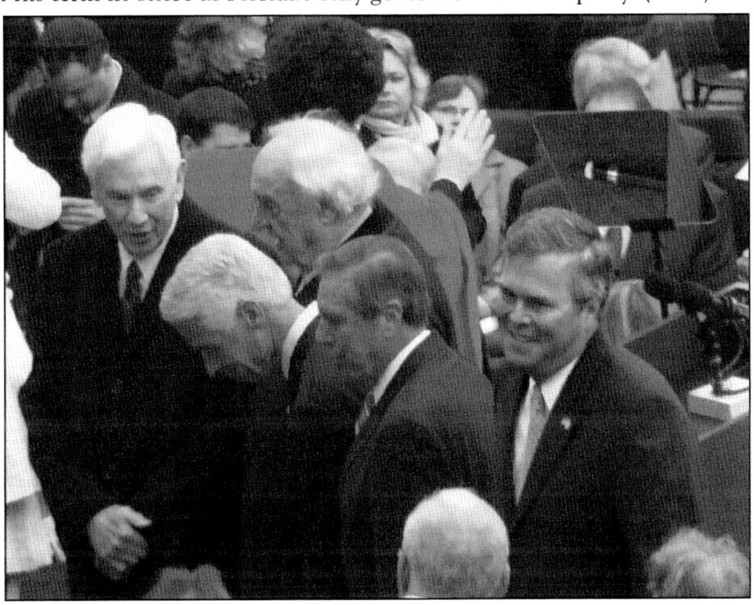

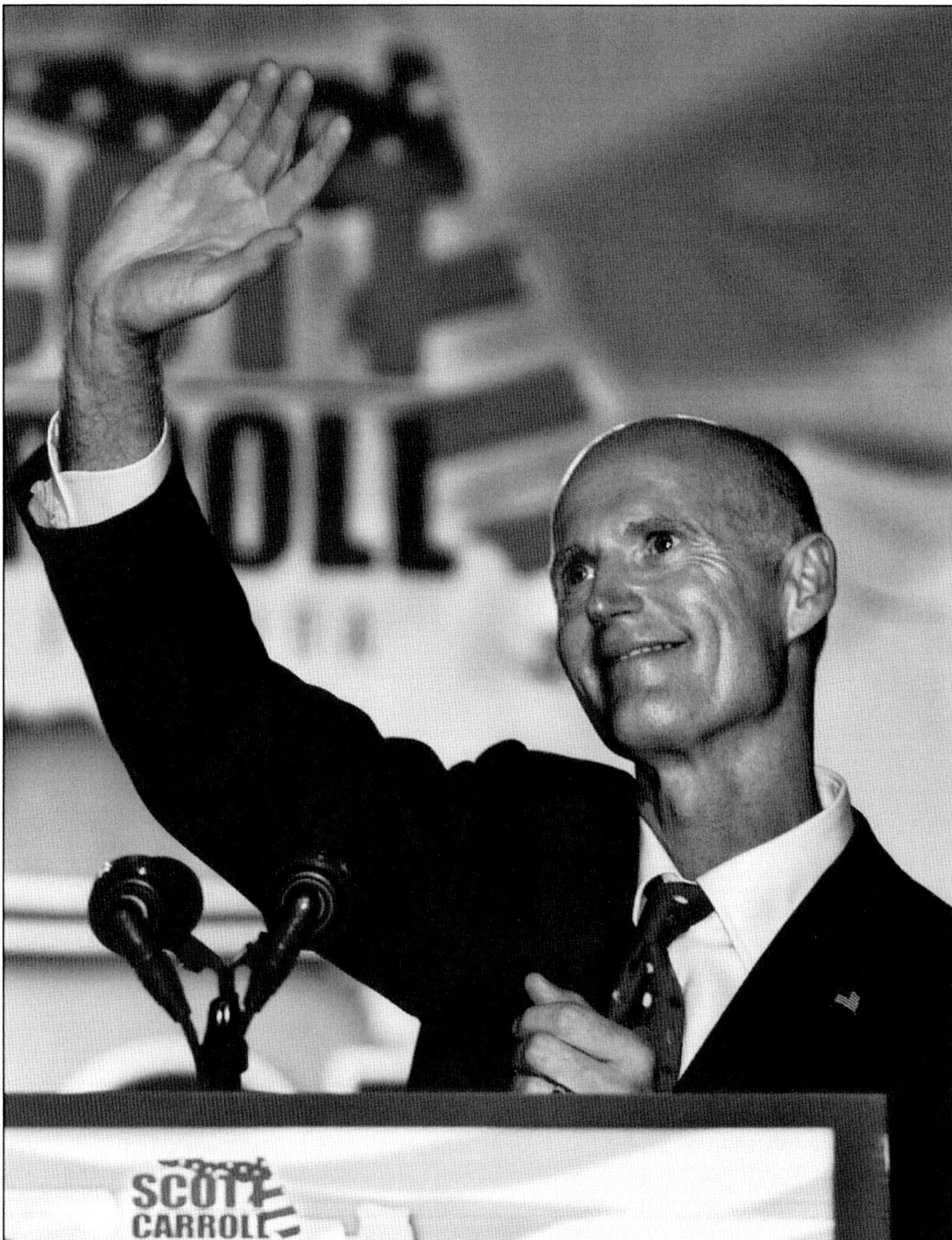

The son of a truck driver and JC Penney clerk, Rick Scott is known as the founder of two healthcare providers, Columbia Hospital Corporation and Solantic Corporation. Scott announced his intention to run for governor in 2010. He defeated Bill McCollum in the Republican primary election and beat Democratic nominee Alex Sink in a close race in the general election, spending roughly $75 million of his own money in the process. (AC.)

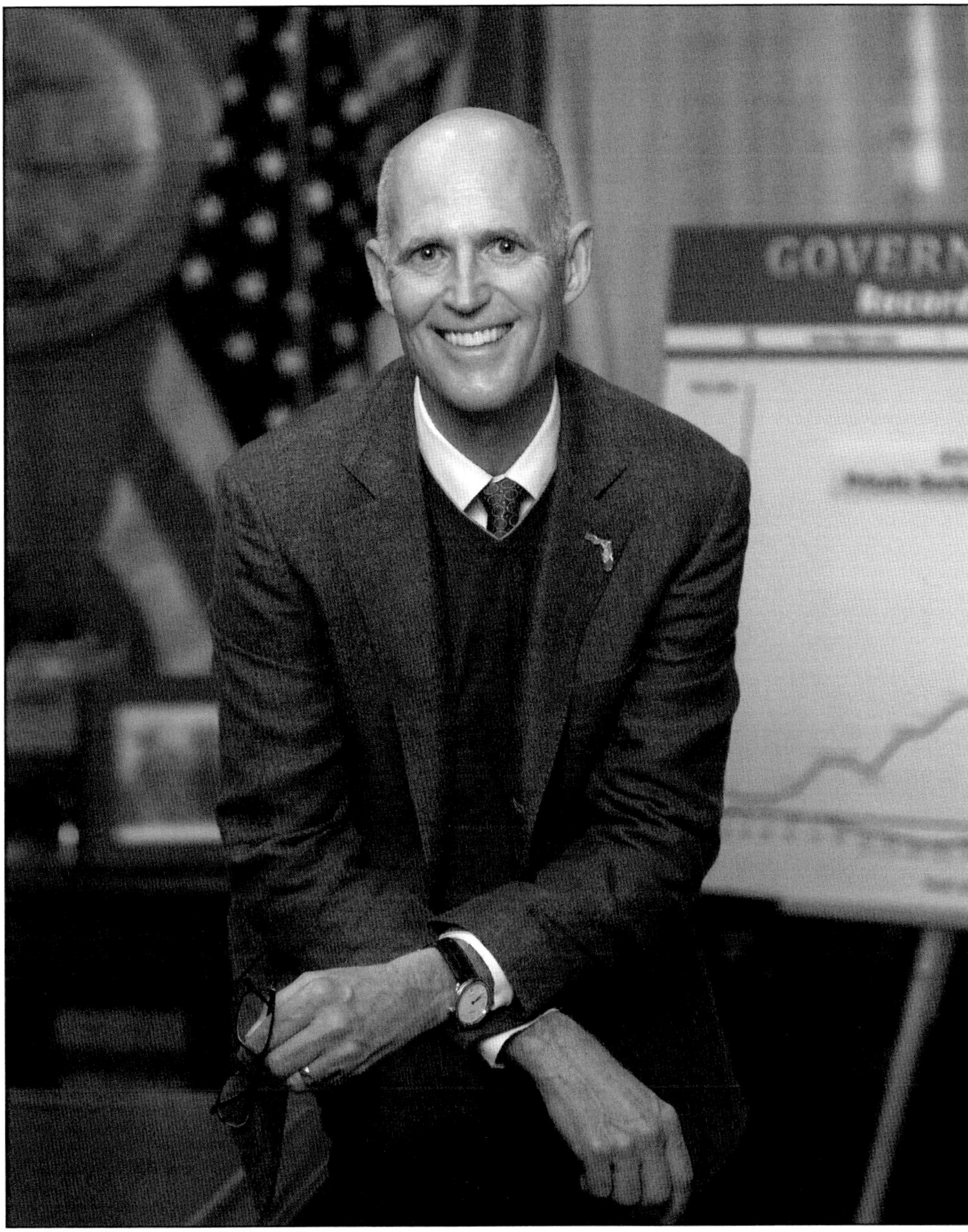

Assuming office on January 4, 2011, Governor Scott devoted himself to creating jobs. During his first three years in office, the State of Florida saw modest levels of job creation. His administration also saw Jennifer Carroll, the first woman and African American to serve as lieutenant governor. In 2013, Carroll resigned from office over her links with a federal gambling racketeering case. In 2014, Carlos Lopez-Cantera was sworn in as Florida's 19th lieutenant governor. The Scott administration experienced a short honeymoon. Scott rejected $2.3 billion in federal funding to develop a high-speed rail line between Tampa and Orlando. The Republican majority in the Florida Senate then approved a letter rebuking Scott and asking the Department of Transportation to continue funding. While his tenure has seen both successes and frustrating pitfalls, it is perhaps too early to judge the legacy of Florida's 45th governor. (Meredyth Hope.)

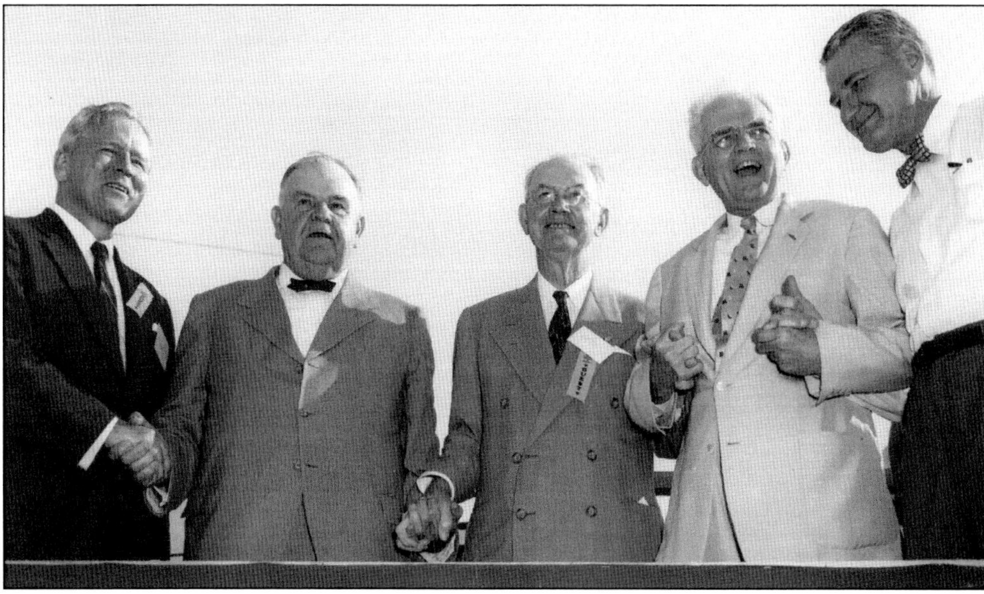

Since its inception, the office of governor has attracted some of the state's most promising figures. However, until the new state constitution was signed into law, a governor could not succeed himself. This severely limited the governor and concentrated power in cabinet members, who were not restricted by term limits. Since being freed from this status as a single-term lame duck, the governors have been able to increase their influence in a number of ways. The splendor of the governor's mansion has aided in the executive's efforts to win support for his agenda. Both the mansion and the governor's capitol office have become important home-court advantages for most administrations. Pictured above from left to right are Fuller Warren, John Martin, Doyle Carlton, Spessard Holland, and Millard Caldwell. The photograph below was taken during a Graham-Mixson event. (Above, SAF; below, WM.)

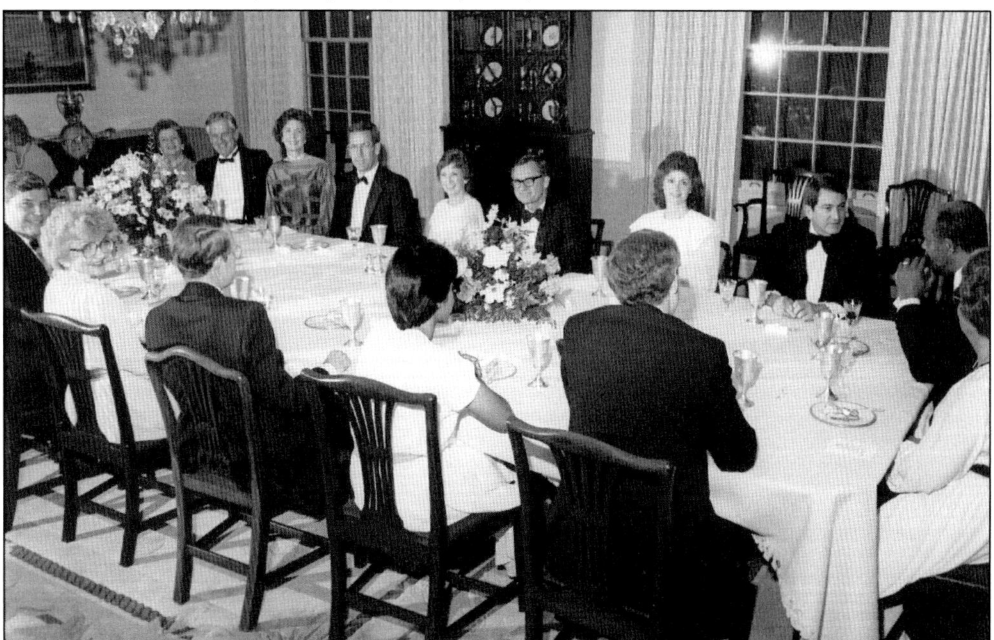

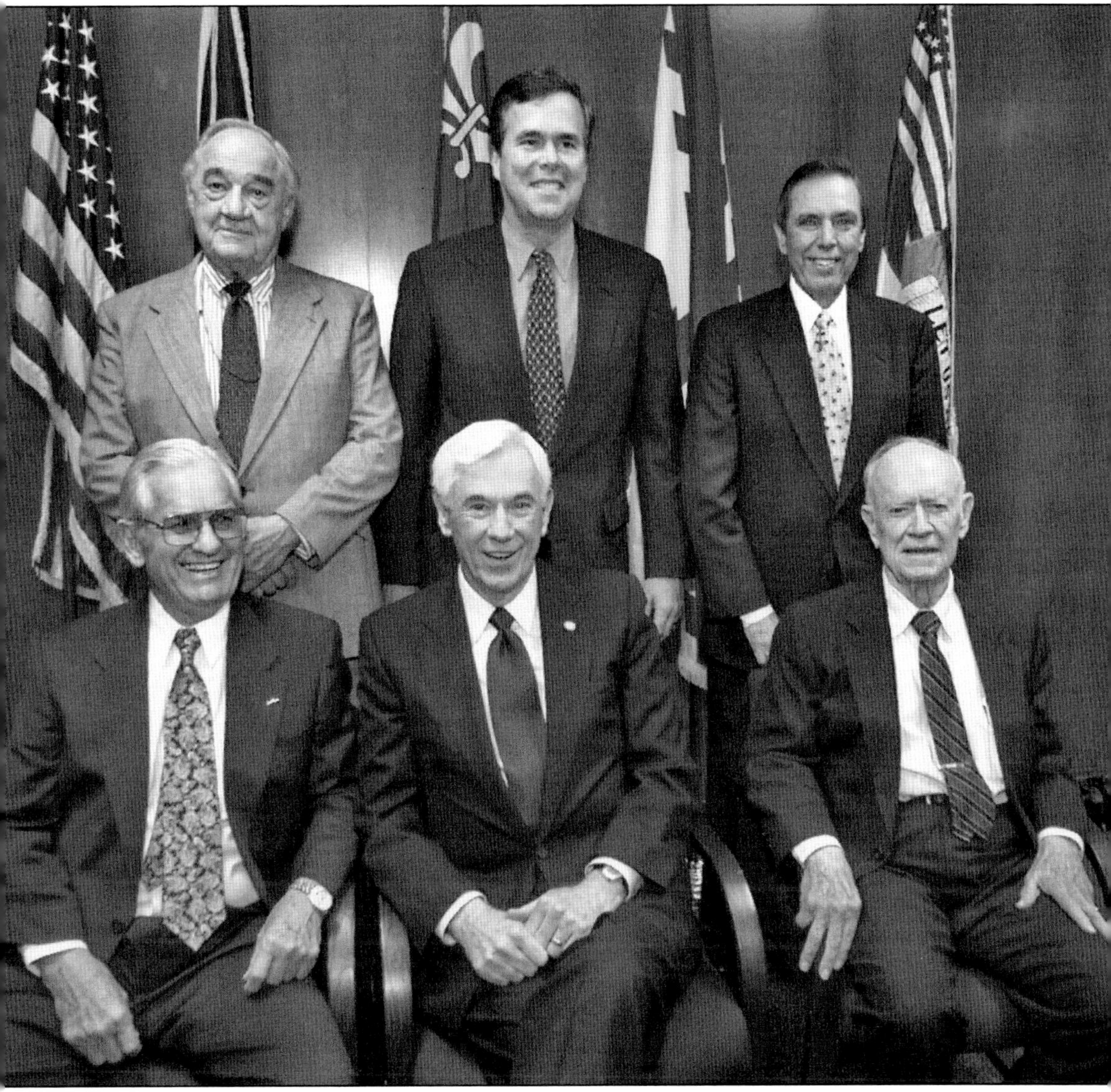

As of 2014, only Reubin Askew and Jeb Bush have served two consecutive terms in office. Governor Bloxham is the only individual to serve two nonconsecutive terms, and Leroy Collins was elected to a full term after serving an abbreviated two-year term. The first territorial governor, William Pope Duval, still holds the overall record, with 12 years in office. From left to right are (first row) Wayne Mixson, Reubin Askew, and Farris Bryant; (second row) Claude Kirk, Jeb Bush, and Bob Martinez. (Courtesy of Mark Foley.)

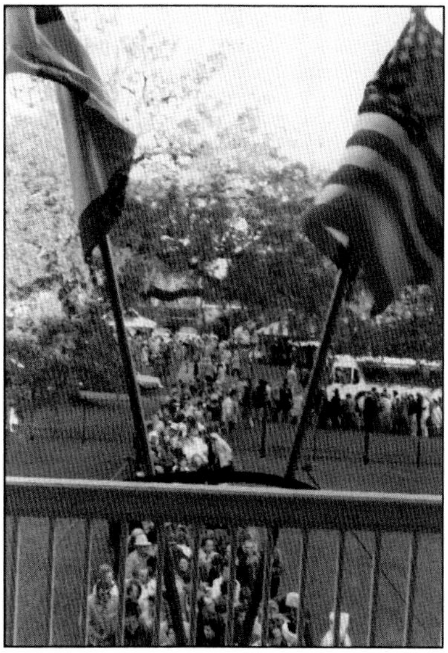

Citizens line up to greet the newly sworn-in governor at the mansion's traditional open house. The public can be a powerful lobbying tool for any governor. Some of Reubin Askew's most ambitious legislative goals became law only after he took his case to the people. Leroy Collins used television better than any other governor to project his message to the state. (WM.)

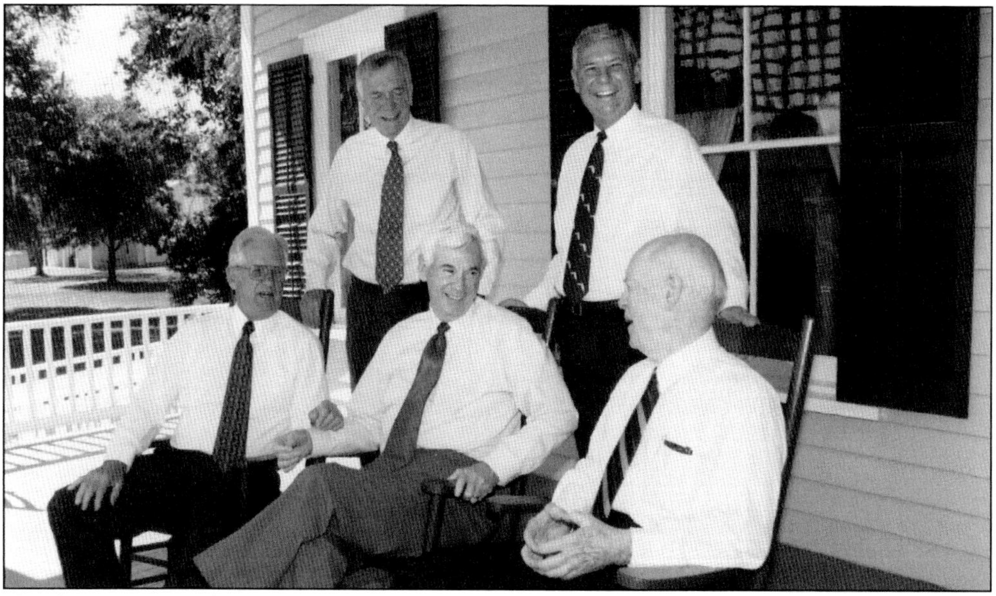

Florida was a typical Southern stronghold for the Democratic Party following Reconstruction. For this reason, 34 of the 45 men elected governor have been Democrats. There have been eight Republican governors, a Whig governor, and a provisional governor. Sidney Catts was elected as a member of the Prohibition Party, but he governed largely as an independent. When Charlie Crist left the Republican Party in mid-2010, he became the state's sole independent governor. In its nearly 200-year history, four occupants have died in office. In addition, three lieutenant governors and two senate presidents have been elevated to the governorship. Jeff Kottkamp served as acting governor for two hours while Charlie Crist was under anesthesia for knee surgery. There have been 14 governors who have served in high-ranking positions within the federal government; one as president, two as cabinet members, one as the director of the National Drug Control Policy, one as an ambassador, one as a special ambassador, and one as a presidential envoy. Pictured from left to right are (sitting) Wayne Mixson, Reubin Askew, and Farris Bryant; (standing) Lawton Chiles and Bob Graham. (WM.)

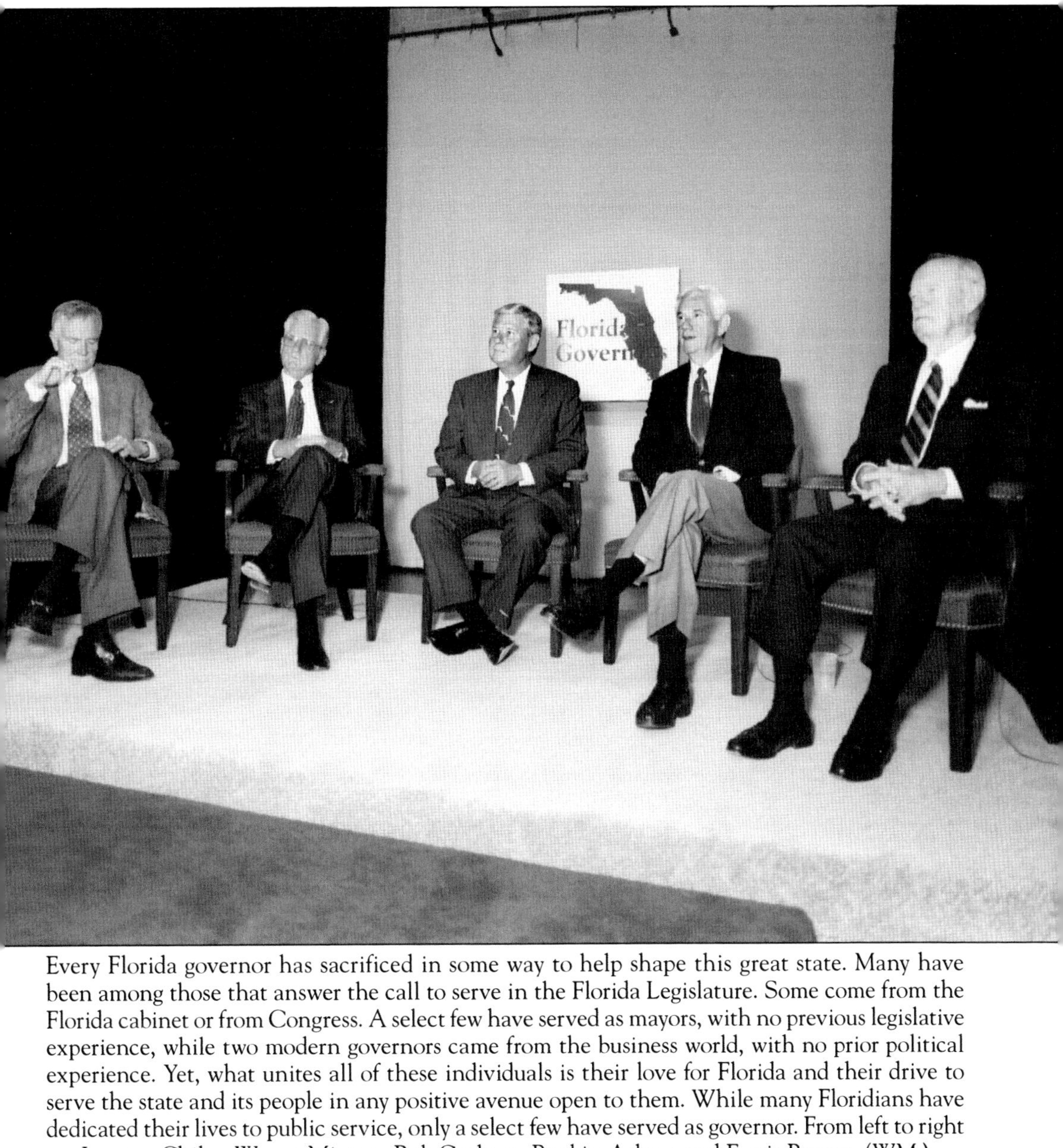

Every Florida governor has sacrificed in some way to help shape this great state. Many have been among those that answer the call to serve in the Florida Legislature. Some come from the Florida cabinet or from Congress. A select few have served as mayors, with no previous legislative experience, while two modern governors came from the business world, with no prior political experience. Yet, what unites all of these individuals is their love for Florida and their drive to serve the state and its people in any positive avenue open to them. While many Floridians have dedicated their lives to public service, only a select few have served as governor. From left to right are Lawton Chiles, Wayne Mixson, Bob Graham, Reubin Askew, and Farris Bryant. (WM.)

INDEX

About the Organization

The state of Florida is truly blessed for its state archives and its efforts over the past few years to present countless items to the general public on its website, Floridamemory.com. The mission of the Florida Memory Program is to provide free online access to select archival resources from the collections of the State Library and Archives of Florida. Florida Memory chooses materials for digitization that illuminate significant events and individuals in the state's history and that help educate Floridians and millions of people around the world about Florida history and culture. The site's Florida photographic collection alone is a searchable database of 185,041 photographs. The video collection has over 157 full-length films from the archives' extensive catalog of moving images, including news, political footage, promotional films, interviews, sports coverage, and films produced by various state agencies. Many of the images in this book were used with permission from both the state archives and the Florida Museum of History. Yet, these images are truly just a small taste of what awaits you with just a click of a mouse.